THE

PARTNERING

SOLUTION

A Powerful Strategy for Managers, Professionals, and Employees at All Levels

William Ronco, Ph.D. and Jean S. Ronco, Ed.M.

CAREER
PRESS

THE CAREER PRESS, INC.
Franklin Lakes, NJ

THE PARTNERING SOLUTION
EDITED AND TYPESET BY KRISTEN PARKES
Cover design by Johnson Design
Printed in the U.S.A. by Book-mart Press

To order this title, please call toll-free 1-800-CAREER-1 (NJ and Canada: 201-848-0310) to order using VISA or MasterCard, or for further information on books from Career Press.

CAREER
PRESS

The Career Press, Inc., 3 Tice Road, PO Box 687,
Franklin Lakes, NJ 07417
www.careerpress.com

Library of Congress Cataloging-in-Publication Data

Ronco, William C.
    The partnering solution : a powerful strategy for managers, professionals, and employees at all levels / by William Ronco and Jean S. Ronco.
        p. cm.
    Includes index.
    ISBN 1-56414-789-4 (pbk.)
    1. Teams in the workplace—Management. 2. Organizational effectiveness. 3. Communications in organizations. 4. Industrial productivity. I. Ronco, Jean S. II. Title.

HD66.R647 2005
650.1'3--dc22

2005040949

We dedicate this book to our partners:
clients and program participants who have
taught us much about the meaning of partnering.

WCR and JSR

Contents

Introduction

Using This Book

This is a "tools" book. Most of the book describes specific strategies, skills, and tools you can put to use in a wide range of applications. The first chapter provides the context for using the tools in an optimal way, outlining the scope and seriousness of the Babel Problem and providing basic information on the method that comprises the Partnering Solution.

To provide a deeper understanding of the situations where the Partnering Solution is useful and the outcomes it can achieve, Chapters 2 and 3 describe partnering case studies. Chapter 2 provides a "partnering album," a series of brief descriptions of 12 different partnering applications. Chapter 3 describes four typical partnering cases in more detail.

Chapters 4 through 8 describe each of the five parts of the partnering agenda in detail:

Chapter 4: Taking Stock. Developing measures of partnering effectiveness.

Chapter 5: Building Trust. Improving the "people chemistry" in partnering situations.

Chapter 6: Clarifying Goals. Why and how to develop performance and communications goals for partnering.

Chapter 7: Implementing Key Processes. Defining and implementing essential procedures to achieve partnering goals.

Chapter 8: Raising the Bar. Using the Partnering Solution not only to solve problems ,but also to explore and develop opportunities.

Chapters 9 through 13 describe processes, training, tools, and concepts that strengthen the Partnering Solution. Running partnering meetings for optimal participation, performance, innovation, and creativity.

Chapter 9: Partner, Heal Thyself. Doing the internal work necessary to make your organization an effective partner externally. Getting your own house in order.

Chapter 10: Improving Meetings and Group Communications Skills. Improving group communications skills to make partnering meetings more effective.

Chapter 11: Improving One-on-One Partnering Communications Skills. Strengthening the one-on-one skills that contribute to partnering results.

Chapter 12: Partnering Leadership. Developing models and practices for leadership that fit with and reinforce partnering.

Chapter 13 (an appropriate number?) is the murder mystery "Death by Outsourcing." We thought that it would be both useful and entertaining to wrap many of the book's core concepts into an unconventional approach to a business case.

Chapter 14 helps readers translate the strategies and skills in the book directly into "Preparing Your Own Partnering Plan."

Our Core Case Organizations

We follow a handful of what we call "Core Case Organizations" throughout the book for two reasons. First, we thought that following a core set of organizations would make it easier for readers to follow the partnering process throughout the series of different issues and tasks we address. We draw on many case examples for brief illustrations, but having a core group to follow through the partnering strategies makes it easier to see how the partnering pieces fit together.

Second, we sought out the core case organizations because we want to make the point that for an organization to develop competence, it is essential for partnering to infuse the organization at many levels. Our core case organizations have high levels of partnering competence and extensive experience with partnering. They illustrate not only how specific partnering approaches work, but also how those approaches fit into a cohesive business strategy.

Our Core Case Organizations include:

❑   Lee Kennedy Co., Inc.: A 150-person construction
    company based in Boston.

❒ SEi Companies: A 140-person mechanical, electrical, and plumbing engineering firm with offices in Boston and Houston.

❒ Foliage Software: A 100-person software development company based in Burlington, Massachusetts.

❒ Keyes North Atlantic: A 60-person electromechanical contracting company based in Newton, Massachusetts.

❒ PCA Architects: A 30-person architecture firm based in Cambridge, Massachusetts.

❒ ADS Financial Services Solutions: A 150-person firm that provides systems integration and software consulting services for banks and the financial services industry.

Lee Kennedy Co., Inc. (Construction)

Lee Kennedy describes his construction company's roots with partnering: "When I started this, I said there's got to be a way to be a contractor without being a Mongol raider. Without realizing it, I got us started presenting a more cooperative face to clients and architects." Tucked in a South Boston location, the Lee Kennedy Co. is entering its 25th year of business with 150 employees and an enviable reputation among clients, architects, and subcontractors.

The company's "Door Award" typifies its in-depth involvement with client partnering. The company annually gives the award to field staff whose actions exemplify its commitment to customer service. (The company also gives a parallel award annually to internal office staff.) The title of the Door Award stems from the work of one of the company's carpenters. Without asking for permission from the company, the carpenter took considerable time to refit a door belonging to a tenant of one of Lee Kennedy's clients, Boston Properties. The carpenter had no obligation to fix the door, he just wanted to provide good service to Boston Properties. The job took so much effort that Boston Properties staff asked him why he was working so hard. The carpenter replied, "Right now, this door is the most important job our company is working on."

SEi Companies
(Mechanical, electrical, and plumbing engineers)

"What business are we in?" CEO Bob Gracilieri likes to ask new project managers when they begin working for SEi Companies, a 140-person engineering firm with offices in Boston and Houston.

"Engineering?" the new recruits respond, a little tentatively.

"No!" Gracilieri replies, bringing his fist down on the table. "We are in the people business, and don't ever forget that!"

Gracilieri explains, "We have to make it very clear to people what we're all about. So many firms in this business try to make it on technical smarts alone, and that's not enough. Of course you have to be very strong technically, but that's not good enough. What we try to do, beyond all our technical expertise, is get our project managers to really listen to the clients, really try to understand them. It's hard because that's not the way engineers are trained, but it's something we have to do."

Foliage Software

Co-CEO Tim Bowe explains, "Our interest in partnering is what drove our extensive reorganization these past few years. We realized that if we focused on technology solutions alone, we might do everything we promised on a project, and still have an unhappy customer." Foliage Software is a 100-person software development, systems integration, and strategy consulting firm based in Burlington, Massachusetts. "So we've moved from seeing the problems we're hired to tackle as technology problems to recognizing them as business problems."

Semiconductor Division Manager Norm Delisle explains how that emphasis affects his work, "I had years of experience managing projects before I came to work here. What's different here is that senior management is always asking me, 'Did you call the client today? Did you call the client today?' Just the idea of constant communications permeates everything here."

Keyes North Atlantic (Electromechanical contractors)

"We have lots of strong customer relationships," Susan Keyes points out, "but not all strong customer relationships are partnering relationships." She is president of Keyes North Atlantic, a 60-person electromechanical contractor in Watertown, Massachusetts, with a strong history of partnering with clients as well as with other members of project teams—contractors, architects, and engineers.

"Partnering relationships," Keyes continues, "are especially interesting to us because those are the ones that push us to do our best work. Those are the ones that treat us as if we were staff for them. It's not just satisfying customers when we partner with them, it's working with them side by side to meet challenges and solve problems. We give them advice, and they give us advice as well. Often, we're able to develop new systems and processes, and everybody benefits."

PCA Architects

"One of the things about partnering is that it's been humbling," David Chilinski confesses.

CEO of PCA Architects, a 20-year-old, 30-person design firm in Cambridge, Massachusetts, Chilinski, explains, "We often get work through referrals and that is very satisfying. What is surprising is to hear that the client who referred us said, '...the reason to hire PCA is that you will have a *great time* working with them.' What's humbling is that it's not our design excellence that brought them, or our on-time, on-budget project management, it's the simple fact that they have a good time!"

David Galler, a principal in the firm elaborates: "Partnering for us also means that we pay attention to the client's business objectives. I think the college dining renovations that we have done are a good example. The new facility is such an attractive place to congregate. We hear that there's increased volume: 30 percent more dining hall volume than before our renovation. That's a big jump, and it has big impacts for our university clients."

ADS Financial Services Solutions
(Systems integration and software consulting)

"The real partnering challenge in our business is to be simple and focused on what the client wants, not on how smart we are," CEO Bill Gallagher reflects. ADSFS is a 25-year-old, 150-person firm that provides systems integration and software consulting services for banks and the financial services industry.

"Our senior consultants have the technology expertise, but they are primarily bankers; all of them have 15 or 20 years' experience working in banks before they join ADS. That helps them stay focused on what the client really needs. Being an effective partner means we have to show our value, not just our expertise. In order for us to be successful in the way that's most important to our clients, we need to be sure that our customers get the solution that's best for *them*."

1

The Babel Problem, the Partnering Solution

Everyone has encountered the Babel Problem, the tendency of all organizations and alliances to fragment into different and often warring factions. The factions speak different languages, hold different interests, and pursue different goals. As a result, the whole shrinks to become less, often much less, than the sum of its parts. The Babel Problem wreaks havoc in the companies in which we work, the associations to which we belong, the colleges that educate us, the hospitals that care for us, and the government agencies that protect us. The first half of this chapter examines the Babel Problem in detail: its pervasiveness, the forms it takes, the symptoms that signal its existence, the root causes that create it, and the economic forces that fuel it.

The second half of this chapter explores the Partnering Solution: its sources, its history, its core content, how it differs from other forms of teambuilding, and why it works. The Partnering Solution solves the Babel Problem. Based on our work in more than 200 projects, the Partnering Solution is a structured method that improves communications and bottom-line performance in organizations and alliances of all kinds: large corporations, small associations, outsourcing, mergers, customer relations, strategic alliances, government, and nonprofit. The Partnering Solution provides insight, strategy, skills, and tools for managers, employees, and members at all levels.

The Babel Problem

The CIA announced that they plan to cooperate more openly with the FBI. They just haven't told the FBI.

—Jay Leno

Remember: When the lion lies down with the lamb is when Marketing will cooperate with Accounting.

—Sign posted over accounting department coffee pot

Some two-thirds of mergers either fail or fall far short of expectations.

—Dennis C. Carey and Dayton Ogden,
The Human Side of M&A

I discovered that the college was run as a kind of organized anarchy.

—College president

The Babel Problem attacks not only large corporations and strategic alliances, but small businesses and civic organizations as well. It affects churches, professional firms, labor unions, hospitals. It wreaks havoc not only with bureaucracies, but also with small groups, teams, and collaborations of just a few individuals.

We lost a major customer. Programming blames marketing, marketing blames support, support blames quality assurance. We're putting much more energy into attacking each other than we are into solving the problem.

—Software company vice president

We were so certain they were the right company to outsource our facilities management to, they have so much experience and look so good on paper. But they just did not understand our priorities, and they were too difficult to work with.

—Bank facilities manager

This is supposed to be a place that follows a Higher Order, the Golden Rule, but our internal politics can be brutal. The worship committee fights with the pastoral task force, and the social committee fights with everyone.

—Church committee member

The merger looked so strong on paper. We all stood to make a lot of money from it. But the two companies failed to work together. We talked past each other, never listened, never worked together. Our cultures were just too different.

—Engineering firm president

Forms of the Babel Problem

The Babel Problem thrives in large organizations and small ones, formal bureaucracies and informal groups. It is so pervasive, so much a part of our daily lives, that we may fail to register appropriate concern when it occurs. The Babel Problem takes predictable forms. Recognizing those forms provides an initial foothold in solving the problem.

Departments at War

In this, the most visible version of the Babel Problem, two organizations or departments that claim to be partnering are actually at war with each other. Often the battles are out in the open: the departments or organizations express their disagreements openly and vocally. They criticize each other openly and perhaps even publish memos and e-mails about each other. When this kind of warfare occurs in alliances, it usually takes place at grassroots levels between people who were not involved in formulating the partnering arrangement, but are responsible for carrying it out. When this kind of conflict occurs in organizations, it often involves departments that attempt to monitor or control other departments, such as quality control, accounting, auditing, and other regulatory departments.

Not My Job

In this form of the Babel Problem, people who work at grassroots levels in organizations that are supposed to be partnering with each other acknowledge the partnering arrangement; however, they don't think that it applies to them. For example, people working in the accounting department of a software company know and even applaud their company's efforts to build strong relationships with its customers. At the same time, though, the department maintains rigid accounting practices that make it difficult for customers to do business with the company. The accounting practices undo much of the partnering work that the company's marketing and technology departments achieve.

If We're the Experts, Why Aren't You Listening to Us?

In this version of the Babel Problem, organizations or departments that are supposed to possess "expert" knowledge approach others in a one-way, top-down manner. This can occur in outsourcing, when a company partners with a service provider that possesses strong technical or professional skills. This version of the Babel Problem also occurs inside organizations when a strong technical department such as research, strategy, or statistics tries to partner with internal user or customer groups.

Quiet Standoff

In this form of the Babel Problem, departments or organizations don't battle openly so much as they ignore each other. Here the issue with conflict is that there is not enough of it. Standoff often occurs when one department's role involves planning for another, as when a corporate office develops strategies and policies for field offices. In alliances, standoff occurs when one organization ignores the relationships it is supposed to be building with the other. Standoff occurs in mergers and acquisitions when organizations fail to make use of the resources their new partner organizations potentially bring to them.

All of these forms of the Babel Problem take place not only in large corporations, government bureaucracies, universities, and hospitals, but also in small companies, professional firms, civic groups, and informal partnerships.

In fact, the Babel Problem can affect an "organization" or "alliance" of just two people. For example, two painters (maybe they are professionals, or maybe they are a husband-wife "alliance") tackle the job of repainting a kitchen or wallpapering a living room. They divide the work to take advantage of the talents and interests each brings to the job. With a brush, one tackles the trim and fine detail, while the other, with a roller, covers the large spaces.

If they don't partner effectively, all four forms of the Babel Problem described here can occur. They may argue about who will work in what area and what to do when the large spaces meet the trim: *That's not my job!* They may feel the need to offer or reject advice and feedback from each other: *I'm supposed to be the expert!* If their arguments about who should paint what and when escalate, they can go to war. But when matters finally deteriorate, they will likely end in standoff.

Symptoms of the Babel Problem

The Bible's portrayal of the Tower of Babel story provides useful insight into the symptoms of the Babel Problem. The Bible has it that the people stopped working on the tower when the Almighty caused them to be "confused" and to "speak in different languages." These conditions describe four symptoms of any fragmented organization or alliance:

Forms and Symptoms of the Babel Problem: Biblical View.
"Fall of the Tower of Babel," Anthonisz, Cornelisz, 1549
Photo: Joerg P Adams
Bildarchiv Preussicher Kulturbesitz / Art Resource NY186232

1. The overall work of the organization stops and the people become confused.
2. In their confusion, the people focus more on the goals of their own immediate group than on the goals of the organization at large.
3. To make matters worse, people in the different groups speak a kind of different language.
4. When people speak different languages, they don't listen to each other.

Beyond these, we observe that a fifth symptom of the Babel Problem is either too much or too little conflict. Healthy, successful organizations and alliances have a reasonable amount of conflict, which is an outcome of normal discourse. An absence of discord, rather than the absence of problems, often signals the denial. It's not that healthy organizations and alliances don't argue, but that they argue well.

Forms and Symptoms of the Babel Problem	
Forms	**Symptoms**
Departments at War.	Work stops or slows.
Not My Job.	People focus on immediate group.
Quiet Standoff.	People speak different languages.
If I'm the Expert, Why Aren't You Listening to Me?	People don't communicate effectively.
	Too much or too little conflict.

Causes of the Babel Problem

The only things that evolve by themselves in an organization are disorder, friction, and malperformance.

—Peter Drucker

Why does the Babel Problem occur? Why do so many organizations and alliances fragment into warring factions? What are the roots and causes of the Babel Problem?

Eight different factors cause the Babel Problem. Each is powerful on its own. But combined, as they often are in real-world organizations and alliances, the factors form a mighty force.

1. *Division of labor.* Robert Michels, one of the first organizational sociologists, theorized that fragmentation in organizations is *inevitable.* His groundbreaking 1920s text, *Political Parties*, observes that organizations must divide labor in order to accomplish anything significant. However, he contends that dividing labor creates different roles and responsibilities, and thus leads inevitably to an organization's members pursuing different self-interests.

2. *People bond emotionally with smaller groups.* Some psychologists believe that people identify more closely with smaller groups rather than with an overall organization because it is easier to form a human connection with the smaller group. The larger organization is more removed, more abstract. Even in organizations that are mid-size or small, people gravitate to groups and subgroups that are smaller and easier to bond with than the organization overall.

3. *People chemistry.* Often the most visible and visceral cause of the Babel Problem is that, at a personal level, the people involved in

an organization or alliance simply do not and apparently cannot get along with each other. People themselves who are entangled in troubled organizations or alliances don't talk about the division of labor or bonds with the smaller group. They focus more on their gut-level dislike and distrust of "the other guys." This kind of conflict arises often in mergers and acquisitions, and in outsourcing situations that bring different organizational cultures together. It also arises in organizations when departments talk, look, and work in ways that differ significantly from each other.

4. *Unclear or conflicting goals.* Even when organizations have articulate goals and alliances have detailed contracts, the goals that percolate down to specific departments and groups can be unclear. Frequently, when departments clash over tactics and details, the conflict traces back to unclear organizational goals. Both departments may have quite a different understanding of the organization's goals, and that difference in understanding fuels conflict in their everyday work.

5. *Insufficient procedures.* Sometimes the chief roadblock is not strategy or people chemistry, but nuts-and-bolts processes and procedures. In recent decades, our organizations have become flatter, less hierarchical, and more informal. This trend enhances innovation and speeds decision-making, but it can also create chaos. Many organizations have less than optimal processes for handing off work between departments, managing employee performance, and resolving differences of opinion across groups.

6. *Misunderstanding the meaning of "customer service."* Service provider firms and internal service departments in organizations have done much useful partnering work under the banner of "customer service." In some cases, this effort has helped insensitive departments and organizations to pay more attention to what their customers really need and to provide a more useful service. In growing numbers of cases, though, both customers and service providers have taken the intention of customer service too far, translating it into simply whatever customers ask for. Though it is important to listen to the customer, the customer is not always right. Productive partnering is more two-way, more collaborative, and may involve challenging the customer as much as simply doing what one is told.

7. *Ineffective leadership.* Leading any organization, even a simple one, can be challenging. In partnering, developing effective leadership can be particularly difficult. How does one lead when there is no formal hierarchy, perhaps even no organization, new alignments,

and untested working arrangements? Every year, hundreds of books and articles are published on leadership, and many offer valuable insight and advice. However, little has been written and established about the nature of effective leadership in partnering situations.

8. *Overall, underestimating the difficulty of achieving alignment.* We observe this phenomenon in nearly every partnering situation. Even in complex alliances and organizations with experienced executives, people consistently and significantly underestimate how much effort it takes to achieve alignment and partnering among the different constituencies.

5 Economic Forces That Fuel the Babel Problem

In the future, all the work on the planet will be outsourced.

—Scott Adams, *The Dilbert Future*

Five economic forces are causing more meetings between organizations, departments, and people who "got along great" for many years working apart. These five forces in our economy provide further fuel for creating the Babel Problem:

1. *Decentralized organizations.* Decentralized organizations dominate our economy to such an extent that it may be difficult to recall how different organizations were not too long ago. In the 1940s and 50s most organizations emphasized control, bureaucracy, alignment, and authority. Most organization charts were tall pyramids with many layers of middle management.

   Currently, decentralized organizations dominate in our economy because they are "leaner," make decisions more quickly, and implement change more rapidly. However, decentralized organizations also breed Babel Problems in that they often do little to integrate their various departments. Decentralized organizations in which departments don't communicate with each other can easily become "Departments at War."

2. *Outsourcing.* Outsourcing is very popular in our economy at present because it enables organizations to get rid of functions that distract from their core mission and competencies,

and has the potential to save the organization money. However, outsourcing often creates Babel Problems in the communications and coordination between service provider firms and customer organizations. Customer organizations can demand too much or too little information from service provider firms, and service firms can focus too much on providing the technical aspects of the service while neglecting the communications that the customer organization needs.

3. *Strategic alliances.* Organizations form strategic alliances with other organizations for a wide variety of reasons: to develop products and services together that neither one could do alone, to join forces against a common competitor or threat, and to increase market share. Each time organizations form a strategic alliance they also create a breeding ground for the Babel Problem, as the new alliance depends on the organizations communicating and collaborating with each other.

4. *Mergers and acquisitions.* Merger activity has been high for several years running. However, mergers have been popular for many years. As long ago as the 1930s, Will Rogers commented on the business world's love of growing by merging and acquiring. Mergers and acquisitions have strong potential to build an organization's core competencies, increase revenues and profit, and build economies of scale.

   At the same time, mergers and acquisitions often breed Babel Problems because they can create "forced marriages" of organizations with very different cultures and values. Mergers that look good on paper can fail when people in both organizations are unable to solve the Babel Problems they face.

5. *Rising customer expectations.* Customers' rising expectations is a fifth source of the Babel Problem. When customers demand more of the organizations that supply them with goods and services, organizations often respond by trying to listen, respond, and build more effective long-term working relationships. Unlike the other four trends fueling the Babel Problem, this one is rooted more in social forces than in organizational structure or strategy. Over the past few decades, individual consumers and organizational customers alike have come to demand more from the organizations.

Solving the Babel Problem:
The Unlikely Roots of the Partnering Solution

The construction industry provides the roots of a method that consistently solves the Babel Problem. Known more for conflict and litigation than cooperation and communication, the construction industry may seem to be an unlikely source for a partnering method. Yet the fragmented, complex nature of large projects also provides the conditions that any successful partnering method must address.

Construction partnering has achieved an impressive track record in the industry in the 30 years since its inception. It provides essential building blocks for a Partnering Solution for other forms of the Babel Problem: outsourcing, mergers, alliances, interdepartmental communications, government, education, sales, support.

This red wine partners well with cheese.

—Ad in the *Boston Globe* food section

What's significant about construction partnering is that, unlike the general intention to partner that the *Globe* ad illustrates, it provides a *method*. Many people and organizations use the word "partnering"—in fact, so many use it that the word can be reduced to shallow levels of meaning. In construction, however, partnering is not only an intention, it is a method. And the method is not only effective, it is simple and efficient.

The pervasiveness, forms, symptoms, causes, and economic sources of the Babel Problem are daunting enough to make it clear that a Partnering Solution will require some significant thought and effort. No easy fix, no magic bullet, is going to put back together the organizations and alliances that the Babel Problem so effectively fragments.

At the same time, a Partnering Solution cannot be so complex that it is unwieldy. In order to be useful, a Partnering Solution must not only resolve the Babel Problem, it must do so in a way that mere mortals can master it. The construction industry rises to meet this challenge with a partnering method that is both comprehensive enough to achieve results and simple enough to achieve widespread understanding and use.

The construction industry roots of the Partnering Solution are unlikely yet understandable. It's not that people who work in construction enjoy conflict, but that, until recently, there was no effective forum for discussion and problem-solving on projects. Most projects involve numerous companies carrying out different tasks: architects, engineers, contractors, and subcontractors. There is a contract and a project manager, but the contract can't anticipate all of the coordination problems. There is a project manager, but he or she has no formal power or authority. With all the organizations involved, conflict and miscommunication are inevitable.

The culture and history of the construction industry posed further obstacles to partnering. Compared with other industries, design and construction lags consistently and conspicuously in training and development, as well as in investing in human capital. Getting any form of meeting to take hold outside those dealing with immediate project concerns broke significantly, almost shockingly, with standard practices.

Yet in spite (or perhaps because) of these problems, the industry has developed a highly effective partnering method. Construction partnering has demonstrated results consistently and positively enough to earn endorsement by the American Institute of Architects, the Associated General Contractors, and the American Consulting Engineers Council. Increasing numbers of government agencies and corporations now require partnering workshops as a condition of project funding.

The Army Corps of Engineers developed the first construction partnering experiments about 30 years ago in its Pacific Northwest region. Frustrated with a growing list of projects over budget and beyond schedule, several Corps managers got the notion to pilot teambuilding on some of their projects. With their own professional roots in engineering, they developed an approach to teambuilding that differed in key ways from teambuilding rooted in the human resources and organization development field.

Since the Corps produced its initial material, various facilitators and managers have adapted and refined it. Still, many current construction partnering efforts share consistent agenda items, content, and structure. Most construction partnering focuses on a partnering workshop or series of workshops. One or two days long, depending on the complexity of the project, the workshop brings together key project players from each of the organizations working on the project. For a typical $30 million building, the group can engage 20 to 30 people: a diverse and usually quite vocal group of architects, engineers, plumbers, electricians, subcontractors, clients, building users, facility managers, government officers, and so on.

The meeting usually follows a highly structured agenda:

- ❏ *Taking stock.* In the first hour or two, participants list what they think will go well on the project and what they think may cause problems. This part of the workshop surfaces the key issues the project will have to address.

❑ *Building mutual understanding and trust.* Before working to address the project's key issues, the most effective partnering workshops work with the Myers-Briggs Type Indicator, DiSC, or other personality profile indicators. Even just an hour or two of work with a personality indicator accelerates participants' getting to know each other and building trust.

❑ *Writing a Goals Statement or Partnering Charter.* After clarifying the project's key issues, participants develop a project Goals Statement that addresses the issues. Typically 10 to15 sentences in length, the Goals Statement includes both quantitative performance goals and more qualitative goals for the ways people on the project should interact. To give the statement clout, participants sign it. Work on the Goals Statement takes an hour or two, depending on the number of people in the group and the extent of differences they attempt to resolve.

❑ *Refining communications processes and procedures.* Participants develop detailed communications processes and procedures necessary to achieve the goals. These procedures usually include mechanisms for handling changes, clarifying issues likely to arise in the field, resolving disagreements, and ensuring that everyone gets the information they need when they need it.

An external, objective facilitator usually runs the meeting to ensure that all the players participate, no one dominates, and the group stays focused on the agenda. To conclude the workshop, participants plan when a follow-up meeting should occur and what issues it should address. In follow-ups, people monitor the plans and commitments they made in the original workshop, address new problems, and explore new opportunities.

At a Construction Partnering Workshop

Arriving first, the three men from the construction firm fill their coffee cups and move quickly to the table in the middle of the room. The engineers and some subcontractors come in next, take their coffee, and also take a table. The owner, facility manager, and a few future tenants arrive, followed quickly by four people from the architecture firm.

In the opening hour, participants work with people from their own firms. Each table lists items on flip charts its members anticipate will go well and others they think will be more difficult. As the groups put their charts up on the walls, it becomes clear that the different groups anticipate similar problems.

Now the group works with the Myers-Briggs Type Indicator. Participants all put their scores on a flip chart page. The facilitator describes what the grid means, then groups together people who have similar personality types. Working with the Myers-Briggs helps people to criticize themselves. With a great deal of animation and storytelling, participants discuss how their types influence their communications on projects.

Just before noon, the facilitator reorganizes the small groups to work on the Goals Statement, placing people with their counterparts from the other organizations. Each group writes two or three quantitative performance measure goals and two or three communications process goals important to the project. The groups refine their statements while eating. Over dessert, the groups present their drafts to the whole group. The whole group reaches agreement on 14 statements. Participants sign the final draft on the flip chart.

In the afternoon, people work in yet another different group, developing policies and procedures necessary to implement the goals. The senior managers draw up an Issue Escalation Process. Field staff work on procedures for managing Requests for Information, which is the paperwork people on the site file with the architect when they have questions. The owner and several of the subcontractors work on procedures for handling change orders. The future tenants, facility manager, and architect discuss how to address their interests.

All the groups end with detailed, specific plans. The whole group discusses when to meet again. Finally, they schedule the follow-up meeting.

The Partnering Solution Method

It is important to note that construction partnering is not just a meeting, not just "venting," "networking," "planning," or "getting to know each other." An intelligent infrastructure and thoughtful agenda provide the foundation for construction partnering to achieve lasting results.

We have led more than 50 successful construction partnering programs and another 50 successful partnering programs outside construction using the partnering method for outsourcing, mergers, strategic alliances, sales, support, and interdepartmental coordination in large organizations. Based on these cases, we define the method inherent in the Partnering Solution as having four steps:

1. *Arrange a meeting of the key people involved in the situation.* In some cases, this may be difficult in itself. Even if meeting initially seems easy, it can be difficult to determine who should attend partnering meetings. Consider who is involved, who holds influence, and who can disrupt things later on.

2. *In the meeting, follow the five-part partnering agenda.* It's important to discuss all five of the items—Taking Stock, Building Trust, Clarifying Goals, Implementing Key Processes, and Raising the Bar. It's also important for each discussion to result in specific action plans.

3. *Schedule a follow-up meeting at the end of the first meeting.* Don't wait until trouble arises. At the follow-up, track the group's progress on its own goals and processes, address new issues, and explore opportunities.

4. *Schedule additional follow-ups at proactive intervals.* Meetings should occur soon enough to anticipate and avert new issues. Use the principal of "preventive maintenance" that automobile manufacturers use.

Beyond the core method of the Partnering Solution, we have also identified a number of factors that enhance partnering effectiveness:

❑ *Improving meetings skills.* Running partnering meetings for optimal participation, performance, innovation, and creativity.

❑ *Increasing one-on-one collaboration skills.* Building grassroots one-on-one skills to advance partnering goals.

❑ *Strengthening partnering leadership.* Developing models and practices for leadership that fit with and reinforce partnering.

❑ *Putting your own house in order.* Getting organizations to be "partnering-ready."

❏ *Rethinking partner selection.* Choosing better partners from the outset.

The Partnering Solution Method

1. *Arrange a meeting of the key people involved in the situation.* This may initially seem easy, but it can be difficult to determine who should attend partnering meetings. Consider who is involved, who holds influence, who can disrupt things later on.

2. *In the meeting, follow the five-part partnering agenda.* It's important to discuss *all five* of the items and to result in specific action plans for each:
   a. Taking Stock.
   b. Building Trust.
   c. Clarifying Goals.
   d. Implementing Key Processes.
   e. Raising the Bar.

3. *Schedule a follow-up meeting at the end of the first meeting.* Don't wait until trouble arises. At the follow-up, track the group's progress on its own goals and processes, address new issues, and explore opportunities.

4. *Schedule additional follow-ups at proactive intervals.* Meetings should occur soon enough to anticipate and avert new issues. Use the principal of "preventive maintenance" that automobile manufacturers use.

Beyond the core method of the Partnering Solution, several other factors enhance partnering effectiveness:

❏ *Improving meetings skills.* Running partnering meetings for optimal participation, performance, innovation, and creativity.

❏ *Increasing one-on-one collaboration skills.* Building grass-roots one-on-one skills to advance partnering goals.

❏ *Strengthening partnering leadership.* Developing models and practices for leadership that fit with and reinforce partnering.

❏ *Putting your own house in order.* Getting organizations to be "partnering-ready."

❏ *Rethinking partner selection.* Choosing better partners from the outset.

Why the Partnering Solution Works

In your typical teambuilding exercise the employees are subjected to a variety of unpleasant situations until they become either a cohesive team or a ring of car-jackers.

—Scott Adams, *The Dilbert Principle*

What makes the Partnering Solution successful? Some teambuilding exercises are indeed as unproductive as the ones that Scott Adams describes. Even teambuilding that is thoughtful and intelligent often fails or falls far short of its original goals. The Partnering Solution succeeds because it differs from most other teambuilding activities in five important ways:

1. *Most teambuilding aims to increase participants' awareness.* The Partnering Solution aims to produce lasting results. Increasing individual awareness is a noble and often valuable goal, but the Partnering Solution also aims to produce lasting, tangible results. The Partnering Solution deals with real issues and develops actual processes and procedures.

2. *Most teambuilding activities begin with a solution—for example, "Let's go white-water rafting." The Partnering Solution begins with participants defining the issues.* Even when participants think they are familiar with the issues, effective partnering workshops all begin with an open discussion of what's working, what isn't, what is likely to work, and what will likely cause problems. Beginning with discussing the issues builds buy-in to partnering activities and agreements.

3. *Most teambuilding activities involve an intact team. The Partnering Solution involves a cross-organization, multilayered group.* Effective partnering involves a vertical cross-section from key organizations—for example, the owner of the architecture firm, the architect who did the design, and the person back in the office who will correct the drawings. The multilayer approach builds in internal checks so that internal issues in the partnering organizations are surfaced and addressed as needed.

4. *Most teambuilding focuses on one type of issue—for example, "trust" or "self-esteem." Construction partnering addresses different scopes of concerns from goals to people issues to procedures.* Sensitivity training, assertiveness skills, and Myers-Briggs workshops all impart useful information; however, none of

these combines work with both "micro" people-issues and more "macro" concerns of strategy and structure as partnering does. Combining focus not only addresses more, but also links micro and macro issues.

5. *Most teambuilding activities are one-time events. The Partnering Solution involves multiple workshops and builds in ongoing work and follow-through between workshops.* Most teambuilding activities attempt to achieve results by the sheer power of the insight they deliver in a one-time activity. Construction partnering attempts to achieve results by tracking action items over the course of the project. When done effectively, partnering de-emphasizes the partnering workshop and stresses instead the ongoing work of monitoring partnering results over the whole project. Making partnering ongoing is essential to ensure lasting results.

How the Partnering Solution Differs From Other Teambuilding	
Other Teambuilding	**The Partnering Solution**
Aims to increase participants' awareness.	Aims to create lasting, tangible processes and results.
Begins with a solution.	Begins with participants defining issues.
Involves one intact team.	Involves multiple layers from several organizations.
Focuses on one activity.	Works at both micro and macro; uses the five-part partnering agenda of Taking Stock, Building Trust, Clarifying Goals, Implementing Key Processes, and Raising the Bar.
One-time effort.	Ongoing.

2

A Partnering Solution Album: 12 Key Case Applications

This chapter has two goals:

1. To clarify what the Partnering Solution is and how it can produce significant outcomes.

2. To enlarge readers' "target" uses of the Partnering Solution. Most people who work with us begin with one or two specific partnering applications. After working with the concepts, however, they often realize that they can appply the partnering methods in several other situations.

Learning From Cases

Human beings, who are almost unique in having the ability to learn from the experience of others, are also remarkable for their apparent disinclination to do so.

—Douglas Adams

One way to clarify what the Partnering Solution is and what outcomes it can produce is with an "album" of typical case applications. In this chapter we briefly chronicle 12 Partnering Solution applications we have worked with. Six of these are "external partnering" between organizations; the other six are "internal partnering" between departments in the same organization.

Each of the 12 cases can occur in three different ways:

1. Problem-solving, as when problems arise between organizations or departments.

2. Exploring opportunities, as when things are working well between organizations or departments.

3. Strong start, or using partnering to kick off a new relationship, and accelerate the development of effective communications and the building of trust.

For example, companies can use the partnering solution to strengthen their relationships with customer organizations when problems occur in those relationships, when things are going well and they want to explore opportunities or when a relationship has ended and they want to learn from it.

Some of the information in this chapter is repetitive because the partnering solution produces somewhat similar outcomes in a wide array of applications. Nonetheless, we repeat the lists of outcomes and component parts of partnering because we have encountered many program participants who have found such examples useful. The examples help them to broaden their own abilities to anticipate where working with partnering methods might be used to improve communications and performance.

12 Key Partnering Solution Applications

Between Organizations		Between Departments in Organizations	
Application	**Outcomes**	**Application**	**Outcomes**
Customer Satisfaction	• Increased customer satisfaction. • Increased repeat business. • More even relationship.	Internal customer (accounting, IT, human resources, facilities, training).	• Improved quality of service and customer satisfaction. • Overall organization performance.
Merger/ Acquisition	• Faster, smoother mutual acceptance of peers/processes. • More effective problem-solving and exploration of opportunities.	"Departments at War" (turf wars, conflict over resources, overlapping responsibilities).	• Resolution of conflict. • More focus on overall organization. • Clarification of goals and roles. • Lasting processes.
Strategic Alliance	• Fully developing the potential of the alliance. • New products and services.	Advisory departments have responsibility but limited authority (statistics department).	• More effective use of advice. • Increase value of advisor group to the organization.
Preferred Vendor	• Increases in savings and quality to customer. • Increased revenues to vendor.	Monitoring departments (audit, quality assurance).	• More effective auditing. • Less conflict. • Better use of monitors' resources.
Project/Multiple Organizations	• Coordination and communication. • Reduced duplicated effort or waste. • Improved service.	Handoffs—for example, between multiple shifts or between departments working in sequences.	• Improved overall production. • Lasting processes for improved communications.
Outsourcing	• Optimal use of service provider expertise. • Reduced conflict.	Multiple departments working together— for example, all the departments involved in getting a software product out and updated.	• Improved communications. • Increased productivity. • Increased revenues. • Better resource use.

Partnering Between Organizations: Customer Satisfaction

A large customer likes the company's product, but dislikes its communications processes and tone so much that the customer begins to look for another supplier.

Typical Scenarios

❏ *Solving problems.* A customer organization registers continuing dissatisfaction and complaints.

❏ *Strengthening a good relationship.* Service or product provider wants to make a good relationship with customer organization even better.

❏ *Strong start.* Service or product provider wants to get new customer relationship off to a strong start.

Typical Agenda

❏ Addressing or anticipating customer complaints.

❏ Achieving optimal customer satisfaction.

❏ Clarifying expectations for customer responsibilities.

❏ Increasing mutual understanding.

Likely Obstacles

❏ Difficult history on either side.

❏ Arrogance on the part of the company providing the service or product.

❏ Inflexibility and complex existing procedures on the part of the customer organization.

Potential Outcomes

❏ Increased customer satisfaction.

❏ Creation of new processes for communications.

❏ Development of new products and services.

❏ Increased profit for service provider.

❏ Increased savings and convenience for the customer organization.

Partnering Between Organizations: Merger/Acquisition

Partnering provides methods and tools to accelerate the building of trust and understanding, and to develop the processes necessary to make the merger work at every level of both organizations.

Typical Scenarios

❒ *Solving problems.* Merger of two organizations looks good on paper but "stalls" when people in the two organizations conflict with each other.

❒ *Exploring opportunities.* Two organizations in merger don't conflict but don't really merge either and continue to work as if the other organization does not exist.

❒ *Strong start.* Both organizations begin merger by clarifying goals and relating the merger to individual job priorities.

Typical Agenda

❒ Concerns about job security and duplication.

❒ Reconciling how different cultures and values of the organizations can work together.

❒ Increasing mutual understanding and trust.

❒ Improving communications.

Likely Obstacles

❒ Fear about job loss and career planning.

❒ Mutual misunderstanding and mistrust (for example, "We just don't like those people").

❒ Pride and arrogance.

Potential Outcomes

❒ Combined strategy, structure, and job integration.

❒ Development of effective processes for essential communications.

❒ Development of new products and services.

❒ Acceleration of building mutual understanding and trust.

Partnering Between Organizations: Strategic Alliance

Partnering provides tools and strategies to translate the goals of the alliance into the everyday jobs of employees at all levels.

Typical Scenarios

❐ *Solving problems.* The organizations in an alliance are locked in conflict with each other.

❐ *Strengthening a good relationship.* A strategic alliance is working well, and could be expanded to include new products or services.

❐ *Strong start.* Both organizations want to get a new relationship off to a strong start.

Typical Agenda

❐ Addressing communications problems.

❐ Clarifying the goals of the alliance.

❐ Relating the goals of the alliance to the daily work of participants at all levels.

Likely Obstacles

❐ Participants' limited experience with alliances.

❐ Inability of participants to relate the alliance to their own work.

❐ Arrogance on the part of either company.

❐ Inflexibility and complex existing procedures on the part of either organization.

Potential Outcomes

❐ Resolution of obstacles and problems.

❐ Effective, lasting communications procedures.

❐ Development of new products and services.

❐ Acceleration of organizations in the alliance working together.

Partnering Between Organizations: Preferred Vendor

Partnering enables the preferred vendor to streamline its ordering processes and demonstrate that it is providing superior savings.

Typical Scenarios

- ❒ *Solving problems.* A customer organization registers continuing dissatisfaction and complaints with service or product provider
- ❒ *Strengthening a good relationship.* Service or product provider wants to make a good relationship with customer organization even better.
- ❒ *Strong start.* Service or product provider wants to get new customer relationship off to a strong start.

Typical Agenda

- ❒ Addressing communications problems and tangles.
- ❒ Clarifying the goals of the relationship.
- ❒ Relating the goals of the relationship to the daily work of participants at all levels.
- ❒ Increasing mutual understanding and trust.

Likely Obstacles

- ❒ No incentive seen by customers to use preferred vendor.
- ❒ Communications procedures from other arrangements not workable for preferred vendor.
- ❒ Arrogance on the part of either company.
- ❒ Inflexibility and complex existing procedures on the part of either organization.

Potential Outcomes

- ❒ Resolution of obstacles and problems.
- ❒ Development of effective, lasting communications procedures.
- ❒ Development of new products and services.
- ❒ Acceleration of organizations in the relationship working together.

Partnering Between Organizations: Outsourcing

Partnering enables the facility's service provider to learn more about the customer's communications needs and develop communications processes to deliver its services.

Typical Scenarios

☐ *Solving problems.* Using partnering to address problems with communications, service quality, or delivery after the outsourcing relationship is in place.

☐ *Exploring opportunities.* Using partnering when outsourcing is going well to improve already high levels of service and to explore new services and innovations.

☐ *Strong start.* Using partnering to anticipate and address communications issues that are likely to arise.

Typical Agenda

☐ Addressing conflicts and miscommunications.

☐ Clarifying outsourcing goals.

☐ Relating outsourcing to the daily work of participants.

☐ Increasing mutual understanding and trust.

Likely Obstacles

☐ Anger and mistrust.

☐ Different communications styles in the two organizations.

☐ Inability of participants to relate outsourcing to their own work.

☐ Arrogance on the part of either company.

☐ Inflexibility and complex existing procedures on the part of either organization.

Potential Outcomes

☐ Resolution of obstacles and problems.

☐ Effective, lasting communications procedures.

☐ Development of new products and services.

☐ Acceleration of the organizations' ability to work together.

Partnering Between Organizations: Project/Multiple Organizations

In multiple organization situations, the Partnering Solution provides structure and skills to get the most from each organization.

Typical Scenarios

❑ *Solving problems.* Using partnering to address communications and coordination problems and conflicts.

❑ *Exploring opportunities.* When the project is going well, using partnering to explore innovations and efficiencies.

❑ *Strong start.* Using partnering at the outset of the project to clarify project goals and establish workable processes.

Typical Agenda

❑ Addressing communications problems.

❑ Clarifying project goals.

❑ Developing communications processes.

❑ Increasing mutual understanding and trust.

Likely Obstacles

❑ Limited experience with alliances.

❑ Inability of participants to relate the alliance to their own work.

❑ Arrogance on the part of either company (for example, "Why do we need you?").

❑ Inflexibility and complex existing procedures on the part of either organization (for example, "We've always done it this way").

Potential Outcomes

❑ Resolution of obstacles and problems.

❑ Effective, lasting communications procedures.

❑ Development of new products and services.

❑ Acceleration of organizations in the alliance working together.

Internal Organization Partnering:
Service Departments (Accounting, IT, and Facilities)

Partnering enables internal service departments and their customers to better understand their differences, clarify goals, and implement more effective procedures.

Typical Scenarios

❒ *Solving problems.* Using partnering to address communications problems and misunderstandings.

❒ *Exploring opportunities.* When things are going well, to improve and streamline systems.

❒ *Strong start.* Using partnering with a new department or a new department manager to clarify goals and establish workable communications processes for all.

Typical Agenda

❒ Improving full implementation of required procedures.

❒ Improving required procedures to make them easier to follow.

❒ Increasing mutual understanding, respect, and trust.

❒ Developing lasting communications processes.

Likely Obstacles

❒ Significant differences in communications style.

❒ Different values and priorities.

❒ Arrogance on the part of either department.

❒ Inflexibility on the part of either department.

Potential Outcomes

❒ Large outcomes for the organization. In the accounting department example, improved communications contributes significantly to improved profitability of the whole firm.

❒ Effective, lasting communications procedures.

❒ Development of new products and services.

❒ Acceleration of organizations in the alliance working together.

Internal Organization Partnering: "Departments at War"

Even in the best organizations, departments occasionally find themselves "at war" with each other. Partnering helps resolve the battles.

Typical Scenarios

❑ *Solving problems.* Using partnering to surface, address, and resolve communications conflicts and misunderstandings.

❑ *Exploring opportunities.* When things are going well, to improve and streamline systems.

❑ *Strong start.* Using partnering with new departments or managers to clarify goals and establish communications processes that manage conflict in a positive way.

Typical Agenda

❑ Reducing unproductive conflict and mistrust.

❑ Breaking deadlocks and communications lockdowns.

❑ Developing communications processes.

❑ Increasing mutual understanding, respect, and trust.

Likely Obstacles

❑ Significant differences in communications styles.

❑ Different values and priorities.

❑ Arrogance on the part of either department.

❑ Inflexibility on the part of either department.

Potential Outcomes

❑ Large outcomes for the organization. In the development and quality assurance example, improved communications contributes significantly to streamlined processes and improved quality and performance in the product.

❑ Effective, lasting communications procedures.

❑ Acceleration of departments working together effectively.

Internal Organization Partnering:
Advisory Departments (Statistics and Design)

Many organizations house advisory departments that, though employing smart people, deliver less than optimal returns to the organization. Partnering can develop more effective methods for engaging and using in-house experts.

Typical Scenarios

❑ *Solving problems.* Using partnering to redefine how an advisory group relates to other departments.

❑ *Exploring opportunities.* When things are going well, explore the advisory relationship and develop enhancements.

❑ *Strong start.* Using partnering with new advisory groups to clarify goals and establish communications processes.

Typical Agenda

❑ Increasing the influence of the advisory department.

❑ Redefining the goals of the advisory department.

❑ Developing communications processes that reinforce the goals.

❑ Increasing mutual understanding, respect, and trust.

Likely Obstacles

❑ Unclear lines of authority in the organization. Limited support for the advisory department and senior management.

❑ Other departments fail to fully acknowledge the department's value.

❑ Unclear organizational charter for the advisory department.

❑ Arrogance on the part of either department.

Potential Outcomes

❑ Advisory group increases the value it delivers to the company.

❑ The research process benefits from increased quality and speed.

❑ The advisory group and the other departments it works with develop improved, lasting communications processes to ensure effective dialog.

Internal Organization Partnering: Monitoring Departments

Partnering helps the monitoring department to maintain its edge while also developing processes that work more effectively to translate its recommendations into viable actions.

Typical Scenarios

❏ *Solving problems.* Redefine how a monitoring group relates to other departments. Develop methods for effective dialog.

❏ *Exploring opportunities.* Explore the monitoring relationship and develop enhancements and innovations in what the advisory group does.

❏ *Strong start.* Clarify goals and establish communications processes in new monitoring groups.

Typical Agenda

❏ Clarifying which aspects of the monitoring group's performance work well and which need improvement.

❏ Clarifying and perhaps redefining the goals of the monitoring department.

❏ Developing communications processes that reinforce the goals.

❏ Increasing mutual understanding, respect, and trust.

Likely Obstacles

❏ Unclear lines of authority in the organization.

❏ Track record of adversarial relationship with the advisory group.

❏ Unclear, changing organizational charter.

❏ Arrogance on the part of either department.

Potential Outcomes

❏ Monitoring group increases the value it delivers to the company.

❏ Monitoring processes improve, increasing in quality and speed.

❏ Departments being monitored internalize the goals of the monitoring process.

❏ Improved spirit of communications.

Internal Organization Partnering: Handoffs and Interdependencies

Partnering provides structure and methods for day shifts and night shifts to develop brief handoff processes that ensure essential communications flow between shifts and improve overall productivity.

Typical Scenarios

❐ *Solving problems.* Break logjams and longstanding rivalries among interdependent groups.

❐ *Exploring opportunities.* Have both departments develop processes to make handoffs even better in order to enhance the overall production and quality processes.

❐ *Strong start.* Using partnering with new handoff situations to clarify goals and establish communications processes.

Typical Agenda

❐ Clarifying what is working well and what needs to be improved in the handoff.

❐ Clarifying and eliciting buy-in to clear goals for an effective handoff.

❐ Developing communications processes that reinforce the goals.

❐ Increasing mutual understanding, respect, and trust.

Likely Obstacles

❐ Often longstanding track record and history of conflict and mistrust between the departments engaged in the handoff.

❐ Each department fails to fully acknowledge the department's value and challenges.

❐ Unclear organizational charter for how the handoff should work.

❐ Arrogance on the part of either department.

Potential Outcomes

❐ Improved processes generate increased overall productivity and efficiency.

❐ Increased morale and job satisfaction.

❐ Lasting, clear processes for effective communications at the handoff point.

Internal Organization Partnering: Multiple Departments

Partnering enables the companies with communications gaps between its departments to develop much more effective alignment among all its departments, and this results in sharp gains in productivity, profit, and morale.

Typical Scenarios

☐ *Solving problems.* Surface and catalog the full range of communications gaps and overlaps across departments. Developing methods for more effective coordination.

☐ *Exploring opportunities.* Enable all departments to further improve coordination and to re-engineer and innovate to enhance overall productivity and performance.

☐ *Strong start.* Introduction new products or large-scale systems in the company to clarify goals and establish communications processes.

Typical Agenda

☐ Clarifying what is working well and what needs to be improved.

☐ Eliciting buy-in to clear goals for improved coordination.

☐ Developing communications processes that reinforce the goals.

☐ Increasing mutual understanding, respect, and trust.

Likely Obstacles

☐ Large scale of project, large group coordination.

☐ Initial inability of departments to relate to all the others.

☐ People identify more with their department than with the overall organization.

☐ Arrogance on the part of any department.

Potential Outcomes

☐ Improved processes increase overall productivity and efficiency for the organization.

☐ Innovation in processes and communications.

☐ Increased alignment of all staff to company goals.

☐ Improved morale and positive organization culture.

Core Case Organizations' Partnering in Different Situations

All of the core case organizations used formal partnering in several different applications, both internally among their own departments and externally with other organizations.

SEi Companies
(Mechanical, electrical, and plumbing engineers)

"We've had experience with the formal project partnering with a number of our larger, more complicated projects," explains CEO Bob Gracilieri. "Those exercises have always helped the specific projects, and they've had larger effects on our firm also. People have always brought the skills and the strategies, as well as the expectations, to other projects they work on.

"We also used a very formal partnering process, 'the Partnering Solution,' in two other ways: both for mergers and for our strategic planning. With mergers, the formal partnering approach helped us to spot some serious flaws and break off one merger. And it helped us clarify and speed up a successful merger. For strategic planning, the formal partnering process helped us develop a business plan that links with our strategic goals, and then translate the plan into individual action items for our principals."

ADS Financial Services Solutions
(Systems integration and software consulting)

"Our current processes mirror the Partnering Solution quite a bit. Our proposal process builds in Taking Stock. We do a lot to Build Trust. And we have what we call the 'Big Q' process that works in detail to clarify goals. We use our own internal processes, working with our project management office, to make sure that we achieve those goals," notes EVP Erik Golz. "And we follow similar processes in our partnering with other service providers. We work with other consulting firms on many projects, and we have developed great methods for working with them.

"There is a potential for our internal project management office to get into a fair amount of 'positive conflict' with the projects they oversee. So we work very hard to make sure that everyone is on board for the department's goals and methods for working with projects. Getting the project managers' buy-in to all this has made the department's work more effective in the end."

Lee Kennedy Co., Inc. (Construction)

"We've done formal construction partnering on a number of projects, and that's always been valuable," remarks Lee Michael Kennedy, president. "We follow almost the same agenda—Taking Stock [and] Clarifying Goals, Processes, and Procedures—for our internal project start-up meetings.

"Internally, we recently made a big change in our accounting department. The old regime was too rigid, too controlling, not effective enough with communicating. It wasn't quite as bad as 'Departments at War,' but there was a lot of conflict. And the conflict was the worst kind of conflict: unproductive. In redefining the accounting processes, we very much followed a partnering set of goals internally."

Keyes North Atlantic (Electromechanical contractors)

"We haven't actually done formal partnering meetings on a job, but we probably should have, especially on our bigger jobs," Business Development Manager Brad Keyes observes. "What we have done, though, is to incorporate the pieces of the Partnering Solution in our regular meetings. In particular, we find that discussing and formalizing goals is a useful thing to do, even on small jobs.

"We've also used a kind of Partnering Solution in working with other companies providing services. As we get bigger, we get more and more opportunities to quickly ramp up to take on larger projects. We bring in staff from a few other firms that do the same kind of work we do. But we have had to develop thorough processes to make sure that they do the work following our standards. Partnering Solution methods have worked very well for that."

PCA Architects

Principal Eric Brown comments, "The part of formal partnering that has had a huge impact on our overall business has been the survey and interview work we did. We had an outside firm conduct surveys and interviews of clients, stakeholders, and unsuccessful proposals, and that generated ideas we have been able to build on for more effective partnering overall.

"The survey results weren't completely surprising, we kind of knew how they would come out. But the details did surprise us, and they gave us information that helps us better understand our clients. We have put some of this to use and we are already seeing positive results. Also, just the act of surveying was positive. Clients appreciated it; they said it showed our commitment to partnering."

Foliage Software

"We actually follow the Partnering Solution steps pretty closely in most of our partnering engagements," notes Semiconductor Division Manager Norm Delisle. "In particular, we do a lot of work with Taking Stock and Clarifying Goals. What's working, what's not working, and what the real goals of a project should be are seldom immediately clear.

"We also have numerous processes and procedures to ensure that our deliverables are on track. And we have to do a lot to build trust and earn our client's confidence in our ability to deliver. In many cases, people in the client organization worry that we are going to put them out of a job. We have to work specifically at building relationships so that people can see the success of the engagement as a win-win situation."

3

4 Classic Partnering Cases

> The four cases in this chapter provide a more in-depth look at how the Partnering Solution works in some of the most typical Babel Problem situations. The 12 cases in the album in Chapter 3 illustrate the Partnering Solution by outlining their variety and the different ways each scenario put the Partnering Solution to work. The four cases in this chapter provide more detail about the Partnering Solution by going into greater depth. The four cases are:
>
> ❏ Between organizations: Customer Partnering and Mergers.
>
> ❏ Within organizations: Departments at War and Quiet Standoff.

In-Depth Cases

The essence of success is that it is never necessary to think of a new idea oneself. It is far better to wait until somebody else does it, and then to copy him in every detail, except his mistakes.

—Aubrey Menen

The cases in this chapter provide Partnering Solution details so that you can copy others' successes and avoid their mistakes. The four cases track how the Partnering Solution works in situations that occur frequently between and within a broad range of organizations:

❏ *New Project/Customer.* A software service provider company lands a new account with a large bank. Using the

Partnering Solution, they can build a strong foundation between the software company and the bank.

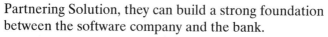 *Merger/Acquisition.* Two engineering firms with different areas of expertise, different client bases, and different regional markets have strong potential to provide a broad range of services. Using the Partnering Solution, they can capitalize on these strengths while also addressing significant cultural and values differences.

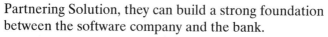 *Departments at War.* It seems that as long as anyone can remember, the architects and their accounting department have been "at war" over procedures, requirements, priorities, and differing communications styles. Using the Partnering Solution, they can reduce conflict, improve the relationship, and increase profitability in the organization.

 Quiet Standoff. The hundreds of statisticians in a global pharmaceutical company are brilliant and hardworking, but underutilized by the company's researchers and marketing staff. Using the Partnering Solution, they can redefine the statisticians' role and the relationship between the statisticians and the departments with which they work.

Beyond enabling you to understand the Partnering Solution and "make it happen" in your own situations, we also want to help you broaden your sense of where you can use the Partnering Solution. Participants in our partnering seminars consistently expand the range of applications they have for the Partnering Solution in the course of the seminar program. They usually begin with one, perhaps two uses for the Partnering Solution. Most often, these are problem and conflict situations.

Engaged in case analysis, discussion, and skills development in the seminar, they usually broaden the range of applications for the Partnering Solution to include situations that are not only blatant Babel Problem standoffs and conflicts, but also more subtle and informal communications and performance issues. Often, they identify situations that are not problems at all, but rather opportunities: situations that are working reasonably well, but could also stand to be improved.

All four cases are fictitious in the sense that the names of the people and companies, and the specific events in each case are fictitious. However, each case is based on real events, often involving a mix of actions and results from several real situations.

4 Classic Partnering Solution Cases

❑ *New Project/Customer.* A software company wins a new account with a large bank. New projects and clients present excellent opportunities to use the Partnering Solution to build a strong foundation, address immediate concerns, accelerate people getting to know and trust each other, and elicit buy-in to partnering at all levels of the organization.

❑ *Merger/Acquisition.* Two engineering firms with different areas of expertise, different client bases, and different regional markets have strong potential to provide a broad range of services. Here, the Partnering Solution provides a method to capitalize on these strengths while also addressing significant cultural and values differences.

❑ *Departments at War.* The accounting department in the architecture firm is supposed to be a service department but is actually "at war" with the rest of the organization. The Partnering Solution provides structure and process to address and reduce conflict, improve the relationship, and increase profitability in the organization.

❑ *Quiet Standoff.* The hundreds of statisticians in a global pharmaceutical company are brilliant and hardworking, but underutilized by the company's researchers and marketing staff. The Partnering Solution can redefine the statisticians' role and relationship with the departments with which they work.

Case 1:
New Project/Customer Partnering

Synergy Software and Global Bank

Every time an organization begins a new project, every time an organization begins work with a new client, the Partnering Solution provides an excellent foundation for a productive relationship. Both organizations enter partnering with extensive experience in their own worlds and with no negative history and no ongoing tangles or problems to unravel.

In our case, Synergy Software lands a new client. This not only means that new revenue will be coming into the company, supporting its growing army of top-ranked software technicians, it also means that there will be new opportunities to push the limits of the technology and develop fresh concepts and approaches.

Similarly for Synergy's client, Global Bank, it's usually positive to be able to work with a technically skilled, experienced service provider such as Synergy. Global has an experienced, motivated IT staff, but it is still limited by its lack of perspective on what goes on in the rest of the world. Working with Synergy can provide not only solutions and manpower, but also an influx of new ideas.

Partnering Challenges/Obstacles

Landing the Global Bank account intrigued Synergy's programmers, analysts, and data architects, but it also worried them. They had heard about Global's poor internal communications, weak infrastructure, and resistance to change from peers inside the organization and from occasional articles in the business press. Software firms that worked with Global described them as a "difficult" client, with different departments giving different and often conflicting commands to the software companies. Though knowledgeable, Global's staff also had a reputation for reacting to external suggestions as if they were being threatened.

For their part, Global's staff had mixed feelings about Synergy. They were aware of Synergy's technical expertise, but concerned about Synergy's reputation for developing elegant technologies their clients did not want or need. They worried about Synergy providing enough information about what they were doing so that Global could provide meaningful input. They worried about their own ability to speak with one voice, to provide Synergy with clear direction.

Partnering Agenda

Not senior executives, but a group of four middle managers, two from each company, proposed the formal partnering effort. Senior executives on both sides were bemused and a little skeptical, but they blessed and supported the partnering because they had confidence in their middle managers. The middle managers decided to invite a large contingent of people to the initial partnering meeting: some of the senior executives from both companies, as well as mid-level and some junior staff who would be responsible for implementing the details of the arrangement.

In the Taking Stock discussion in the meeting, people from both organizations openly discussed all the concerns they had raised privately about how the work between the two organizations would take shape. Global's IT staff members led the charge, voicing their concerns about getting the solutions they needed. Synergy's consultants responded quickly with their worries about getting timely approvals from Global's complex organization.

Participants wrote and signed a Goals Statement that responded to the concerns they raised. In the Goals Statement, they developed quantitative goals for Global's turnaround time on requests for information and approvals. They also signed off on a satisfaction goal for Global's IT staff. Some participants were reluctant to sign the Goals Statement initially, but they all joined in after the majority expressed their support.

The group then worked at developing procedures that would enable them to achieve the goals. This aspect of the meeting took the most time. Several small groups of people from both organizations developed outline drafts of how one procedure might take shape. They presented their drafts to the whole group for input and left with detailed plans for implementing the processes in the coming months.

The group moved onto discussing their personality profiles. They were interested but not really surprised to discover that more than half of the group, of about an equal proportion from both organizations, fit into one personality type category from the Myers-Briggs Type Indicator. The type they fit into, ISTJ, is noted for its reliability, persistence, attention to detail, as well as for its stubbornness, resistance to change, and tendency to under-communicate. They agreed that this information should remind them to work extra hard to be more flexible and communicate more than their first impulses may lead them to do.

The group concluded by planning a follow-up meeting six months after the initial meeting to track their progress on their goals and processes.

Partnering Results

At the follow-up, participants noted that they were making reasonable progress on the goals. None of the processes they anticipated at the initial meeting were taking shape exactly as the group had anticipated, but all of the processes were working in encouraging ways. At the meeting, the group refined the processes and addressed a few new problems that had arisen—communications roadblocks and technology issues.

Looking back on the partnering work six months later, the group agreed that the partnering work:

❒ Surfaced all the issues that concerned people on both sides.

❒ Clarified mutual goals that all the participants thought were important to achieve.

❏ Enabled the group to develop their own processes and responses to the issues.

❏ Accelerated people getting to know each other and building mutual understanding and trust.

❏ Produced processes and procedures that have lasted over many months.

❏ Provided the foundations for a strong, positive partnering relationship.

Case 2: Merger/Acquisition Partnering

East Coast Engineering and Dawes & Lee

Mergers and acquisitions provide fertile ground for partnering work. Using the Partnering Solution with a merger or acquisition can turn a failed merger into a success or move a success to higher levels of performance.

However strong their potential may be, mergers and acquisitions often pose substantial challenges, as the two organizations involved often fail to connect with each other. People in both organizations worry about how the merger is going to affect them, and so they withhold information and participation. Often the mergers with the strongest potentials also encompass the greatest differences between the two organizations involved: different values, work styles, communications, and priorities.

In this case, the new merged organization consisting of East Coast Engineering and Dawes & Lee has the potential to land bigger, more complex, and more interesting jobs than either firm could expect to win on its own. The merged organization, if working well, also would be able to even out both organizations' fluctuating workload. When one office has a backlog of work, it would be able to draw on the other. Finally, the merger could get both offices into regional markets that have strong demand for their respective services.

East Coast initiated the merger. Operating from its base in midtown Manhattan, the firm had built itself up in its 26-year history to a staff of 140 engineers divided about equally among electrical, plumbing, heating, telecommunications, and new technologies work. Despite its success as a firm with a national client base, East Coast lacked the experience with emerging "green" sustainable engineering methods that Dawes & Lee had been demonstrating. Based in Atlanta, the 40-person regional firm had emerged as a leader in this important new market segment.

Partnering Challenges/Obstacles

Striking differences in communications, work style, and priorities marked the two firms to a point that attempting to put them into one organization seemed impossible at first. East Coast Engineering exemplified the New York approach: work hard, push your technology agenda, confront the client, and confront each other. "Hey, it doesn't mean we don't get along, it's just the way we do things," one manager observed.

Though they thought they were prepared for it, Dawes & Lee's engineers were surprised by East Coast's style, and more than a little concerned. "This will never work," a senior engineer commented. "We expected them to be assertive, but these people are animals. We will lose our clients, and even if we didn't, we would lose our dignity."

Partnering Agenda

The presidents of East Coast and Dawes & Lee each assigned a mid-level manager to develop the partnering agenda. Reluctantly at first, but with greater comfort as they got to know each other, the two communicated frequently by phone and e-mail. They planned two two-day partnering meetings. The first would be held in New York and the follow-up, two months later, in Atlanta. Participants would address the immediate conflicts, clarify goals, and outline several key communications processes in the first meeting, leaving with initial agreements and specific plans to try. They would use the second meeting to track progress, make necessary repairs, and chart a longer-term plan.

Three of the six Atlanta engineers who came for the first meeting had never been to New York before. Uncomfortable at first, they warmed to the pace, the scale, and the people by the end of the three-day visit. "They may not sound like us, but they really are, if you can just get below the surface a little," one of them reflected. "I could never work here every day, but it is fun, at least for a little while," another added.

Ten people from the New York office worked with the six from Atlanta in the partnering meeting. They met in a conference room at 8 a.m. and worked through to 6 p.m. both days. During breaks and lunches, they toured the office, meeting individually with engineers at their workstations and discussing project details, challenges, and new technologies the office was experimenting with.

The group worked through the partnering agenda, reaching specific conclusions for each. For Taking Stock, they took another look at the financial reports, assessing the merged firm's potential to enter new markets and capture new clients. The group concluded that the projections were cautious and that the merged firm could probably beat them.

For goals, the group reached quick agreement on timelines to bring Atlanta's "green" expertise to New York and for New York to train Atlanta in its marketing methods. The group struggled more with goals for how they wanted to treat each other. "You people are too sensitive— grow up!" an exasperated New Yorker blurted at one point. Ultimately, they agreed to goals to treat each other with respect, clarify their expectations with each other, and provide needed information quickly at all times. Working with the personality profiles, the group was surprised to discover that, despite their regional differences, many of them were the same "type." "No wonder we were squabbling," a junior staffer from Atlanta remarked, "we're all stubborn."

Partnering Results

Several months later at the follow-up meeting in Atlanta, participants noted that the processes they had been working on for importing Atlanta's "green" expertise and sharing work between the offices were working well— much better than expected. However, the processes for joint marketing and business development were taking a longer time to get off the ground. Reviewing the goals written at the first meeting, the group agreed they had made progress on all fronts but still had work to do. While they worked on tuning up the processes and clarifying the goals, the group also had to agree that, despite their concerns, they were getting along much better than they had anticipated. "Working through the partnering agenda helped us build the trust we need to make the business and engineering sides work," a senior engineer concluded.

Case 3: Departments at War

The Accounting Department and the Designers

Accounting is "at war" with the designers. Audit is in conflict with operations. Sales and marketing are tangled up with each other. Quality assurance and production are arguing over standards. It seems that every organization hosts some aspect of "Departments at War." This version of the Babel Problem afflicts not only large bureaucracies, but also smaller and more informal organizations. Committees in a church argue violently about choices for new furniture and lighting. Factions in a community group divide the group in their conflicts about the group's brochures.

Based in Chicago, Signature Design is a 40-year-old, 200-person architecture firm. The firm is successful professionally, with a consistent track record of winning national and international design awards. But the firm has struggled financially, seldom achieving its goals for profitability. Failing to make a profit for the past three years, the firm has been running at a growing deficit.

Chief designers in the firm place the blame for its financial problems on its accounting department. They say the seven-person department is rigid and focused on minutiae. They say the accountants don't understand the "real" nature of the design business, that they don't listen to the architects or comprehend their priorities. The accountants claim that the designers cause their own problems, that they are too arrogant (or perhaps too lazy) to use the resources the accountants are trying to provide. The accountants' requests for the designers' accounting information are curt and borderline hostile. The designers' responses to the requests are slow, incomplete, and often sarcastic.

Partnering Challenges/Obstacles

The designers openly, even proudly, admit that they are not "numbers people." They joke about their ineptitude with accounting tasks, their tendency to make mistakes with even the simplest addition and subtraction tasks, and their resistance to using project budgeting tools. They discuss their personal problems with managing finances, their unbalanced checkbooks, chronically late tax returns, and unworkable filing systems.

The accountants freely and openly admit that they frequently don't understand what the architects are talking about. They confess that they "tune out" when the architects start talking about design concepts and theory. They acknowledge that some of the standard accounting processes they use may, in fact, really not be necessary or suited for architectural practice.

Partnering Agenda

Signature's new chief financial officer proposed the formal partnering work to the firm's six design principals. The CFO came from a smaller firm that had smoother relationships between accounting and its architects. He was aware of Signature's situation as well as its history of using up CFOs. In the past seven years, no CFO had lasted more than a year in the job.

The CFO planned the partnering meeting with the one principal who was most interested in the firm's finances, also enlisting input from several project managers and one of his own staff accountants. He developed a partnering agenda for two half-day workshops spaced a month apart. To enable the designers to maintain their billable hours and client contacts, he scheduled the workshops in the early evenings.

To prepare for the meeting, the CFO developed a brief customer survey of the designers' satisfaction with the accounting department. The survey results contributed to the sober tone at the outset of the meeting, documenting high levels of mutual dissatisfaction. The results also helped to reinforce the perspective that the problems between the designers and the accountants were essential to resolve in order for the whole firm to succeed.

It took the group nearly an hour to write a Goals Statement that everyone could agree on. The accountants pushed for clear timeliness goals for the architects to follow in sending them project budget, expense, and time-sheet information. The designers advocated for more qualitative goals concerning how the accountants talked to them.

The group started to work on streamlining the reporting processes that the designers found so cumbersome. Surprising the designers, the accountants immediately acknowledged that the forms they were using asked for levels of detail that were not really necessary. They divided into three groups, with two accountants in each, to work on making the forms more realistic.

More important, the group devised a major shift in the whole framework of their communications, moving from accounting's "We have an open-door policy, come see us if you have any problems" to "We will have scheduled meetings, planned to occur before problems arise." Several participants did not think this proactive approach would work because it seemed too formal, but most thought it would enable accountants to spot problems while they were still small and easy to address. Everyone agreed to try it for a few weeks to see what it produced.

In the final hour of the meeting, group members explored their personality profiles. They noted how the architects and accountants' profiles differed completely, and in ways that would fuel their miscommunications and conflicts. The CFO reminded both groups that the preferences were not licenses to neglect important tasks, and both groups responded with expressions of intentions to work harder at the tasks that needed to be accomplished.

Partnering Results

At the follow-up meeting, the group reported that they were making excellent progress on their goals. The designers had been meeting nearly all their financial reporting requirements, and the streamlined forms were providing the accountants with the information they needed. More significantly, the change from meet-as-needed to scheduled meetings had surfaced numerous small problems the accountants were able to resolve quickly. "Each time I found a new problem, I wondered what would have happened if we had been meeting 'as needed,'" one of the accountants commented. "This approach is much better, and it keeps the tone of our communications positive."

Case 4: Quiet Standoff

The Clinicians and the Statisticians

There's little conflict when statisticians advise clinicians in the pharmaceutical company that their multimillion dollar research project may not pass review by the Food and Drug Administration. The conversations are collegial, polite, brief, often even friendly. But the calm tone of the discussions can mask their ineffectiveness and failure to address serious problems. When clinicians ignore a statistician's advice, the result can be catastrophic. The clinicians can proceed with plans that are faulty and, ultimately, quite expensive to repair. Once in awhile, the faulty plans slip through FDA scrutiny and propel a flawed drug into the marketplace. There, it may produce life-threatening side effects.

Quiet Standoffs exist in many organizations and alliances. Any situation where people and departments are in advisory roles, where they have responsibility but limited authority, provides fertile ground for a Quiet Standoff. Typical examples include safety departments, financial advisors, quality committees, planning departments, and "watchdog" committees.

Quiet Standoffs also exist when departments doing similar work fail to share information and communicate adequately with each other. The FBI and CIA have been engaged in a kind of Quiet Standoff for many years, resulting in devastating intelligence failures for the nation. On a much smaller scale, one of the more striking Quiet Standoffs we encountered involved two departments providing similar services for a large consulting firm. Their Quiet Standoff surfaced on the day when they met in a client's office and realized they had competed and bid against each other for a major project.

In our sample case here, a statistics department tries to redefine its role in a large pharmaceutical company. Spread throughout the company's research facilities around the world, the hundreds of statisticians in the group are hardworking, but underutilized by the company's clinicians, researchers, and marketing staff. Executives would like to see the statisticians become more proactive and more involved in the research process. They would like to see researchers make better use of the statisticians, and they would like the statisticians to be more active partners in the research process.

Partnering Challenges/Obstacles

Many recommendations that the statisticians make cost the clinicians in increased project spending, or worse, delay the project. The clinicians claim that the statisticians provide input that is "interesting" but often impractical. They contend that the statisticians are overly cautious and frequently obscure, that they recommend extensive statistical work because they like the work, not because it is really needed.

The statisticians claim that the clinicians are not cautious enough, that the company rewards them too much for making their schedule and not enough for statistical prudence. Unlike a "Departments at War" situation, people discuss these problems reluctantly and quietly. They temper their concerns and criticisms with praise for each other's high levels of technical knowledge, dedication, and hard work. From a distance, it seems that relationships between the two groups are cordial. They attend group social events and barbecues, and play Frisbee together every Thursday.

Redefining the statisticians' role is a major initiative for the company because the research process strongly and directly affects the company's bottom line. The company initiated partnering between the statisticians and clinicians shortly after the FDA denied approval to a major study. The denial cost the company tens of millions of dollars. Senior managers reviewing the project's internal history were surprised to find that, months earlier, memoranda from the statistics group voiced the exact concerns that the FDA later concluded. The company appointed a working group of eight statisticians and seven clinicians to improve dialog between the departments.

Partnering Agenda

Meeting twice a month for several months, the group began by studying the track record of their dialog, a task that proved difficult because of the frequent movement of people from one project to another. Nonetheless, a concerted effort made it clear that numerous project delays and failures could be traced back, not to problems with the science, but with the dialog between the two departments.

The working group initially struggled with developing goals that provided useful guidance for their problems. The group members agreed easily that the primary goals were to both ensure patient safety and to maximize efficiency. But they disagreed on more detailed goals. How long was long enough? How big a sample was necessary? The group did make some headway in focusing on the statisticians' role. Clinicians initially drafted goals that placed the statisticians in a policing role, but the statisticians thought it was important to participate more as equal team members.

To achieve their goals, the group developed processes to ensure that statisticians were involved in projects earlier in the planning and research design phases. They also clarified key milestones in the research process when the groups could meet informally to exchange ideas before they got locked into a formal decision. The group worked briefly with their personality profiles, but they thought the work was useful because it pointed out that nearly all of the group members were "introverts." They laughed at this, but also used it. Acknowledging that they often under-communicated, they increased their initial plans for frequency and length of meetings between the groups.

Partnering Results

Brought into the research design and planning process earlier than usual, the statisticians were able to make a few important suggestions. On one project, their input saved hundreds of thousands of dollars as they were able to suggest more streamlined approaches that still maintained validity. On another project, the statisticians' early input brought to an early halt a research design that was fundamentally flawed. This input led to cost increases, but the discussion was positive and cooperative because it occurred early enough in the discussions the level of emotions was low. In both cases, both sides agreed that the process for early involvement was valuable.

4 Classic Partnering Cases and Their Results	
Type of Partnering	**Outcomes**
New Client/New Project Partnering: Synergy Software and Global Bank	• Surfaced all the issues that concerned people on both sides. • Clarified goals that all participants thought were important. • Enabled the group to develop their own processes. • Accelerated people getting to know each other, building mutual understanding and trust. • Produced processes and procedures that have lasted over many months.
Merger:East Coast Engineering and Dawes & Lee	• Processes for importing Atlanta's "green" expertise and sharing work between the offices were working well. • Both offices used "green" skills and methods. • Four projects had shared work successfully between the two offices with few miscommunications or gaps. • The processes for joint marketing and business development were taking a longer time to get off the ground. • Reduced conflict; increased trust.
Departments at War: The Accounting Department and the Designers	• Increased number of designers doing financial reporting. • Streamlined forms working effectively. • Accounting had identified dozens of small problems in the scheduled meetings and addressed the problems easily. • Process of scheduled meetings in place. • Increased profitability resulting from better reporting. • Reduced conflict, more positive communications.
Quiet Standoff: The Cliniciansand the Statisticians	• Lasting process for earlier statistician involvement in the research process. • Positive project results stemming from earlier statistician involvement in projects. • Improved tone of communications. • More effective research process— more valid and more efficient.

4

Taking Stock: Assessment Strategies and Tools

"Taking Stock" is the first part of the Partnering Solution. In this task, the people in the group for a new partnering arrangement discuss how they anticipate the arrangement will go. In ongoing partnering, people assess how the arrangement is working. Either way, this work taps into the "wisdom of the group" and stretches everyone's perspective beyond their immediate concerns.

Anchoring Partnering in Reality

I believe in looking reality straight in the eye and denying it.

—Garrison Keillor

Effective partnering begins by attempting to look reality straight in the eye, not denying it, and building on it. We call this "Taking Stock." Neglecting or ignoring the partnering tasks of Taking Stock will build serious flaws into any partnering efforts that follow, no matter how well those efforts may be designed. Conversely, if Taking Stock tools are developed and used well, they provide a strong foundation for partnering that is not only free of problems, but pushes the potential of the partnering relationship.

Taking Stock consists of a set of tools to measure and assess a partnering relationship, to identify what's working well and what isn't, and to surface new opportunities the relationship can explore. Taking Stock tools are simple, inexpensive, and easy to work with. They provide essential data about partnering performance and expectations.

These four Taking Stock tools can help people in partnering situations:

☐ *Group Discussion: Perceptions.* The first thing the group does at a partnering workshop in an ongoing partnering situation is to discuss how the relationship is working. Groups should do this in partnering situations including customer partnering with an ongoing customer, an ongoing strategic alliance, or work with an internal service department such as an accounting department and its internal customers. In this type of discussion, the partnering group lists major aspects of the relationship that are working well and other major aspects that need to be improved.

☐ *Group Discussion: Predictions.* In a new partnering arrangement, people do not yet have perceptions of each other or of the arrangement, but they do have insights, concerns, and hopes. Thus, in a new partnering arrangement, the Taking Stock discussion consists of having the group discuss its expectations and best guesses about major factors that are likely to go well in the arrangement and other major factors that are likely to be difficult. Groups should do this in partnering situations including new projects and clients, mergers and acquisitions, and new alliances.

☐ *Satisfaction Surveys.* Brief, well-designed customer satisfaction surveys provide valuable clarity for Taking Stock discussions in numerous partnering situations: customer satisfaction, outsourcing, internal service departments, and so on.

☐ *Mutual Perceptions Surveys.* These surveys are useful in partnering arrangements among organizations or departments that generally hold equal levels of status and power; for example, in Mergers/Acquisitions, Departments at War, and Quiet Standoff. Further useful data is provided by 360-degree communications surveys of key individuals in each of the partnering organizations. Data from the 360-degree survey surfaces information about individual communications styles. It often provides recipients of the data with information about specific aspects of their communications approach. The specificity of 360-degree survey data makes it useful in providing insights that people can turn into specific, realistic actions.

Taking Stock Generates Important Outcomes

Taking Stock tools generate different, important kinds of outcomes for partnering: valid information and increased buy-in to partnering solutions.

The information provided by Taking Stock anchors goal-setting and provides guidance for prioritizing key actions and processes that the partnering needs to develop. Customer partnering that responds to valid data about customer sentiment is much more likely to address the most significant issues than customer partnering that responds to several random complaints and testimonials.

Information also contributes to more productive discussions because it takes the sting out of personal criticisms. It's much easier for people to maintain their dignity while reviewing critical survey data than it is for those same people to respond to critiques of their individual performance. Many people say they welcome criticism and suggestions, but few people respond positively when the criticism comes.

More than providing useful information, the process of Taking Stock also increases buy-in to Partnering Solutions. Dozens of studies of technological change identify one key factor as the chief reason that people resist using new solutions to problems, even when the solutions are clearly beneficial: in order for people to optimally implement a solution, they need to be involved in defining the problem. Taking Stock tools involve people in a partnering relationship in defining the problems in the partnering.

Taking Stock taps into the "wisdom of the group." This philosophy believes that groups possess huge resources in terms of their own experience, learning, and resources. The purpose of Taking Stock is not to impose a solution from some external source, but rather, to work with the group at hand. Taking Stock helps a group to surface and organize the insights and resources it already has.

At a more practical level, Taking Stock also plants the seeds for other partnering tasks; tasks that generate actions. People develop goals for partnering to achieve in response to the issues and opportunities raised in Taking Stock. The processes people develop to help achieve the goals often address problems and opportunities originally surfaced in Taking Stock.

Finally, Taking Stock provides the basis for measuring learning and improvement. After a group has developed goals and implemented new processes to achieve the goals, it should be possible for Taking Stock measures to create metrics to determine whether the processes have been successful.

On the other hand, if Taking Stock of the results of partnering actions months after the original partnering work indicates improvement, it is then both possible and likely for partnering to raise the bar. Once Taking Stock work shows gains in problem areas, it's only natural for people to began exploring opportunities, pushing the envelope, and examining new horizons.

Overall, then, it is important not to think of Taking Stock as a straight-line kind of process, as in "identify the problem, then solve the problem." The full potential of Taking Stock emerges when people use it more as a general process of inquiry, part of ongoing learning and continuous improvement rather than a one-time solution to a one-time problem.

Why People Neglect Taking Stock

Despite the importance of Taking Stock, managers who attempt to strengthen partnering relationships often skip this essential step. They cite these reasons:

❏ *We already know what our problems are; don't be negative.* Elaborating on them any further is just too much negative energy.

❏ *We really do think we know what the problems are.* Due to the sheer volume of information they receive, managers who receive frequent complaints, comments, and criticisms about partnering can understandably think they know what the problems are. These people certainly do have information, but the information they have is unlikely to accurately represent the whole other organization. In fact, and this is a crucial point about Taking Stock, feedback that comes in unsolicited is highly unlikely to accurately reflect the sentiment of the larger group. Unsolicited feedback is likely to overemphasize very high and low sentiment, people who are either very pleased or very displeased. This kind of data ignores the silent majority, a group that may outnumber the vocal majority. Developing action plans to respond to a vocal minority is clearly a risky partnering strategy.

❏ *We may not know what our problems are, but we don't really need to know.* The important thing for us is to take action. We don't want to suffer from paralysis-by-analysis.

❏ *We may not know perfectly what our problems are, but we know enough.* We have some data, some information.

❏ *It would be nice to know more about our problems, but our priorities at this time have more to do with taking action.* Maybe we'll get around to these Taking Stock activities later on, but right now we're too busy.

Each of these points can delay or even eliminate work on Taking Stock, and that's a big problem. Working at partnering without using the Taking Stock tools is like driving a car at night without turning on the lights. Knowing what's there may cause worries and anxiety, but not knowing can create far more damage.

How to Run an Effective Taking Stock Discussion: Predictable Problems and Tips

It's difficult to capture in writing the energy and emotion in a Taking Stock discussion. In new partnering situations, this is often the first time people in the different organizations have met each other, so they are hopeful, interested, and anticipating. In ongoing partnering situations, people often know each other, and the emotion is usually more negative. There are problems to address, issues to resolve. There may be some skepticism and frustration in the air as well.

Despite the fact that participants have usually received material describing what will happen at the meeting, some are surprised by the discussion. Some attend anticipating they can sit in the back and take a passive role while a few executives hash out the issues. They don't resist invitations to contribute, but it's not always what they expected or are prepared to do.

The first few minutes of discussion usually interests attendees. For many people, this is the first time they may have thought about what happens in the partnering relationship outside their own perspective. Thus, it's often possible to hear, right at the outset, comments such as, "Why didn't somebody tell me that?" and "That's going to affect my work!"

Simple group discussions of partnering strengths and weaknesses provide the lowest-effort, highest-return way for people working with partnering to try a Taking Stock activity. People in the partnering group simply discuss what's working well and what isn't. If it is the beginning of a new project or relationship, they discuss what they think will go well and what will be more difficult. This kind of meeting need not take much preparation, advance work, or expense.

However, leading a Taking Stock discussion so that it produces the information it has the potential to produce can be very difficult. Groups discussing problems and issues encounter recurring, predictable problems in discussions. Chapter 11, which discusses how to improve meetings, provides detailed information on the problems groups encounter and guidance in developing facilitation skills that address the problems.

For this chapter, it is important to note that, unless carefully facilitated, Taking Stock discussions are entirely likely to turn into unproductive "venting." Taking Stock of partnering performance, participants in a partnering workshop are likely to dwell on their criticisms and complaints, and neglect the positive aspects of the partnering relationship. Several vocal people, a minority of the group, are likely to dominate the discussion. Most people will remain silent or very quiet.

Drawing on the principles in Chapter 11, these are some guidelines to ensure that the discussion is productive in a Taking Stock exercise:

- ❏ To frame the discussion, don't ask the group, "What are your concerns?" or tell them, "List your problems." If the leader asks the group about their concerns or problems, that's what they will provide.

- ❏ A better question for a more balanced, productive discussion is: "What number, on a 10-point scale, do you think describes the overall productivity of the partnering relationship?"

- ❏ A productive follow-up question is: "What are the three most important things that are working well in our partnering, and what are the three most important things that need to be improved?"

- ❏ To make sure that every person in the group participates, either call on one person at a time in some kind of order, or form the whole group into smaller subgroups, usually threes and fours. It's often easier to ensure that people participate fully in a small group than in a large one (see details in Chapter 11).

- ❏ Record participants' responses on flip charts, not in notes that one person keeps. Flip charts make every person's ideas accessible to everyone else, and they provide the content for meeting minutes. Some groups reduce the actual chart to letter-size paper and circulate the charts without having them typed.

Facilitating a Taking Stock Discussion in a "Departments at War" Partnering Situation

"This ought to be rich," Jim LaPlante muttered to Brendan Michaels, his counterpart in the leasing group of Memory Systems' Real Estate Department. "Getting us into a room with those dim-wits from the audit department—how are we going to get anything accomplished in this meeting when we can't work with those people on a regular day?"

"Beats me," Brendan replied. "Don't they know that audit has been locked in mortal combat with us? Don't they know that audit has stopped us from leasing any of the land the company owns for the past three years? It's one thing to be concerned about safety, but audit has shut us down completely."

Brendan paused to listen to Ed Tyman, a human resources manager who worked with both departments, start the discussion. Ed assured the group that they could start the meeting sitting right where they were, in small groups with others from their own department. Brendan, Jim, and the eight other people from the leasing group sat on one side of the room. The six people from the audit department sat at their own table on the other side. Each table had a flip chart positioned nearby.

Ed approached the flip chart near Brendan and drew a line down the middle of the paper, then wrote a brief heading on the left side of the line. The heading said, "Things Audit Does to Frustrate Us." As soon as they were able to make out the words, everyone laughed. Then Ed wrote another heading on the right side of the chart "Things We Do to Frustrate Audit." This time the group smiled but stopped short of audible laughter. Ed walked over to audit's chart and posted similar headings: "Things Real Estate Does to Frustrate Us" and "Things We Do to Frustrate Real Estate."

"I'd like you, both groups, to take 15 minutes to list six or seven items in each column. Try to focus on the most important things, not just the minor annoyances. And try to be honest about both columns. This will create the agenda we will use for partnering goals and processes, so make sure you hear from everybody in your group."

For a few minutes, no one seemed to move. Then, simultaneously, both groups started filling in the columns on the left, the columns about what the other group did to frustrate them. Both groups displayed a lot of enthusiasm for their complaints, listing their first few complaints with a great deal of energy. But then rather quickly, they seemed to lose steam. By the time the groups had the left columns only half full, they began to note an item or two on the right side. Leasing listed "We give them incomplete information" and "Our memos are nastier than they need to be." Audit listed "We ask for some information we really don't need" and "Our memos are nastier than they need to be."

First to notice what the other group was writing, the audit group laughed when they noticed that leasing had listed the same comment about "nasty" memos that they had listed themselves. Stopped by audit's laughter, leasing joined in as they noticed that much of what audit listed as their frustrations were items leasing had listed as knowing they did to frustrate audit. In fact, both group's right columns matched, almost perfectly, each other's left columns.

"An excellent beginning," Ed concluded. "Let's take a short break. When we get back, I'd like you to change seats so that there are a few people from each group at each table. Then we will work on developing shared goals."

Why Survey?

Beyond discussions, several different types of surveys can enhance both the information and buy-in that Taking Stock can accomplish. Surveys provide benefits and outcomes that can be especially valuable:

- ❏ *Rational.* Listening to a group discussion, it can be difficult to accurately gauge individuals' emotions. People who sound angry about an issue may have just been annoyed at the time of the discussion.

- ❏ *Specific.* Having people rate their feelings on a five-point scale provides a much more accurate reading of sentiment than any amount of informal listening to the group could possibly provide.

- ❏ *Representative.* It's difficult in a group not to pay too much attention to the people who are speaking loudest and to neglect the quieter members. Surveys equalize opinions; all respondents' surveys hold equal weight.

- ❏ *Measurable.* By translating perceptions and opinions into numerical scales, surveys provide more accurate, clearer measures. After all, Taking Stock is supposed to include work with measuring the performance of the partnership. Surveys measure more effectively than discussions can.

- ❏ *Benchmarks.* As time goes on, it will be useful to know if and how a partnering arrangement has improved. Survey data makes this kind of comparison possible.

- ❏ *Involvement at the foundation.* When people work on formulating a survey and listing questions, they are really defining the terms of a partnering arrangement's success. Having to ask oneself what to measure in a partnering arrangement increases one's sense of involvement in the arrangement.

❐ *Improvement impulse.* Most people we have worked with respond to survey data of any kind with an impulse to improve. If the data is disappointing, people want to make it acceptable. If the data is good, most people want to figure out what to do to make it great.

Not only do surveys provide these benefits, they are relatively easy to design and administer. In most partnering situations, a well-placed survey or two will significantly enhance the quality and impact of Taking Stock and of the partnering performance overall.

Survey Applications in Partnering

It is possible to use surveys in all 12 of the types of partnering we outlined in Chapter 2. The three major types of surveys used for partnering in all these situations are:

❐ Customer satisfaction surveys.

❐ Organization or department surveys.

❐ 360-degree communications surveys.

How Different Types of Partnering Can Use Action Surveys	
Type of Partnering	**Type(s) of Surveys**
Customer Satisfaction	Survey of customer satisfaction with product, company, or service.
Merger/Acquisition	Survey of employees' opinions in each organization regarding the merger.
Strategic Alliance	Survey of employees' opinions in each organization regarding the alliance.
PreferredVendor	Survey of customer satisfaction with vendor. Survey of vendor's staff perceptions of the customer.

Chart continued on next page.

Type of Partnering	Type(s) of Surveys
Project/Multiple Companies	Survey of employees of each organization's perceptions of the project.
Outsourcing	Survey of customer satisfaction with service provider. Survey of service provider's perceptions of the customer.
Internal Customer (accounting, IT, human resources, facilities, training)	Internal customer satisfaction with service department.
"Departments at War" (turf wars, conflict over resources, overlapping responsibilities)	Employees in each department's perceptions of each other.
Advisory Departments— have responsibility but limited authority (statistics department)	Employees in each department's perceptions of each other.
Monitoring departments (audit, quality assurance)	Employees in each department's perceptions of each other.
Handoffs (between multiple shifts or between departments working in sequences)	Employees in each department's perceptions of each other.
Multiple Departments Working Together (all the departments involved in getting a software product out and updated)	All employees' perceptions of the project and/or of the overall group.

**In addition to the above, 360-degree communications surveys may be useful in all forms of partnering.

Avoiding Six Recurring Mistakes in Partnering Action Survey Method

The key word in partnering Action Surveys is the word "action." The point of many surveys is to calibrate opinions, predict markets, or assess perceptions. The point of an Action Survey is to enable people to act. Action Surveys are more like Polaroid snapshots than 35 mm portraits: clear enough to see and understand, but not detailed just for the sake of detail.

When working with Action Surveys in all forms of partnering, people make many recurring mistakes that lead to misinterpreting the data:

1. *Not including the customer in formulating the questions.* People being surveyed always provide a useful reality check on the wording of questions and the mechanics of getting surveys distributed and collected.

2. *Letting the survey expand beyond one page.* The longer a survey is, the less likely it is that people will respond.

3. *Having the survey lose focus to satisfy diverse and perhaps confusing goals.* The more unfocused a survey is, the less likely it is that people will respond.

4. *Not pre-testing a draft survey on a small pilot group of people who will receive the final survey themselves.* People who will be surveyed provide the most accurate reading of the clarity of survey questions.

5. *Confusing "a lot of responses" with valid statistical results.* Assuming that because one has received "a lot" of responses that the responses accurately represent the overall group of respondents leads to misinterpreting the data. A small sample, often of just 20 respondents, can more accurately reflect the sentiment of the larger group than 100 responses that "just come in." Responses that "just come in" are most likely to reflect the opinions of people who have strong opinions, either very positive or very negative.

6. *Not getting back to respondents.* It's important to communicate survey results back to respondents in part out of courtesy and ethics. Respondents took the time to complete the survey; they are entitled to hear what one intends to do with the results. Further, failing to get back to survey respondents likely will taint any future survey efforts. Respondents who receive surveys later on begin their responses with an edge of frustration and suspicion resulting from the information vacuum following their prior survey experience.

Responding to these problems, the following are brief guidelines for developing and using action surveys:

❑ Involve the customer in formulating and testing the questions.

❑ Keep the survey short and focused.

❑ Tabulate the surveys that come in, but then add a carefully structured sample that reflects key characteristics of the overall group (for example, size of account, volume of work, complexity of work, years of experience, and so on).

❑ Devise several action steps in response to the survey results, and test the action steps on carefully selected focus groups.

❑ Report the results of the survey and focus groups back to all respondents.

❑ Survey again in about a year.

Customer Satisfaction Survey Template

The following is a template for an effective customer satisfaction survey, along with typical data in a customer survey situation. By "typical," we mean that the survey depicts response patterns and comments that we have observed in a number of different types of partnering situations. This type of survey would be useful in partnering situations with existing customers, in outsourcing, in organizations with service departments (such as accounting and IT), an in facilities' relationship with their internal customers.

Partnering Customer Satisfaction Survey Template (Typical Hypothetical Results Based on 20 Respondents)								
The Service Provider	**Effectiveness**				**Importance to Me**			
	Very High		Very Low		Very High		Very Low	
Technical Expertise								
1. Has strong technical skills.	6	8	3	3	4	4	11	2
2. Provides innovative solutions.	5	9	2	2	3	3	12	2
3. Is adequately trained technically.	8	4	1	2	4	3	12	2
4. Uses new technologies effectively.	7	5	2	1	4	7	7	3

Chart continued on next page.

	Very High			Very Low		Very High			Very Low	
5. Performs effective technical work overall.	8	7	3	2		4	4	11	2	
Business Value										
6. Effectively balances technical and business priorities.	3	4	6	4	3	7	8	5		
7. Understands what adds value.	1	3	4	8	4	8	4	8		
8. Provides solutions that add value.	1	2	5	7	5	9	3	7	1	
Customer Partnering										
9. Provides adequate, timely information.	3	5	7	5		8	3	3	5	
10. Understands customer priorities.	1	3	8	6	2	8	4	5	3	
11. Responds to customer priorities	1	4	7	5	3	11	4	5		
12. Responds effectively to customer input.	1	4	8	4	3	10	5	4	1	
13. Listens effectively.	3	5	9	2	1	9	4	5	1	
14. Overall partners effectively with the customer.	2	4	6	5	3	9	3	5	2	
Overall										
15. Overall, I am satisfied with the service provider.	4	4	4	4	4	8	7	5		
16. I would recommend the service provider to others.	2	3	9	4	2	5	5	9	1	

Chart continued on next page.

17. The Service Provider's three greatest strengths are:
   - They know what they're doing technically.
   - Well-trained; lots of experience.
   - Interesting ideas.

18. The Service Provider's three greatest weaknesses are:
   - They don't understand our priorities; don't try.
   - They don't (can't?) listen.
   - They think they are still in school. We are a business!

19. The three most important improvements the Service Provider should make are:
   - Remember who pays their salary. Learn to be more responsive.
   - Communicate, communicate, communicate.
   - A little less arrogance would go a long way.

Analyzing and Using Survey Data

What do these results mean? How could a partnering group use them to develop useful actions and planning?

These are the issues people usually grapple with as they try to interpret survey data, along with our thoughts on how to address them:

❑ *Keeping criticism in perspective, viewing all feedback as positive.* It is easy to write this, but it is difficult to live it. Many people ask for feedback and genuinely want it. Still, when the feedback comes, it is difficult for most people to remain objective. Most people get defensive, and that is understandable. But it is also essential to maintain objectivity about the survey results if one is to derive value from them.

❑ *Interpreting the "Importance to Me" columns.* These columns create extra work for people filling out the survey and for people tabulating the results, but they provide very valuable insight. The survey questions are not all equal to each other; some are more important than others. The columns that post respondents' priorities are essential to understand and to respond to. It's not that they are right or wrong (although some people say that "perception is truth"), but that respondents' priorities are important to consider when formulating action plans.

❑ *Boiling the survey results down into meaningful, practical insights and actions.* Though the survey is brief, it provides a wealth of data. Before trying to analyze the results, it is useful to try to identify the four or five questions that matter most for the particular situation.

❑ *Understanding how a group of respondents can hold widely contrasting views on the same question.* On the sample survey, for example, the 20 respondents are equally divided in their perceptions of the service provider's overall effectiveness. This probably does not mean, as people who receive data often speculate, "We must have split personalities." More likely it could mean several different things: that the service provider treats different customers differently, that different customers have different needs, that some customers have different values, or some of all these.

❑ *Assessing the meaning of the open-ended comments.* Open-ended comments such as those in the last three questions of the survey are always interesting, often colorful, and occasionally inflammatory. ("What do they mean, 'arrogant'? I'll show them.") It's easy for people being criticized to fixate on the written comments. However, it is important to start with the numerical results and use the open-ended comments more as "color" to add tone and shades of meaning to the overall structure the numbers provide.

Features of the Survey Template

Several features of the survey template are important to note, as they help ensure that the survey provides useful results:

❑ *One-page form.* The complete survey fits on one page. This is important because a number of respondents stop completing surveys after completing a page.

❑ *Focus on key issues.* Once people start working with surveys, they often find it interesting to add questions. Before long, the survey includes many questions that are "interesting," but do not necessarily produce results that can be used. More people answer short surveys: every question that is added to a survey reduces the percentage of people who respond. Thus, it is important to keep surveys short.

❑ *Two responses for each question.* Respondents designate their perceptions of both the service provider's effectiveness and the importance of the question to them.

The dual responses are important because they often surface differences between what the customer thinks is important and what the service provider thinks is important.

❐ *Five-point scale for each response.* It's important for surveys to pick up shades of difference in respondent sentiment. There's a big difference between a far-left column response and a second column response for "Effectiveness."

❐ *Clear categories.* Statements for rating are categorized into different concerns so that respondents can clearly see the point of each section.

❐ *Open-ended questions.* The survey includes both 16 categories to be rated and three open-ended statements where the respondent can fill in his or her own thoughts and ideas.

It is easy to lose sight of these features in developing a survey as the planning often becomes increasingly complex. However, these features tend to shape surveys that produce useful data, so they are important to preserve.

Organizational Surveys

Partnering situations such as Mergers, Strategic Alliances, Departments at War, and Quiet Standoff often benefit when their Taking Stock work includes surveys of both organizations in the partnership. In all these cases, the Taking Stock discussion benefits from working with quantitative data from a group. People use the survey to crystallize key issues and test the group's sentiment. The general format and structure of these surveys follows the same design principles as those used for customer surveys.

It's possible to use an organizational survey on one's own organization or to calibrate one's opinions about the other organization in the partnership. To illustrate the categories and questions in either, we use the following sample survey.

Organization Survey Template (Useful in Mergers, Strategic Alliances, Departments at War, Quiet Standoff, and so forth.) *Use blank spaces to insert questions for your own partnering situation.									
	Effectiveness					Importance to Me			
	Very High				Very Low	Very High			Very Low
Job Satisfaction									
1. My job is challenging and interesting.									
2. I am paid fairly for the work I do.									
3. I have adequate career development opportunity.									
4.									
5. Overall, I am satisfied with my job.									
The Organization's Leaders									
6. Articulate clear vision and goals.									
7. Communicate effectively with the organization.									
8. Function effectively as a team.									
9.									
10. Provide effective leadership overall.									

Chart continued on next page.

	Very High			Very Low	Very High			Very Low
The Organization Overall								
11. Effectively utilizes new technologies.								
12. Manages employee performance effectively.								
13. Provides adequate training.								
14. Effectively involves employees in decision-making.								
15. Provides a supportive working environment.								
16. Effectively coordinates different departments.								
17. Manages change effectively.								
18. Consistently delivers high quality.								
19. Consistently delivers high value.								
20. Partners effectively with the customer.								
21.								
22. Overall, runs effectively.								

Chart continued on next page.

23. The organization's three major strengths are:
    a.
    b.
    c.
24. The organization's three major weaknesses are:
    a.
    b.
    c.
25. Three important changes the organization should make are:
    a.
    b.
    c.

360-Degree Surveys

Some aspects of partnering success have to do with organizations, some with strategy and plans, some with customer satisfaction. Some aspects of partnering success depend on much more personal issues: the simple relationships and communications among people at grassroots levels. This is where partnering that looks good on paper can break down, as people simply cannot find common ground for working together. Fortunately, 360-degree surveys provide a useful tool for this aspect of partnering.

The 360-degree survey finds an individual's communications style and effectiveness. The individual typically gives the survey to six to 12 people with whom he or she works. They complete the survey and return it to a third party, usually either a consultant or a human resources department. The third party tabulates the results and provides the individual with a summary report. The report contains data and comments, but does not include any way to trace the respondents. The data is anonymous and confidential.

The 360-degree survey has become increasingly popular for management and leadership training because it provides participants with valuable data and insight. It can be difficult for people being surveyed to come to terms with the criticisms that the surveys sometimes include. (In consulting and seminars, we sometimes joke that we provide a small bottle of Scotch or Bourbon along with the survey results.) However, the hundreds of people we have worked with in 360-degree surveys say the experience provided valuable insight. The surveys make communications concerns more specific and easier for people to identify and to address.

In partnering, 360-degree surveys can be useful when partnering success really depends on peoples' ability to get along with each other and when the partnering group is small, usually less than 20 people. Specific examples include:

- ❏ *Mergers/Acquisitions.* The management team, eight people from each organization, survey the people they work with from the other organization.

- ❏ *Outsourcing.* Nine people from the customer organization and nine people from the service provider survey each other.

- ❏ *Departments at War.* Six people each, from the two departments working together, survey each other.

- ❏ *Customer Partnering.* Nine people each, from the customer and service provider organization, survey each other.

The 360-degree survey is not useful in every partnering situation. If high levels of distrust and conflict exist, the data that comes in may be warped, biased, inaccurate, or misleading. If the people leading the discussion of the results do not possess strong facilitation skills, the meeting can degenerate quickly. And if there is any question about these, we find it is better to err on the side of caution than to take risks that cause damage that cannot be repaired.

For people who are comfortable with the 360-degree survey tool, it is important to take extra care in working with 360-degree data in order to get the most from the insight it can produce:

- ❏ *Ensure confidentiality and anonymity.* It is important to do this in all surveys, but even more so with 360-degree surveys. People who are being surveyed should be able to discuss the mechanics of how the surveys will be distributed and tabulated so that they are comfortable the process preserves respondents' anonymity.

- ❏ *Use a skilled facilitator.* People receiving 360-degree survey results usually need help from an objective third party experienced in working with 360-degree data in order to interpret their survey results. In addition, the facilitator must have the skills to be able to structure group discussion so that people can address problems in a positive way.

- ❏ *Focus on key items.* As with other surveys, it is useful with 360-degree surveys to focus on the handful of questions that matter most.

- ❏ *Focus on developing action plans.* More than with other surveys, it is easy to overdo the analysis of a 360-degree survey and neglect developing thoughtful action plans. With a little focus, it is usually possible with any set of 360-degree survey results, to develop an action plan consisting of three or four key, specific changes.

	Effectiveness					Importance				
360-Degree Survey Template for Numerous Partnering Applications (Mergers, Outsourcing, Customer Satisfaction, Departments at War, Quiet Standoff) Please mark "X" twice for each question, once for the person's Effectiveness and again for Importance of the issue.										
	Very High				Very Low	Very High				Very Low
Informational/ This individual:										
1. Knows what's going on in the partnering relationship.										
2. Knows what's going on in the industry.										
3. Provides others with adequate information.										
4. Is accessible.										
5. Is approachable.										
6. Communicates clearly and completely.										
Interpersonal/ This individual:										
7. Treats others with respect.										
8. Initiates relationships appropriately.										
9. Maintains relationships effectively.										
10. Values diversity.										
11. Listens effectively.										

Chart continued on next page.

	Very High			Very Low		Very High		Very Low	
12. Works effectively with others' ideas.									
13. Participates effectively in meetings.									
14. Communicates directly.									
15. Sets a positive tone in communications.									
16. Works effectively with others overall.									
Strategic Partnering/ This individual:									
17. Effectively formulates goals and vision.									
18. Effectively communicates goals and vision.									
19. Actively supports partnering goals.									
20. Works effectively with all departments.									
21. Focuses appropriately on the overall partnership, not just on his/her projects.									
Partnering Leadership Effectiveness/ This individual:									
22. Works hard.									

Chart continued on next page.

	Very High			Very Low		Very High				Very Low
23. Manages time effectively.										
24. Follows appropriate priorities.										
25. Demonstrates strong concern for quality.										
26. Maintains a high level of ethics.										
27. Thinks effectively "outside the box."										
28. Strives for continuous improvement.										
29. Overall, leads effectively in our partnering.										

30. This person's three most important partnering communications strengths are:
a.
b.
c.

31. This person's three most important partnering communications weaknesses are:
a.
b.
c.

32. The three most important things this person should improve in partnering communications are:
a.
b.
c.

Core Case Organizations' Experience With Taking Stock

ADS Financial Services Solutions
(Systems integration and software consulting)

"An in-depth kick-off meeting is necessary to provide a strong foundation for effective partnering," Vice President Erik Golz explains. "The meeting usually takes a half day or more, and it involves people from different levels in our organization, the client organization, and whatever other organizations we are partnering with on the project.

"Taking Stock in these meetings starts with the proposal and looks ahead. We use the proposal as a work plan for the project and work through all the issues in detail. We make sure people understand all the assumptions. We anticipate all the tactical issues necessary to make the proposal work, how we're going to communicate, who is going to have to communicate with whom."

Lee Kennedy Co., Inc. (Construction)

President Lee Michael Kennedy explains, "We do a Taking Stock discussion at the beginning of many of our projects. For example, working on library construction, we draw on the individuals inside our own organization who have extensive experience working specifically with libraries. We bring them into meetings with our new library clients and have them tell the new clients what's worked well and what hasn't in past projects.

"Nine times out of 10, our new clients haven't heard of the things our staff knows. For example, there are entire categories of common building materials, things you might think it would be fine to use, that you simply cannot use in libraries because they would damage the books. Certain kinds of carpets, wall coverings, even some wood products are all out of bounds for library projects."

Foliage Software

Semiconductor Division Manager Norm Delisle comments, "The Taking Stock aspects of the partnering we do on projects is especially important. What's working and not working is often a complicated issue, dependent on what client you are working with. We typically find that we have to involve stakeholders beyond our initial point of contact in order to get a complete picture of what's going on in the organization.

"Some of our Taking Stock also takes place at the end of projects. We make it a habit to bring the project team together and review what went well and how we could improve things in the future. During this work, over and over again, we have found ways to make improvements as we go forward."

Keyes North Atlantic (Electromechanical contractors)

Service Manager Stanley McConnell notes, "A lot of our Taking Stock discussion focuses on the building code. The content of the code usually provides a baseline for what we do: it spells out the legal and safety requirements.

"In a first meeting with a client, we talk about what the code requires and what it will allow you to get away with. Other contractors try to scare clients and tell them that the code requires everything, but they are often stretching the truth. In truth, sometimes the code is very restrictive, and sometimes it is too lenient. We do a kind of Taking Stock by really looking at the real code requirements with the client. We discuss what might go well and what is likely to be more difficult. Often, we encourage clients to do more than the code requires, but we find that it's important to begin with the truth."

SEi Companies
(Mechanical, electrical, and plumbing engineers)

"We do Taking Stock discussions at the beginning of most projects. They are very effective in flushing out problems and opportunities that are likely to occur on the project," reports Mark Warren, a principal of the firm. "We've also done extensive surveys—clients, stakeholders, unsuccessful proposals, even the leadership 360[-degree] surveys. They've all been useful, all contributed to our partnering.

"Beyond those discussions, we've also actually developed an entire service that's all about Taking Stock. The service is called 'commissioning,' it's a kind of audit of the client's engineering systems: are they working up to the levels they are supposed to? We are really Taking Stock of their systems. There's not a lot of profit in this service, but it provides valuable information for the client, and it strengthens our ability to understand what the client really needs."

PCA Architects

Eric Brown, a principal of the firm explains, "We've also done all the surveys. We surveyed clients, stakeholders, unsuccessful proposals, and leadership 360s. The unsuccessful proposals survey produced interesting results, and [they were] very useful.

"We've tried Taking Stock types of discussions on several projects and had great success. We recently did one between two phases of work on a big project. The discussion enabled some of the people on the team to raise the deeper issues they had in working with each other. One member of the team felt that several others were not trusting him, and excluding him from information he needed. The others did not realize this, and the discussion enabled them to develop a better process for exchanging information on the next phase of the project.

"It's funny, because we had plenty of regular ongoing project meetings with the same group from the beginning. But blocking out the Taking Stock discussion provided the time and place so that the issue got surfaced and resolved."

5

Building Trust

Do the people get along? Do they trust each other, understand each other? Can they communicate? This, the "people" component, figures into the success of every partnering arrangement. After Taking Stock, it is useful to work at this second task of the Partnering Solution, Building Trust. It is influential and important, yet extremely difficult to quantify and work with. Yet it is also quite possible to intentionally build trust in partnering, to accelerate people understanding and appreciating each other. It's easy to say "we value diversity," but hard to do it in one's everyday work. Working at Building Trust can help.

Ninety percent of the art of living consists of learning to get along with people one cannot stand.

—Stanley Goldwyn

Some of the most potentially successful partnering arrangements put people together who are all too likely to be unable to stand each other. The unlikely, quirky combinations of organizations and departments also often have the strongest potential to produce some of the most striking results: creative people with finance people, risk-taking organizations with cautious organizations, as well as scheduled groups with spontaneous ones.

Although participants can usually see the value of these arrangements in principle, they can have a hard time living with the arrangements on a daily basis. What starts out as stimulating and interesting can easily become provocative and hostile.

Interpersonal issues also arise in partnering situations that do not involve such diverse groups. Even people who basically see things eye to eye can stumble on disagreements and differences of opinion. Most people recognize the likelihood for conflict to arise in their marriages when couples attempt to tackle joint tasks. As a result, few married couples would attempt to hang wallpaper together. And married couples have usually had more time to select each other than most partnering groups have.

Of the five parts of the Partnering Solution, Building Trust is surely the most difficult to quantify and the most complex to pin down. Taking Stock involves numbers and measures. Clarifying Goals produces strategic documents. Implementing Key Processes puts procedures into place. Raising the Bar increases performance. But Building Trust? That addresses a different set of concerns, a whole dimension of alliances and organizations that accounting, strategy, processes, and methods are likely to neglect.

Yet Building Trust is an essential part of partnering. Without trust and mutual understanding, some of the most promising partnering arrangements fail or fall far short of their potentials. And when trust and mutual understanding increase, bottom-line partnering performance usually increases as well. Because of the qualitative nature of the work done for Building Trust, some of our partnering clients have declined to work with it. They either could not see the value or did not feel that the work was needed.

In one case, a state agency acknowledged that the Building Trust work would be interesting, but felt that the other items on the partnering agenda were more important to focus on in meetings. After listening to our reasons for doing the Building Trust work, the agency relented and agreed to try it in the first of a series of projects. They assessed what the work did in the first workshop and then quickly determined that Building Trust should become a required part of the partnering agenda.

Why Building Trust Is Important

"I could never work with that kind of person," the facilities manager muttered to a friend at the end of their get-acquainted meeting with the financial managers. The senior managers of the facilities firm had agreed to partner with the financial firm to expand their range of services, increase revenues, and attract more customers. But most of the facilities managers felt the same way as the person mentioned here, they took a personal disliking to the financial managers. They commented on the ways the finance managers dressed ("all that designer logo showy stuff"), the way they spoke ("all those 10-dollar words"), and the way they smiled ("smug SOBs, aren't they?").

Building Trust is an important part of partnering work because effective partnering requires extensive amounts of problem-solving in the field at grassroots levels. Even when partnering agreements are highly detailed, new and unforeseen circumstances inevitably arise. Many loose ends remain, waiting to be tied up, not by senior managers, but by people working at grass-roots levels. In all situations, much of the work of partnering is done informally as people who are placed in relationships with each other try to make the best of the situation.

Mutual understanding and trust have several different kinds of effects on partnering results. On the downside, if trust and mutual respect are missing, there will be negative impacts for partnering results. People may hold back and fail to share needed information with each other. If they do try to work together, they are likely to be ineffective at solving problems or exploring opportunities together.

On the upside, if trust and mutual respect are strong, there will be positive impacts for partnering results. People will share information willingly and, in so doing, provide their counterparts with fresh information and insight. When it comes to solving or exploring problems together, people who trust each other are more able to focus on the issues and come up with productive, innovative results.

Why Building Trust Is Necessary

"In my day," an elderly banker assured us, "we didn't have to go in for this building trust kind of thing. It happened on its own because people worked together and got used to each other."

In some cases, this approach could still work now. But there are also three major reasons for not "letting nature take its course" and, instead, making an explicit effort to build trust:

1. *Time.* People in any situation might come to understand and appreciate each other on their own over time, if left alone. But partnering does not always have the luxury of being able to take all that time. There are projects to complete, services to provide, and bills to pay. One reason people work with Building Trust tasks is to accelerate the process of people getting to know each other.

2. *Expectations.* Senior managers expect people working at grassroots levels in partnering to quickly develop trusting working relationships. That kind of trust resembles a house with no foundation. It looks okay and stands upright. But lacking a foundation, the house is vulnerable when storms arise. A second reason people work explicitly with Building Trust tasks is to dig a solid foundation to support the working relationships.

3. *The divorce rate.* For decades, the divorce rate has hovered around the 50 percent mark. Unlike most partnering arrangements, people who get married usually choose each other and seldom have to make a profit. If divorce-scale conflict evolves in 50 percent of marriages, it should be no surprise that conflict also arises in partnering arrangements.

These three challenges of time, expectations, and the inevitability of conflict together strongly suggest that any help intentional Building Trust work can provide would be valuable.

Using Personality Profiles to Build Trust

- ❏ The Myers-Briggs Type Indicator.
- ❏ The Predictive Index.
- ❏ The DiSC.
- ❏ The Fundamental Interpersonal Relationship Orientation (FIRO) instrument.
- ❏ The RHETI Enneagram test.

These are some of the most popular in a growing number of personality profiles, surveys, and questionnaires that categorize respondents into different "types" of people.

We advocate using personality profiles to build trust as part of partnering. Other activities can certainly contribute to Building Trust, and we provide some information on those at the end of this chapter. But we focus on using personality profiles in this chapter because we have seen this approach to Building Trust achieve success in a wide variety of cases. It is also possible to use the profiles ineffectively and even, in rare cases, to inadvertently create problems with them.

But the overall gains outweigh the risks and problems to such an extent that it is worth trying to use the personality profiles as an integral part of the Partnering Solution whenever possible. In this section we provide guidelines and case examples so that readers can avoid the problems and understand how to use personality profiles to achieve the most important results for partnering.

There is an industry of personality profiles, a veritable feast of surveys, instruments, and indicators awaiting people who want to learn more about themselves and others. People use these instruments for an array of tasks besides the tasks they are useful for in partnering; tasks such as career counseling, marriage counseling, childrearing, and teambuilding.

Some companies try to use these tests to screen prospective employees or as criteria for promotion. ("We know what kind of people we want around here, Finch," and so on.) However, there is widespread and well-justified debate about whether any of the instruments is so accurate that it can predict job performance. (We are on the side that argues that the tests cannot.)

We advocate using the profiles for partnering not because they identify problem people or make it possible to zero in with pinpoint accuracy on specific problem communications, but, if used correctly, the profiles significantly strengthen the work of building trust.

There is a parallel between the way partnering arrangements can use the profiles and the way that marriage counselors use the profiles in their work with couples who are about to tie the knot. The marriage counselors don't use the instruments to reverse the choices people made in each other. As one counselor explained, "I don't use the personality profiles to eliminate arguments, I use them to help people to 'argue better.' By that I mean, I use the profiles to get people to better understand and appreciate each other, and to really listen to each other."

Working often with personality profiles in partnering applications, we observe that they actually produce a number of different results that contribute not only to Building Trust, but to other aspects of the Partnering Solution. Taking the one or two hours necessary to provide members of a partnering group with basic understanding of a personality profile usually results in these important outcomes:

- ❑ *People talk in depth about their values, identity, and deeper selves.* Discussing the question, "Which type am I?" leads people to surface information about their values, priorities, habits, and deeper selves. These are not typical agenda items in a business meeting, but they contribute significantly to building mutual understanding and trust.

- ❑ *People criticize themselves.* When most people read the descriptions of their "type," they agree with the critical and cautionary information. "This profile says I'm pretty judgmental," a partnering workshop participant comments. "Well, I can tell you that's an understatement. I can be impossibly judgmental at times!" This good-natured kind of comment does more than add humor and perspective to any workshop. It also provides others with "ammunition" to use if the person offering the self-criticism demonstrates the behavior. ("Wow, you really are judgmental!") Beyond that, offering the self-criticism makes it somewhat less likely that the person will give in to the behavior. ("My impulse is to pass judgment on that issue, but I just described how judgmental I am. Maybe I should relax a little.")

❑ *People learn that the things others do to frustrate them are not intentional, that it's just "who they are."* This is not at all to say that people should use personality profile information as an excuse. ("It says here that I tend to under-communicate. Yup, that's the way it is. You're going to have to learn to live with that.") However, when people don't understand why others do things or how others think, a part of them sometimes guesses that the person demonstrating the behavior is doing it intentionally, just to get to them. Working with personality profiles at least removes this concern.

❑ *People begin to think of themselves more as "in relation" to others than as alone.* Often, in any meeting, people focus on one question: "How does the thing that we are discussing now affect *me*?" Working with personality profiles, people focus more on the question, "How does this affect *the group*?"

In addition, personality profiles provide an important tool for people in a partnering group to gain new perspective on the group. In fact, it's also possible to use personality profiles to gain valuable insight into the overall, larger organizations involved in the partnering.

Using the Myers-Briggs Type Indicator to Build Trust

To better illustrate how using personality profiles can contribute to Building Trust, we use case examples with the Myers-Briggs Type Indicator (MBTI). We choose this profile for the case examples because it is the most widely used personality profile, so more readers will be familiar with it. We also find that the MBTI focuses on information that is especially relevant for partnering: information about how people are likely to communicate and function in relationships.

Further, we find the type labels in the MBTI less prone to misuse than those in other profiles. For example, "intuitive," a typical MBTI category label, does not imply either a positive or negative reaction. By contrast, the profile called the DiSC uses labels such as "analytical" and "driver." It can be difficult, when using the DiSC with scientists, for a participant to own up to the fact that the instrument does not label him or her as "analytical." It's awkward, among salespeople, to not wear the label of "driver."

The most widely used of the personality profiles, the MBTI is available in at least a half-dozen forms of varying length and complexity. One form alone sells four million copies a year. The mother-daughter team of Isabel Briggs Myers and Katherine Cooks Briggs, both laymen in the field of psychology, developed the instrument in the late 1940s. Educational Testing Service, purveyor of the SATs and other standardized tests, began to publish the test in the early 1950s. After that, the profile took on a life of its own, as people in a wide range of places began to use it for an even wider range of applications.

The popularity of the MBTI continues to increase, with new applications and writing emerging every year. At present, Amazon.com lists more than 100 titles whose primary purpose is to use the indicator for a particular application such as parenting, teambuilding, career guidance, marriage counseling, or personal enrichment.

The MBTI instrument sorts people on four dimensions: Introvert-Extravert, Intuition-Sensing, Thinking-Feeling, and Perceiving-Judging. The instrument follows the theories of Carl Jung, which stipulate that most people have a natural inclination, or "preference," on one side of each these dimensions. It's not so much that one is either on one side of the dimension or the other, but rather that one is placed on a continuum from one to the other. Thus, one may have a strong, moderate, or weak preference for Introversion. (The opposite of a preference is one's "shadow.")

Each dimension contains information relevant for partnering, and some of the key combinations of the dimensions provide especially relevant insight.

Introversion – Extraversion (I-E)

People with an Introvert preference are energized by their own internal thoughts and feelings. People with an Extravert preference are energized by interacting with other people and with their surroundings. This fairly simple distinction links with a number of others: Introverts are more comfortable working alone, more independent, less likely to outreach to others. Extraverts think by talking, prefer to work with others, and outreach to others comfortably and easily.

Implications for partnering. In this dimension, the big implication for partnering has to do with communication. Introverts tend to under-communicate and underestimate the need to communicate. Extraverts tend to over-communicate and overestimate the need to communicate. These tendencies affect partnering in several ways:

❐ If a partnering group includes a majority of Introverts, it may underestimate the need to meet and may plan meetings to occur too infrequently.

❐ If a partnering group includes a majority of Extraverts, it may overestimate the need to meet and may meet too often.

❐ In a mixed partnering group, Introverts will likely frustrate Extraverts by under-communicating and Extraverts will likely annoy Introverts by over-communicating.

Intuition – Sensing (N-S)

People with an Intuition preference "see the big picture." They think in images, metaphors, and symbols. They are comfortable with abstract thinking, new ideas, change, and concepts. They work on multiple tasks and struggle to complete any of them. People with a Sensing preference see details. They think in facts, specifics, and details. They are comfortable with practical thinking, consistency, and pragmatism. They work on one task at a time and prefer to follow a logical order.

Implications for partnering. This dimension of the MBTI has two implications for partnering: the issues people argue about and the ways in which they argue. Intuitives tend to value and argue on behalf of trying new ideas, advancing change, and operating at a conceptual level. Sensors tend to value and argue for paying more attention to details, following established procedures, and operating at a practical level. These tendencies affect partnering in several ways:

❐ Intuitives may underestimate the importance of routine, details, and consistency.

❐ Sensors may overestimate the need for consistency and resist change that is needed.

❐ If a partnering group includes a majority of Intuitives, it may overestimate the need to plan and not devote sufficient attention to implementing their ideas.

❏ If a partnering group includes a majority of Sensors, it may resist change needlessly, spend too much time focusing on details, and neglect longer-term planning.

❏ In a mixed partnering group, Intuitives will frustrate Sensors by focusing on conceptual issues that seem impractical to Sensors. Sensors will frustrate Intuitives by paying too much attention to small details and resisting change.

❏ In most conflicts and arguments between the two, Sensors will tend to "win." They usually recall facts that Intuitives never saw in sharp focus in the first place. Also, Sensors tend to argue logically, arraying their facts in neat, sequential precision, while Intuitives tell stories, relate anecdotes, and wander off point.

Thinking – Feeling (T-F)

People with a Thinking preference make decisions through logical analysis. One joke is that when asked if they are hungry, Thinkers reply with the question: "I don't know, what time is it?" People with a Feeling preference make decisions more by a "gut" feeling. To the same query about being hungry, they might reply by discussing in detail the feelings of hunger they are experiencing. Thinkers communicate more often by criticizing, and they struggle with praising adequately and sincerely. Feelers communicate more often by encouraging, and they struggle more with asserting themselves, conflict, and disagreement.

Implications for partnering. This dimension of the MBTI has major implications for partnering in the ways people connect at a deep level. Thinkers tend to focus on the qualitative aspects of partnering, neglecting the qualitative and human sides, and alienating Feelers in the process. Feelers work with, but can also get lost in, the human elements of partnering. Thinkers in a partnering group can inadvertently hurt the feelings of Feelers—and perhaps not care about it! Feelers can annoy Thinkers by their emotional reactions to what Thinkers might assume are simple issues. These tendencies affect partnering in several ways:

❏ If a partnering group includes a majority of Thinkers, it may underestimate the Feeling reactions of the plans it makes; consequently, incurring resentment by people who feel the group is cold, unappreciative, and insensitive. Thinking groups can also be overly negative and pessimistic in their planning.

❐ If a partnering group includes a majority of Feelers, it may dwell on feelings issues and avoid conflict. Feeling groups may take an overly optimistic stance about progress and downplay real problems facing the partnering.

❐ In a mixed partnering group, Thinkers will likely frustrate Feelers with their critical comments and Feelers will likely irritate Thinkers with their emotionality.

Perceiving – Judging (P-J)

This dimension is about planning and passing judgments. People with a Perceiving preference like to keep their options open, view planning as an obstacle, and seldom make strong judgments. Perceivers are more spontaneous, more flexible, and more live-and-let-live. People with a Judging preference like to accomplish tasks, settle things, and move on; view planning as essential in order to accomplish things; and judge people and things readily. Judgers are more scheduled, more rigid, and more focused on getting things done according to plan.

Implications for partnering. The implications of this dimension for partnering have more to do with action than with communications. Perceivers tend to neglect planning and rely on spontaneity to get things done. Judgers tend to plan a great deal and rely on organization and structure to get things done. These tendencies affect partnering in several ways:

❐ If a partnering group includes a majority of Perceivers, it may underestimate the need to plan, schedule, structure, and organize its work.

❐ If a partnering group includes a majority of Judgers, it may overestimate the need to plan, plan too much, and plan with too much rigidity.

❐ In a mixed partnering group, Perceivers will likely frustrate Judgers by diverging from plans to which they have committed. This can be extremely upsetting for Judgers, who will likely say that the Perceivers are "unreliable" and "untrustworthy." Judgers will frustrate perceivers by planning too much and by sticking with plans that, over the course of time, lose their relevance. Perceivers will likely express their dissatisfaction less than Judgers will, but Perceivers will act by losing enthusiasm and allowing commitments to slip through their fingers.

Myers-Briggs Type Preferences and Their Likely Implications for Partnering		
Type	**Contributions to Partnering**	**Potential Problems**
Introvert	Focus on task. Discretion.	Under-communicates. Secretive.
Extravert	Alert to external issues. Creates energetic environment.	Over-communicates. Indiscrete.
Intuition	Sees big picture issues. Works with concepts.	Neglects key details. More planning than action.
Sensing	Attends to key details. Orderly and organized.	Resists change. Neglects big picture.
Feelings	Provide encouragement. Recognize, address feelings issues.	Avoid conflict. Get "lost" in emotions.
Thinking	Objective, fair. Unswayed by emotion.	Cold, negative. Critical, challenging.
Perceiving	Flexible, responsive. Easygoing.	Irresponsible. Unpredictable.
Judging	Drives to completion. Scheduled and focused.	Rigid, judgmental. Overly serious.

Putting Myers-Briggs Into Action (By Type)

It's a good thing for people in a partnering group to simply learn about their own type and the types of the others in the group. It's a better thing to engage the group in two kinds of discussions, one about their interpretation of the information for themselves, and another about their interpretation of the information for the whole group.

Once people know what types they and the other members of the group are, it is useful to have all the group members respond to the following questions. They can write their responses or just discuss them. It's often stimulating to group people with others who are similar types as they develop their responses. The questions are:

1. Overall, how accurate is your type description in describing you?

2. What are five things that you *value*—that is, place a high priority on—that your type would help to explain?

3. What are five things that you are *naturally good at*—for example, aptitudes, natural talents, and abilities—that your type would help to explain?

4. What are five things that others *criticize you* for that your type helps explain?

These specific questions are important to address for partnering. The first one allows people to accept whatever level of the MBTI information they'd like without having it forced on them. It also enables them to clarify that perhaps they are really a mix of two or three types. The second question is extremely important. People typically don't talk openly and clearly about their values, yet their values drive many of their actions. The third question gives people an opportunity to enjoy the positive aspects of their type. The final question opens up the self-criticism that adds levity to the group and provides information that will often be useful as the group tries to accomplish tasks together.

Putting Myers-Briggs Into Action (Whole Group)

Beyond its ability to help people better understand each other on an individual basis, the MBTI can also help people in a partnering group make some smart guesses about the likely strengths, weaknesses, issues, and opportunities of groups. In order to do this, each person in the partnering group posts his or her MBTI scores on a grid that lists all 16 MBTI types (16 possible combinations of the eight types). In doing this, it is useful to list each person's name and his or her score on each of the four letters that represent Introvert or Extravert, Intuition or Sensing, Feeling or Thinking, and Perceiving or Judging.

Once the names and scores are listed on the chart, the group then uses the chart to predict how the group is likely to handle predictable issues that are likely to arise in the course of partnering work. This exercise is a larger group version of the kind of discussion that counselors have with couples anticipating marriage. In the partnering version, the group discusses the question:

What does the mix of MBTI types say about us as a group?

1. Is there a clear majority of one type that dominates the group? Or are there clear majorities or groupings?

2. If there are, what are the groupings, the similarities, the dissimilarities?

3. Which, if any, types are not included in the partnering group? (Often, the types that are missing from a group say

as much about the group as the types that form the majority or plurality.)

What does our MBTI type grid predict or suggest about us as an *overall group*?

4. What partnering tasks are we likely to value?
5. What partnering tasks are we likely to be naturally good at?
6. What partnering tasks are we likely to struggle with?
7. What partnering tasks are we likely to neglect?

What does our MBTI type grid predict or suggest about issues among subgroups and individuals within our larger group?

8. Who is likely to get along with whom else? (Like types tend to get along more comfortably than disparate types.)
9. Who is likely to conflict and disagree with whom else? Are there clusters of people who will be in predictable conflict with each other?
10. If there are groups that will predictably be in conflict, what kinds of issues are the conflicts likely to focus on?
11. Who is the group most likely to ignore or reject? (Groups tend to ignore and/or reject people who differ most from the majority of the types in the group.)

Sample Group Profile on Myers-Briggs Type Table

This Departments at War partnering situation involves a finance department attempting to provide services to and partner with a design department.

Ian, Jeremy, Lois, Justin, Bob, Beth, and Ted are in a design department. Kathy, Dave, Nancy, Joan, George, Harry, Lydia, Gary, and Jan are in the finance department.

(This fictional mix reflects the actual mix in similar, real partnering situations.)

ENTJ	INTJ	ENTP	INTP
Ian – H, M, M, M	Jeremy – M,H,M,L Lois – M,M,L,H	Kathy – L,M,H,M	Justin – H,M,L,M
ENFJ	**INFJ**	**ENFP**	**INFP**
Bob – H,H,L,M	Beth – L,M,H,M	Dave – H,H,L,L	
ESTJ	**ISTJ**	**ESFJ**	**ISFJ**
Nancy – M,M,L,H Joan – L,L,H,M	George – H,H,M,L Harry – M,M,H,H Lydia – H,H,M,L	Ted – L,L,M,M	Gary – H,H,M,L Jan – H,M,M,L
ESTP	**ISTP**	**ESFP**	**ISFP**

Keys to interpreting the table:
Preference Scores
H = High
M = Moderate
L = Low
Thus both George and Harry score in the ISTJ type box; however, George's Introvert preference is more pronounced than Harry's. Harry's Judging preference is more pronounced that George's.

Interpreting the Sample Grid

Using the sample grid as content for the discussion questions on pages 102–103, the responses would be:

1. Is there a clear majority of one type that dominates the group? Or are there clear majorities or groupings? *With the exception of just one or two people, there are two clear divisions.*

2. If there are, what are the groupings, the similarities, the dissimilarities? *The design department consists mostly of Intuitives; the finance department consists mostly of Sensors.*

3. Which, if any, types are not included in the partnering group? (Often, the types that are missing from a group say as much about the group as the types that form the majority or plurality.) *There are no people in the bottom row. This is the "SP" temperament, characterized by attention to detail without rigidity. Some people label these types as a "Crafts" temperament.*

What does our MBTI type grid predict or suggest about us as an *overall group*?

4. What partnering tasks are we likely to value? *With so many Judging people, the group is likely to value scheduling, planning, and closure on tasks.*

5. What partnering tasks are we likely to be naturally good at? *Same answer as 4.*

6. What partnering tasks are we likely to struggle with? *Tasks that benefit from more open scheduling and less planning. The group will also struggle with any tasks that require unanimity as the Sensing – Intuitive split is likely to fuel differences of opinion on many issues.*

7. What partnering tasks are we likely to neglect? *Tasks that involve spontaneity, play, leisure, taking breaks, and that cannot be effectively planned and scheduled.*

What does our MBTI type grid predict or suggest about issues among subgroups and individuals within our larger group?

8. Who is likely to get along with whom else? (Like types tend to get along more comfortably than disparate types.) *The people in the top two rows (mostly the designers) are likely to see things the same way. The people in the bottom two rows are likely to see things similarly.*

9. Who is likely to conflict and disagree with whom else? Are there clusters of people who will be in predictable conflict with each other? *The Sensing – Intuition split is likely to*

reinforce existing conflicts between the designers and the finance staff.

10. If there are groups that will predictably be in conflict, what kinds of issues are the conflicts likely to focus on? *While favoring change and new ideas, the Intuitive design staff is likely to pay insufficient attention to detail, documentation, and established rules. While resisting change and new ideas, the Sensing finance staff is likely to neglect long-term planning and be overly rigid about rules, policies, and procedures.*

11. Who is the group most likely to ignore or reject? (Groups tend to ignore and/or reject people who differ most from the majority of the types in the group.) *In this sample, there is really no one who is completely isolated. However, one would worry that the ISFJ and INFJ, who can be least engaged in group discussions, might be left out of group decisions and problem-solving.*

Other Trust-Building Activities

Beyond working with personality profiles, nearly any social or recreational activity can help partnering groups accelerate their building of trust and mutual understanding. Golf matches, bowling, white-water rafting, scavenger hunts, pizza lunches, and sports events can all help people spend time together and get the information they need about each other to foster increased understanding and trust.

Some specific activities can create troublesome side effects. For example, groups that have tried to use paintball games for teambuilding report that it sometimes leads to a kind of competitiveness and physicality that offends participants. And some social activities don't really do enough to put people together in interaction. For example, one group that rented bicycles for participants to use on a short city tour reported that, though enjoyable, the cycling made it impossible for participants to converse with each other.

The most successful trust-building activities generally are those, such as bowling, which put people into small groups, make it easy to talk, make it easy to change groups around several times, and don't involve overly serious competition or physical contact.

It is important to note that it is possible to get extra mileage out of any social or recreational activity for Building Trust if, in addition to the activity itself, the group discusses a short list of "teambuilding questions" afterward. For example, after going bowling, the partnering group discusses these questions:

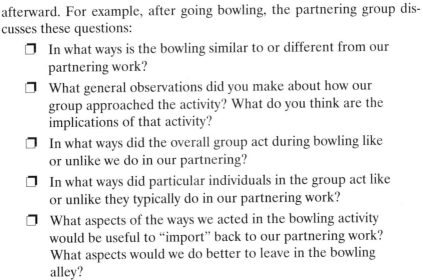

- ❐ In what ways is the bowling similar to or different from our partnering work?

- ❐ What general observations did you make about how our group approached the activity? What do you think are the implications of that activity?

- ❐ In what ways did the overall group act during bowling like or unlike we do in our partnering?

- ❐ In what ways did particular individuals in the group act like or unlike they typically do in our partnering work?

- ❐ What aspects of the ways we acted in the bowling activity would be useful to "import" back to our partnering work? What aspects would we do better to leave in the bowling alley?

Having the group discuss these questions enables it to tap into its innate "wisdom," the common set of resources and insights that it operates from. In many cases, groups behave in any activity much as they do at work. Engaging in the activity, removed from a work setting, the group can more clearly observe its processes. For example, when groups tackle a team activity such as sailing, they often retain their core processes. The same people dominate, control, withdraw, work behind the scenes, and so on. Group members may not be able to see such process issues clearly in the course of their everyday work because they are naturally more focused on their results than their processes.

Many times, also, a group's process in a recreational activity does not really reflect its behavior at work. When this is the case, it is no good trying to force analogies and comparisons that do not hold up. Just having the recreational activity available as a source for observing the group and thinking about its process can be valuable in itself, though. Helping any group learn to observe more clearly its processes can enable the group to manage the process to achieve higher levels of communications and performance.

Summary of Personality Typing

When deciphering the meaning of the personality profiles and the sample applications in the previous sections, it can be easy to lose oneself in the specifics. What type am I? What type is my group? What type is my client organization? What type is my spouse? My children?

These are compelling questions, but it is important to reiterate how they apply to partnering with three points:

1. It is possible for people in partnering relationships to build mutual understanding and trust on their own without working at it. However, many partnering arrangements benefit if the trust-building process can be accelerated by working at it explicitly, as a discrete partnering task.

2. Although the work of building trust usually progresses more quickly when it is approached as a preventive measure, it is also often both possible and necessary to work at building trust in response to problems that arise. In such situations, we use the personality profiles and recreational activities in much the same way as outlined in the previous sections. However, there is more work to do in these cases because it is necessary to go back and make repairs before it is possible to move ahead and build new trust.

3. A number of social and recreational activities can help partnering groups build trust, but personality profiles in particular provide a great deal of insight in return for a minimal investment of time and effort.

Core Case Organizations' Experience With Building Trust

SEi Companies
(Mechanical, electrical, and plumbing engineers)

"Our guys are engineers; it's not in their nature to do a lot of socializing," CEO Bob Gracilieri explains. "Most of our professional staff is introverted; we tend to work alone. We tend to under-communicate. It's not just us, it's our whole profession. We are not smooth talkers, we are the guys at the party who are standing alone in the corner.

"But we know all that. We've worked with the Myers-Briggs and we all are pretty objective about those tendencies and the problems they can create. So we work extra hard to make sure that we communicate, make contact, provide extra information. Building trust really comes down to making contact and exchanging information, so we work extra hard at it. It's still not natural to us, but we have gotten much better at it over the years because we can see that it makes a difference."

ADS Financial Services Solutions
(Systems integration and software consulting)

"To begin with, we recognize that Building Trust is a big part of partnering," says EVP Erik Golz. "Trust is necessary, and it doesn't happen automatically just because you talk about it. It's something you have to identify and work at. One way we work at it is to do events that involve the whole project group. A lot of it is around meals and sporting events. Any setting where you can put people together and let them find out 'He's not such a demon after all,' helps build trust back on the project.

"I have to make sure that it happens in managing my staff, too. It can be hard to control personalities. My counterpart in the organization we partner with and I both have to intervene at times and make sure our staffs get along with each other. It doesn't mean there's any kind of fundamental flaw, it's just a thing that you know you have to address. Then, the trust flows from that work."

Lee Kennedy Co., Inc. (Construction)

"People might be surprised to know how much effort I put into working with the personality profiles to build trust," CEO Lee Michael Kennedy comments. "People think, 'Construction workers thinking about personality profiles?'

"But we've actually done quite a bit with the profile on projects. And what would be even more surprising to people: I can't agree more that this is the most essential part of partnering. The essence is how to build trust among people who haven't worked together before, people who don't know each other. The Myers-Briggs gives all the participants self-awareness. It makes you aware of your own deficiencies. For example, when the Myers-Briggs material suggests that you may not be a good listener, it reminds you to listen to others. You can't partner if you don't listen."

Keyes North Atlantic (Electromechanical contractors)

Keyes North Atlantic CEO Susan Keyes has worked with the MBTI in training programs in the company and on her own for more than 15 years. She points out, "Figuring out which clients are Sensing and which are Intuitive is a lifesaver. You'll lose a client over that difference more than anything else. If a Sensing client wants lists and you don't hear that or don't give them, they'll perceive you as being dishonest. We've tried to develop a writing style that intentionally meets the communications needs of both Sensors and Intuitives, and we use it with e-mail as well as formal correspondence.

"I also think e-mail has helped to build trust. Some of our competitors don't use it; they don't like it. But I think e-mail builds trust and, intrinsically, it supports partnering. It's informal, fast, and there's a track record. It creates a feeling of a real person. Any time the person out there is a real person, you're more likely to build trust."

Foliage Software

"Our White Papers contribute a great deal to Building Trust," explains co-CEO Ron Rubbico. "There are over 70 White Papers on our Website, addressing technical issues of real interest to our customer base. Each paper has enough depth to add value and demonstrate real competence, but is concise enough to be approachable. Moreover, they all go through a rigorous internal review process to ensure high quality. About 30 members of our staff have written the papers, so the effort is spread through the organization.

"The papers work to build trust because they demonstrate to new clients that we can provide something valuable before we walk in the door. Before we had all the papers, we routinely spent a half hour of each client presentation building credibility. Now with the papers, most prospects know who we are, so we can get to work much more quickly.

"That having been said, it's demonstrating results that builds trust more than anything. On our engagements, we typically produce our first deliverables within the first couple of weeks. Our client's confidence in our ability to deliver is greatly increased when they see the rapid progress we are able to make."

PCA Architects

Eric Brown, a principal of the firm, explains, "We do a lot of parties, a lot of social events on projects. Maybe it's because that's our business: designing dining halls, restaurants. There's always food around. I think it's also because some of our senior people came from firms that were impersonal, and they vowed it would be different here. The social events definitely build trust with the whole project team.

"Working with the Myers-Briggs helps us, too. We haven't done that on projects, but we use it internally. For me, the biggest use of MBTI is realizing how I affect each other [person]. It's gotten me to understand some of the more introverted clients we work with and tone down some of the extraverted parts of what I do so that we have a stronger connection."

6

Clarifying Goals

After Taking Stock and Building Trust, Clarifying Goals is the third step in the Partnering Solution. In some cases, people might be tempted to skip this step, it may seem unnecessary. But the work of Clarifying Goals, producing a written Goals Statement, signing the statement, and using the statement thoughtfully increases partnering effectiveness.

The Work of Clarifying Goals

You've got to be very careful if you don't know where you're going, because you might not get there.

Yogi Berra

Yogi knew about the importance of goals: about both their ability to help you figure out where you're going and their ability to help you get there. Written and used thoughtfully, partnering goals can help partnering arrangements on both these counts.

Most partnering arrangements begin with some goals before a partnering group meets. Beyond these, it is very important for the partnering group to write its own Goals Statement, making the original goals more specific. The Goals Statement usually addresses two kinds of goals: performance (quantitative) goals and communications (qualitative) goals.

Writing a Goals Statement is just the beginning of the work of clarifying goals. The Goals Statement can provide valuable focus, harmony, and metrics that the partnering arrangement can use for many months.

Deriving the full value of the tool requires that it be written and implemented thoughtfully. Following these steps is a beginning:

❐ *Engage the whole partnering group.* Some partnering groups give the work of clarifying goals over to a limited group of senior managers. This approach may be efficient, but it is not very effective. Engaging the whole partnering group always brings fresh insight and useful new perspectives to the Goals Statement. And engaging the whole group in writing the goals solidifies their commitment to fully implementing the goals long after the partnering workshop has ended.

❐ *Link the partnering goals to the insights achieved in the Taking Stock work.* Taking Stock clarifies the issues and opportunities partnering faces. Clarifying Goals answers the question: "How would you, the partnering group, like to address these issues?" It's not that all of the partnering goals need to address the issues identified in Taking Stock; many worthy partnering goals may stand on their own. But some part of the Goals Statement should address the major issues that Taking Stock identified.

❐ *Draft five to eight performance goals and five to eight communications goals.* The distinction between *performance goals* and *communications goals* is useful. Both are important in order for partnering to succeed. Performance goals are quantitative, technical, and professional. They may include items such as revenue, profit, and quality. They are usually easy to quantify and measure. Communications goals are more qualitative. They have more to do with how members of the partnering group treat each other, what characteristics they want the group to have. Though more difficult to count, they usually can be quantified in some way.

❐ *Develop a "balanced scorecard" for both performance goals and communications goals.* It's useful to keep the concept of "balance" in mind when writing goals. In other words, performance goals should include a range of goals from profit to quality, from productivity through craftsmanship. Communications goals can include items about both taking partnering seriously and being sure to have fun while doing it.

❐ *Make sure that the goals address outcomes and not methods.* When discussing communications goals, partnering groups sometimes consider drafting a goal that "We will meet every month." This is not a goal, it is about a procedure. If the group did meet every month, what would they hope that would accomplish? They usually say that meeting every month would ensure that all group members got the information they need in a timely way. That is more like a goal. And focusing on that goal often leads back to reconsidering the procedure. For example, if we really want all group members to get the information they need in a timely way, maybe we need to meet weekly instead of monthly.

❐ *Use the ASMART form for writing all goals.* Many groups fall short in this area, proposing partnering goals such as "We will achieve high levels of quality" or "We will achieve excellent customer satisfaction." These goals may be inspirational, but they are not helpful to provide focus for ongoing partnering work. ASMART is the acronym for Agreed upon, Specific, Measurable, Attainable stretch, Results-oriented, and Time-bound. Using these descriptors for writing goals makes them more specific, and making them more specific makes them more usable. An ASMART goal for the topic of quality might be "We will achieve quality levels of 99.5 percent." An ASMART goal for customer satisfaction could be "We will achieve 90 percent excellent customer satisfaction and no significant complaints within three months of the initiation of partnering."

❐ *Refine the Goals Statement until all the members of the partnering group are willing to sign it.* Having all the members of the partnering group sign the Goals Statement can be a very useful way to ensure that they are fully committed to the content of the goals. Telling the group at the outset that you will be asking them to sign what they write usually results in their taking the Goals Statement work particularly seriously. Getting to a point that all group members are comfortable signing the statement may take awhile. In many cases, it is useful to draft a Goals Statement in an initial partnering workshop. Between the initial workshop and the follow-up session, a small, representative group revises the draft to make it smooth and coherent. This also provides an opportunity for all the members of the group to get comfortable with what they are signing and to provide one more vehicle for them to make revisions.

❏ *Have all the members of the partnering group sign the Goals Statement.* It's possible to make just a bit of a ceremony of this, as it does represent important agreement and a foundation of understanding in the group. Groups can sign the Goals Statement as it is written on a flip chart page, or they can sign a printed version.

❏ *Use the Goals Statement as a scorecard.* Once people have agreed to goals, it is often worthwhile to have the group score each goal to reflect their perceptions of how well the group is doing at reaching its own goals. People can write a number from 1 to 10 after each goal to register their scores. It's often interesting to have each individual write with a different color marker so that they can see who holds what perceptions. It's usually very useful to repeat the scoring exercise every few months to chart the group's progress and surface any problem areas.

❏ *Use the Goals Statement to communicate partnering goals to everyone involved in the partnering arrangement.* Often, the people in a partnering group represent much larger groups: customers, employees, and managers. The Goals Statement provides details on the partnering arrangement that are likely to be of interest to anyone who is going to be touched in some way by the partnering in any organization.

❏ *Put the Goals Statement in key places for maximum impact.* In construction partnering, partnering groups usually make copies of the Goals Statement to be framed and hung in the construction trailer, over the coffee pot. Sometimes they copy the statement onto the large metal sign posted outside the project. One especially meaningful place they put the Goals Statement is in employees' pay envelopes; reminding all, every two weeks, that this is a partnering job.

❏ *Use the Goals Statement to track and monitor individual performance.* On one of our first construction partnering projects, the construction company's site superintendent had a communications style that grated on others in the group. The project was for a hospital, and the group's original partnering goals highlighted the need for people to communicate in a professional manner. The job was near other hospital facilities, so the hospital staff and many patients could hear conversations on the construction job. When the construction company placed the site superintendent on the job, the company's president explained the partnering goals and what they might mean for the superintendent's well-known, vocal style. Although the site superintendent vowed to "be good" and "tone it down," he proved to be unable to keep his promise. When the company moved him to a more isolated job, he didn't resist.

❏ *Update and refine the Goals Statement.* As partnering evolves, it's worth taking the time to update and revise the Goals Statement. In ongoing partnering, this should be done at least annually. It should be done more frequently, perhaps quarterly, in situations where some kind of change has altered the partnering arrangement.

The Work of Clarifying Goals: Writing, Implementing, and Full Involvement

❏ Engage the whole partnering group.

❏ Link the partnering goals to the insights achieved in the Taking Stock work.

❏ Draft five to eight performance goals and five to eight communications goals.

❏ Develop a "balanced scorecard" for both performance goals and communications goals.

❏ Make sure the goals address outcomes and not methods.

❏ Use the ASMART form for writing all goals.

❏ Refine the Goals Statement until all the members of the partnering group are willing to sign it.

❏ Have all the members of the partnering group sign the Goals Statement.

❏ Use the Goals Statement as a scorecard.

❏ Use the Goals Statement to communicate partnering goals to everyone involved in the partnering arrangement.

❏ Put the Goals Statement in key places for maximum impact.

❏ Use the Goals Statement to track and monitor individual performance.

❏ Update and refine the Goals Statement.

4 Principles for Writing Goals That Deliver Optimal Results

Just writing a Goals Statement of nearly any kind provides useful results for partnering. However, writing goals that deliver optimal results takes a little more effort and thought. It's important to begin with the ASMART framework mentioned on page 113, but that is only the beginning. Following several additional principles while writing the goals can turn a good Goals Statement into a *great* one:

❏ *Focus on identifying several key outcomes, and build the Goals Statement around them.* Usually, two or three of the statements on the Goals Statement lists are more important than the rest.

❏ *Take the time and effort to identify intelligent, tangible outcomes for goals that initially seem intangible.* For example, many partnering groups begin with a goal such as: "We will communicate well with each other." This is a noble, but not very useful, goal. Making it more useful involves answering the question: "If you were communicating well with each other, what kinds of things would be happening?"

❏ *Make sure that all the goals are an "Attainable stretch."* This descriptor comes from the second "A" in "ASMART." Attainable stretch means that achieving the goal will require some extra "stretch" effort. However, it is also important that people regard the goal as being possible to achieve in some way, or else they will consider it to be more of a good intention than a real goal.

❏ *Approach the whole Goals Statement exercise with the intention of both creating limits and boundaries and of breaking through limits and boundaries.* Useful goals do both. Some of the goals establish clear focus and create metrics that can be used later on to hold people accountable. Others should serve to inspire and motivate people.

Sample Goals Statements: From Average to Excellent

The following two Goals Statements illustrate both the typical issues people address when working on goals and the differences between average goals and excellent ones.

Outsourcing Goals Statement Between Service Provider Firm and Customer Organization *First Draft*	
Performance Goals	**Communications Goals**
Provide low-cost service to the customer.	Treat each other with respect.
Provide high-quality service to the customer. Provide predictable workflow for service provider.	Communicate problems and issues quickly, openly, and directly to the appropriate person.
Use the service provider's capabilities for maximum value.	Provide needed information in a timely manner.
Enable the customer company to focus on its core competencies.	Respect each other's values and cultures.
Make it possible for the service provider to make a reasonable profit.	Have fun; make it enjoyable. Develop the positive potential of the partnering arrangement.

Outsourcing Goals Statement Between Service Provider Firm and Customer Organization *Revised Draft*	
Performance Goals	**Communications Goals**
Provide service to the customer at a cost 50% lower than the average in the region.	Survey the partnering group every three months on all these items using a 10-point scale.
Provide high-quality service to the customer with projected error rates of less than 10% within three months and less than 5% within six months.	Aim for a level of 8 out of 10 scoring their average satisfaction for all the items, and for no items scoring below 5.
Customer provides information to service provider with at least one month notice on any changes in workflow that would affect manpower on the project.	Treat each other with respect. Communicate problems and issues quickly, openly, and directly to the appropriate person.
Use the service provider's capabilities for maximum value such that the value of the services the customer receives is 33% higher than the simple dollar cost.	Provide needed information in a timely manner. Respect each other's values and culture. Have fun; make it enjoyable. Develop the positive potential of the partnering arrangement.

A Personal Note:
The Unlikely Importance of Clarifying Goals

The whole notion of Clarifying Goals seemed unnecessary to us at first. We came very close to omitting this part of the Partnering Solution when we first facilitated partnering workshops for construction projects for two reasons.

First, we could not image that there was any need for the group to clarify goals. Like most construction projects, this one had a contract several hundred pages in length, spelling out specifics and contingencies at a level of detail that left nothing whatsoever to the imagination. What could be left to clarify? The goal of the project was to build the building and follow the contract.

Second, we recoiled at the process for developing a Goals Statement that the Army Corps of Engineers, authors of the partnering material, was suggesting. They recommended that the members of the group not only write the goals, but also sign the statement. The writing part was okay, but the signing part seemed gimmicky to us, the kind of things friends tease us about when they ask us about our work. "And what do you have the group do after they sign the Goals Statement?" We could imagine them kidding us. "Is that the part in the meeting where you have them hold hands and sing Kumbaya?"

But the Corps material expressed strong recommendations to lead the group through the steps it outlined. In addition, several clients who had participated in other partnering meetings spoke highly about how the Corps's structured approach had resulted in a document that generated substantial positive impact on other projects.

So we suspended our own skepticism and went ahead as the Corps suggested. For my efforts, we received two rewards far beyond anything we expected. First, the process did, in fact, generate significant positive outcomes on the project we tried it on. Second, and more importantly, we learned several principles about writing and using goals that continue to positively affect every project we work on.

In this chapter we describe mechanisms and processes to help you write and use Goals Statements in your own partnering efforts. More than that, though, we also want to communicate the importance of this work and the potential it has to enable partnering of any kind to perform not just at but well beyond expectations.

Content Outcomes of Clarifying Goals

The work of Clarifying Goals produces both a tangible item, a written Goals Statement, and process effects for the partnering relationship. The Goals Statement produces important outcomes for the content of partnering, information that refines and alters the partnering relationship. The Goals Statement is usually no longer than a single page, listing 10 to 20 partnering goals. The partnering group writes the Goals Statement by first working in small groups. The small groups each develop a few goals they believe are important for the whole group to support. The small groups present their draft goals, and the whole group discusses and refines them.

The Goals Statement usually involves two kinds of goals: performance goals and communications goals. Performance goals reflect quantitative, nuts-and-bolts aspects of partnering. Typical performance goals address productivity, profit, quality, revenue, cash flow, punctuality, technical performance, error rates, and so on. Communications goals address more qualitative issues, focusing more on how the people in the partnering group would like to get along with each other. Typical communications goals include "Treat each other with respect," "Communicate all differences of opinion quickly, openly, and to the appropriate person," and "Have fun."

More important than the piece of paper for the Goals Statement, the work of Clarifying Goals also produces useful information and mechanisms for people at all levels to buy into the partnering arrangement. The information that Clarifying Goals provides is the information generated when the partnering group makes general partnering agreements more specific and clear.

Few, if any, partnering groups begin with a blank slate of goals. Nearly all have goals of one kind or another spelled out in legal contracts and formal agreements. Some of these agreements may be quite detailed. No matter how detailed an initial partnering agreement may be, however, the group of people charged with implementing it will inevitably have their own ideas about how they can best translate the intentions in the agreement into everyday reality. It's not that the partnering group contradicts the intentions of the formal agreement senior managers reached to initiate the partnering. It's more that they elaborate it, specify how it can be done best, and detail how they can carry out the work they are being asked to do.

Some examples of how the work of Clarifying Goals evolves illustrate the importance of this aspect of the Partnering Solution:

❏ In a software company partnering with a customer, both organizations know that the partnering work should result in increased customer satisfaction. But it is the work of Clarifying Goals that establishes survey methods to assess satisfaction and standards for specific satisfaction levels.

❏ In a merger partnering, both companies have a goal that the merger will bring them interesting new work they would not have been able to land on their own. The work of Clarifying Goals together specifies how much work in each office and divides the work among different key markets.

❏ In a Departments at War situation, both departments buy into an initial goal that they would like to work together more effectively. Working on Clarifying Goals, the partnering group sets a target of accelerating the completion rate of the tasks the two groups must work on together.

What's really going on in these examples? Clearly, Clarifying Goals does not consist of simply adding extra decimal places to numbers that already exist. Clarifying Goals determines the extent to which the formal partnering agreement will come to life. What's an acceptable customer satisfaction goal? Ninety percent? Excellent ratings. Eighty or 70 percent? Setting the specific standards for customer service satisfaction can sway the meaning of a general goal to "improve customer satisfaction" across a wide range.

Process Outcomes of Clarifying Goals

Clarifying Goals also produces process outcomes for partnering beyond the content outcomes it has in refining and specifying general goals. Working on Clarifying Goals provides a powerful vehicle for participants in the partnering group to buy into the partnering process.

A moment occurs in many partnering workshops; a turning point that illustrates how working on Clarifying Goals enables participants to buy into the partnering process. It's an hour or two into the partnering workshop. Participants have already had the discussion about Taking Stock and they've done some work with the personality profiles. They know each other's personality types. They've had a few laughs about the group's type chart, but they are also thinking a bit about the implications of the group's type mix for its ongoing success. The group is polite and civil, perhaps even positive and enthusiastic.

The facilitator introduces the work on the Goals Statement and rearranges the seating so that participants are seated in small groups with their peers and counterparts at similar levels in the partnering organization. The facilitator explains that each small group should write two or three each of performance and communications goals.

And then, in most cases, the group sits in silence for a few minutes.

It's a strange silence, not exactly uncomfortable, but noticeable all the same. It's not that the work of Clarifying Goals is a surprise, most group participants knew that they would be writing a Goals Statement. Working with peers in their own organization, they may have even seen some examples of statements before the meeting.

The silence is a key moment for buy-in. It is the moment when many participants first fully accept their own responsibility for making the partnering arrangement work. They're sitting, asking, "Me? What goals can I suggest to make the partnering work?" They seem surprised to be addressing the question. They discussed problems and opportunities in Taking Stock, and they gained useful insight in Building Trust. But in those two tasks they did not really have to step up and take initiative at a personal level. Now the question before them is: "Okay, you've identified the problems and the people. Now what do you plan to do about it?"

Although groups respond slowly to the question, they do respond. Slowly at first, and then with more conviction, they begin to write goals for performance and communications. As they do, it's easy to see that they are also increasingly accepting responsibility for the success of the partnering relationship.

Making the Goals Statement a Living Document

Most organizations have statements describing their Vision, Mission, Values, and Goals, and those statements have great potential. Many are well written and thoughtful. Some are downright inspirational. But few organizations put the same level of thought and energy into using these statements as they do into writing them. Partnering groups that write Goals Statements face this same challenge: getting the Goals Statement out to the partnering workshop and into the everyday life of the organization, making the Goals Statement a living document.

Why do so many organizational Vision, Mission, and Goals Statements remain on the shelf? Understanding the answer to this question can help partnering groups increase the impact of their own Goals Statements:

❏ In any situation, people struggle much more with implementing goals than they do with formulating them. Even at a personal level, such as trying to lose weight, stop smoking, or start exercising regularly, it's much easier to formulate the goal than it is to carry it out.

❏ There is something about the work of formulating a goal that makes it seem like the job is finished once the goal is formulated. At a personal level, the joke that illustrates this point is the one about the overweight person who spends hours setting interesting, intelligent goals for losing weight and then celebrates with a big dinner.

❏ Organizations have more difficulty than individuals in implementing goals. Many organizations struggle with getting employees to align their work efforts and priorities with the organization's goals. (See Chapter 9 for more detail on this problem and strategies for solving it.)

❏ In partnering, it's not so much that the people writing the Goals Statement are shortsighted, undisciplined, or lazy; rather, the problem is that their current job definition does not include taking responsibility for implementing goals. In many cases, it may be difficult to discern who, in either of the organizations, could take responsibility for ensuring that the organizations implement partnering goals.

Considering these issues, partnering groups may be tempted to throw in the towel and not even attempt to implement their goals. However, we have observed numerous partnering groups succeed in translating partnering goals into everyday actions, even when the organizations involved in the partnering arrangement have been ineffective in general in aligning individual employee effort with overall organizational goals.

The most effective things partnering groups can do to bring their Goals Statements to life are:

1. *Make the Goals Statement visible.* Goals may be intangible, but Goals Statements can be made visible. They can be posted on walls, hung over coffee pots, copied and placed in employees' pay envelopes, emblazoned on baseball caps, embroidered on T-shirts, and copied onto letterhead. Yes, some of these items lack sophistication, but they do serve the larger purpose of keeping partnering goals current in people's thinking.

2. *Make partnering goals a discussion topic in regular meeting agendas.* Experts who work with visualization and goal-setting for individuals advocate that people who want to achieve a goal read, think about, meditate on, and focus on their goals in a disciplined way several times each day. Partnering groups can translate this technique for their own purposes by discussing partnering goals regularly at meetings. Anytime a partnering group meets, it's worthwhile to devote some time to discussing the partnering goals: Which goals are being met? Which goals are not being met? What can the group do to increase success in attaining its own goals? It's also worthwhile to get the partnering goals topic on the agenda in other related meetings in both of the partnering organizations.

3. *Work to get partnering goals to influence individual performance and pay metrics.* In Chapter 9 we advocate that organizations use quarterly performance discussions instead of annual appraisals. The quarterly approach is more effective for a number of purposes, and it is especially useful for partnering because it provides a means to introduce and monitor new partnering tasks. Short of changing an entire organization to quarterly performance discussions, it is still possible to do something meaningful with pay and performance to implement partnering goals. All it takes is ensuring that, in some way, employee pay reflects partnering goals. It's not necessary to pin a person's entire salary on the achievement of partnering goals to make this effort effective. All it takes is for the amount of money involved to be at a level that catches employees' attention. It's amazing what even relatively small amounts of pay differentials can do to convert partnering goals into everyday employee behaviors.

4. *Designate several people in the partnering group as "Goals Coordinators."* It's a maxim in business that, if you want to get something done, you must either create a new job title for it or formally make it part of somebody's job. In partnering, this can mean designating one person from each organization as "Goals Coordinator." This person's tasks include tracking and coordinating the three tasks mentioned in this list—making the Goals Statement visible, getting the goals into regular meeting agendas, and moving the goals into employee performance metrics.

Core Case Organizations' Experience With Clarifying Goals

Keyes North Atlantic (Electromechanical contractors)

"Our written work is really key to clarifying goals on our projects. People laugh at our long proposals," CEO Susan Keyes notes. "They compare our eight-page proposals with the cookie-cutter proposals that most other companies send out—the one-pagers.

"But we do the longer proposals because it enables us to try to clarify the goals of the project. This might not seem necessary, and I suppose it's not for many people. But it is for us because it's understanding, clarifying, and meeting the client's goals that is most essential for partnering. When we work at a goals level, it often helps the clients to redefine what they really want and need. If we just talk about equipment and schedules, it's easy to miss what the client really needs, it's easy to miss important opportunities to do better. If we start by emphasizing outcomes, it clears up equipment issues and expectations pretty quickly."

PCA Architects

"David Chilinski, our president, is famous for his focus on goals. He always tries to get the clients talking about what they want the design to do for them," firm principal Eric Brown explains. "Sometimes it gets us into trouble initially. Clients come in and they want to talk about furniture, color, atmosphere, materials. It's understandable—all those things are interesting, so their initial reactions to David's interest in outcomes is sometimes less than enthusiastic.

"But after a few minutes, they always see the value of the focus on outcomes, and they always have a lot to say. A lot of times, they find out that they are not really so clear about the outcomes they have in mind for a project. They come to see that spelling out project performance goals more clearly, helps them get the project they really want."

ADS Financial Services Solutions (Systems integration and software consulting)

"When I go to my doctor, I know what I need. I tell him I have the flu, I need antibiotics," CEO Bill Gallagher confesses. "He listens patiently, ignores my self-diagnosis, but asks me about my wife and family, my golf game, the weather, the Red Sox. What he's really doing is listening, diagnosing. In the end, I seldom get the antibiotics I thought I needed. Instead, I get what I really need.

"We have a process that does this same thing in our partnering with clients, our 'Big Q' process. The Q stands for *qualifying*. After our initial contact, and before we write a proposal, the 'Big Q' is a comprehensive couple of hours. We ask the client 20 different ways '*Why* are you doing this project? What do you really want this project to *achieve*? What are the *outcomes*, what are the *opportunities*? What *impact* will it have on your business?' It may seem unnecessary and repetitive to some people; they feel that they already spelled things out pretty clearly. But it really helps to both build a strong partnership and get clarity on the joint objectives."

SEi Companies
(Mechanical, electrical and plumbing engineers)

Firm principal Mark Warren notes, "We've done those very detailed Goals Statements on the jobs we did for EMC, the Goals Statements that have detailed project performance specs and detailed goals for project communications. Everybody on the project signed the Goals Statements. It took a lot of work, but it definitely helped the job and the working relationships.

"It's also standard practice to develop formal goals when we work on the 'green' projects, the sustainable buildings that use energy-conscious design. The LEED process requires it. It's very participative from the owner's standpoint. It's a published process, part of becoming accredited. It gets you to focus on the project goals, the green goals, to clarify how you are going to measure performance when the building is completed."

Lee Kennedy Co., Inc. (Construction)

"We've done the formal goals statements on some of our projects and they are useful," observes Pamela Bailey, a project manager. "In house, our kick-off meetings focus a lot on project goals. Everybody goes to these meetings: the estimator, the project manager, the superintendent.

"The goals discussions always surface important issues. Many times it's the first time the project superintendent becomes aware of what the project really is, what the owner wants to get out of it, what the architects want to get out of it. This happened on a job we did for a college theater that is in the register of National Historic Places. The meetings up front made it clear that this was not a typical project, that it demanded a whole new level of craft and care. Most of the time, superintendents are concerned mostly with schedule and budget, but here we had to be concerned with history and preserving the building, with history and heritage."

Foliage Software

"We have to do a lot of work with Clarifying Goals on most projects," comments co-CEO Tim Bowe. "The goals of our projects are seldom clear at the outset, and when they seem to be, it often turns out that different departments in our client organizations have different goals. We have to ask a lot of questions: What are you building? Why are you building it? What do you believe that building it will really accomplish? What do you really want?

"It can be difficult to do all this because it can mean not necessarily giving the customers what they initially say they want. In order to really clarify goals, we often have to challenge the customer and help them clarify the goals. We often have to step back. And we frequently have to work inside the customer organization to get different departments together to make sure they all support the common goals."

7

Implementing Key Processes

After Taking Stock, Building Trust, and Clarifying Goals, the Partnering Solution moves to develop and implement several key processes or procedures. Processes convert goals from wishes and intentions to everyday routine. It doesn't take many of these processes to make partnering successful, but it does take a few. This chapter describes several processes that are useful in many partnering situations.

The Nature and Importance of Processes

True freedom is not the absence of structure.... But rather a clear structure that enables people to work within established boundaries in an autonomous and creative way.

—Erich Fromm, *Escape From Freedom*

Initially, it may seem that the effort in partnering to create processes and procedures is an attempt to re-create the same rigid bureaucracies and mindless organizations that caused the need for partnering in the first place. Processes and procedures in partnering do help create some order and predictability, some organization and routine. But their goal is not to constrain but, rather, to liberate. Useful processes create enough structure so that people can focus on more creative concerns.

Processes and procedures are the mechanisms that turn partnering goals into predictable, ongoing realities. In most partnering efforts, the group identifies three or four key processes that, if working well, enable the partnering arrangement to achieve the Partnering Goals the group developed. Processes are not intentions ("We will really work harder to improve communications") but, rather, specific methods to ensure that people meet their intentions ("In order to improve communications, we will meet weekly on Wednesdays and discuss these six agenda items").

Processes play an essential role in creating lasting partnering success. Long after a partnering workshop, the processes that were established in the workshop are what live on. When people move from the partnering project onto other work, when new people join either organization, when one of the partnering companies encounters a special challenge, the processes are what keep the partnering arrangement stable and intact.

When we encounter conflict and distrust in a partnering situation, the root cause is often the failure or absence of a process. People holding different assumptions about how a process should work come to view others' behavior as indicative of their lack of integrity, when what is really going on is that they are simply following what they thought was the agreed-upon procedure.

The importance of the RFI (Request For Information) in construction partnering provides insight into the importance of processes. Many other kinds of partnering, such as software development, use some variation of the RFI process. The construction RFI is an "official" form created by the American Institute of Architects to log changes made to designs. When a construction worker encounters a condition in the field that he cannot interpret, he sends the architect an RFI. People write RFIs because the material the architect specified is no longer being manufactured, because they can't understand the architect's drawings, or maybe because they think they have a better idea.

Many contractors groan when the subject of RFIs comes up at construction partnering meetings. "Why do we have to discuss this? We all know what RFIs are! We've worked with them for years!" But as the group begins to talk about how they will use RFIs on that particular job, significant differences usually emerge in how people write, read, track, and log RFIs. Some people claim that one should use RFIs as infrequently as possible in order to maintain good working relations, that it is preferable to handle RFI issues verbally. By contrast, others contend that it's a good thing for the project for everyone to write many RFIs. That way, there are fewer gray areas and an assurance that good documentation will help clear up any conflicts. The differing philosophies and approaches make it obvious that it is essential for the group to develop its own plan for handling RFIs in detail.

There are two major implications in construction for all partnering situations of the RFI example. First, partnering groups that think they agree on how a process should be handled often discover that they do not, and that it is necessary to devote some effort in order to reach agreement. Second, processes that seem small and mundane can have major effects for overall partnering success. When the processes aren't working well, they can cause confusion, mistrust, and resentment. When the processes are working well, they can make it possible for partnering arrangements to move far beyond solving problems to opening up the creative possibilities of the partnership.

It is essential to link the processes to the partnering goals. Most people have ample experience with situations where others tried to implement a new process that seemed perfectly clear and worthwhile, only to have the people who were supposed to implement it neglect, ignore, or resist the process outright. Once people have developed partnering goals, however, the task of Piloting Processes follows logically. And because the processes come from the group, they are much more likely to implement them with full acceptance.

In an initial partnering workshop, it is never possible to fully identify which processes the partnering arrangement needs or to plan those processes to ensure that they will work perfectly. However, it is possible to identify a handful of processes that seem essential and plan them with enough detail to try them for a few weeks. After trying them, it is then possible to refine the processes so that they function even more effectively.

Five key processes that are useful in a wide range of partnering situations are:

- ❒ Clarifying individual roles and responsibilities.
- ❒ Mapping individual information needs.
- ❒ Tracking and managing small changes.
- ❒ Planning a meeting schedule and agenda.
- ❒ Involving senior management support/conflict resolution.

The sections that follow provide details on each of these.

Clarifying Roles and Responsibilities

One process that is key to the success of any partnering arrangement and is often difficult to accomplish is a process that translates partnering goals into individual actions. Making this translation is often essential to partnering success. For example, in the software company that wants to partner more effectively with customers, technicians will probably take on more consulting and communications tasks. In a Departments at War internal standoff between departments, employees in both may have to back away from roles that put them into conflict with each other and take on tasks that involve communicating more information more often.

While it is essential to translate partnering goals into individual actions, a number of factors make the translation difficult:

❑ Many organizations struggle with this issue on their own. Because it is difficult for simple organizations, it can be expected to be difficult for alliances.

❑ People may say they don't mind change, but few organizations of any kind could boast that they've never had employees who balk at taking on new tasks because "I wasn't hired to do that."

❑ Partnering often requires people to do more tasks that involve increased or improved communications. These tasks can be easy to agree to, but unclear to define and carry out.

❑ Taking on new tasks often places people outside their comfort zones with roles and responsibilities they do not enjoy and may well neglect.

❑ Taking on new tasks often also involves letting go of old ones. Many people don't like to stop doing things they are skilled at.

❑ Even when people agree wholeheartedly with partnering goals, they simply may not be able to see how those goals trickle down to their own everyday tasks. They may feel that others in their own group are better suited to carry out the tasks, or they just may not be able to see the link between partnering-in-principle and what they themselves do at 10 a.m. on Tuesdays.

Partnering Process Tool 1: Goal-Based Work Plan

A simple spreadsheet called a Goal-Based Work Plan provides a useful tool to strengthen the link between partnering goals and individual effort. The Work Plan describes an individual's job in a way that highlights the three major issues people disagree about in changing their priorities: the tasks they are supposed to carry out, the priorities that weight the tasks, and the outcomes expected for each task. The form is clear and brief, fitting all the relevant information onto one page.

People working to improve partnering can use the form in a number of ways that help individuals increase alignment with partnering goals:

❐   In customer service partnering: Individuals in a partnering group draft the Work Plan for a category of workers, such as the software company staff, who interact with a customer organization. The partnering group, consisting of both some software company staff and some customer staff, jointly agree on the Work Plan that guides the job definitions of the software company staff who interact with the customer.

❐   In Departments at War: People on each side of the battle draft two Work Plans, one for their own group and one for what they think the other group should do. They compare notes and try to agree on Work Plans that are acceptable for both sides.

❐   In mergers: On a management team planning a merger, people on each side of the merger plan what they think their own Work Plan should include. The whole group comments on each individual. Individuals refine the Work Plans to reflect the input.

❐   In service departments: People in both the service department and the internal customer group outline what they think their Work Plan should be. Then each side makes modifications based on input from the whole group.

In all these cases, most of the discussion will focus on people adding tasks that involve increased and improved communications, sharing information, and working together on tasks people previously worked on alone. In the end, for most people in most cases, there is little relative change in their job overall, just adding a few tasks that take less than a half day per week or less. However, trying to make these small additions can trigger large reactions. The narrative case that follows illustrates both the Work Plan form and the reactions people may have to adding partnering tasks to their jobs.

Case 1: Aligning the Finance Manager's Job With Partnering Goals

"Oh no," Michael worried, noting the tag line of the incoming e-mail from corporate. "It looks like another one of those official memoranda to us finance managers, telling us we need to be 'adding value,' or some such management nonsense. Don't those people have enough to do without bothering us all the time? We know we're supposed to be partnering with the business unit managers and we're okay with that. But don't they know we have real work to do? Finance work, for example?"

Michael opened the e-mail just to at least check if there was anything truly necessary in it; no sense putting one's job in jeopardy. Glossing over the text, what he saw confirmed Michael's suspicions that this was more management nonsense that had little meaning for him. He was not trying to be rebellious. If anything, he thought he was being conscientious, focusing on the job he was hired to do.

Phrases jumped off the e-mail, catching Michael's attention:

❏ "Finance managers must be more proactive."

❏ "We should be partnering more effectively."

❏ "We should be working to become equal, strong members of the management team."

❏ "We should build relationships with the line managers and business units."

❏ "Finance managers should be initiating more ideas and bringing them to the team."

❏ "We must do a better job of demonstrating value."

"Okay, okay, I get the point," Michael reflected. "I'm not sure I like it, but I do get it. I can see some relevance to what's being said here. These are all things that could stand some improvement. But I have a few issues, too. First of all, what happened to the finance and accounting work that we are supposed to do? Is that gone completely? Second, why is all this outreach and relationship-building up to us? Why doesn't the company tell the other members of the project team to outreach to us? In my next life, maybe I'll come back as a different member of the management team, and then people will appreciate me.

"And finally, when are we supposed to do all this extra work? I'm already maxed out on the usage of my time. I've got people on the project team telling me what to do, I've got the work I know I should do that they neglect to ask me about. Of course, the fact that they always call me too late doesn't help matters either. I could do a much better job for them, and in much less time, if only people would involve me in the process sooner. I get so many last-minute calls. And then, people ask for too little. They ask me to check their addition when they should be involving me in the financial planning from the outset.

"I think the problem is that they are all self-centered; the only work they think about is their own. The fact that most of them have some accounting training makes it even worse. After they've had Finance 101, they think they can do what I do. They think that they don't need me. The trouble is that they don't understand what I do and what I could do. How can I demonstrate value if they keep calling me too late?"

Michael reached for a spreadsheet form he had copied from a stack his wife had brought home from her job at the software company. Kayla had described to him how her company used the form to help clarify job priorities and outcomes. It seems her company actually had people update and revise the form every three months because, they claimed, peoples' job priorities shifted so frequently and it was important to be clear about how things should change. "Maybe if I take a few minutes working with that form I can clear up some of my own thinking about how things are changing on my job," Michael thought.

With just three columns and about 10 rows, the form looked simple enough. The instructions noted that he should first fill in the column marked "Tasks," dividing his job into eight to 10 major tasks. About half of those tasks should be technical/quantitative, and the other half should be more qualitative/people-based. Once he completed that list, he would divide 100 percent among the tasks to reflect the priority weighting of the tasks. Finally, he would list several measurable outcomes for each task. "This looks like it may take a few minutes, but it also looks like it will be worth the time," Michael reflected.

Michael had no trouble listing the first few quantitative, analytical tasks:

- ❏ Collect financial data.
- ❏ Track project budgets.
- ❏ Interpret data.
- ❏ Prepare and write reports.

The communications tasks stumped him for a few moments, but then he began listing:

- ❏ Provide support when asked.
- ❏ Correct errors in reports.
- ❏ Rein in project team.
- ❏ Police/Enforcer.

The priorities part came easily once Michael realized that "priority" in this case did not imply the amount of time it took to perform a task, but rather, in principle, the priority the task should hold in his overall job. He estimated 80 percent overall for the technical tasks and 20 percent for the communications tasks. Yes, the communications tasks were important, but it was also important to keep them in perspective.

The outcomes were more difficult. It was relatively easy to list outcomes for the quantitative, technical tasks, but more difficult for the communications tasks. What outcomes should one expect in exchange for providing support or for reining in the other project team members? Michael toyed with outcomes such as "gratitude" and "clear conscience," but decided to direct his sarcasm to other activities.

Michael printed out the spreadsheet and reviewed his efforts. Then he looked again at the e-mail memo from corporate. "Maybe I am being a bit rigid about all this," he reflected. "Maybe I haven't really made much of an effort to translate our corporate goals for finance partnering with the business units into my own job. It's true I am a finance professional with all the experience and scars to prove it. But maybe it's time to take my professional development in the direction of my customers instead of just operating inside the boundaries of my own training. At some point, and maybe it's this one, it has to be time to take off the blinders and connect with the others on the project team."

With that perspective in mind, Michael set about drafting a second version of his Work Plan. He kept some of the task labels he originally used, but changed some of the outcomes. For example, for the task labeled "Collect financial data," he added an outcome that the data presented should be user-friendly and valuable to the customer. He had heard project team members complain about the "cumbersome and incomprehensible" table formats for many years and dismissed the comments, reasoning that they could learn to read the data if they made the effort. But he began to question that stance now, considering the possibility that he could play some part not just in presenting the data, but in formatting it to improve its value.

For other tasks, Michael realized that the label he had been using to describe the task was probably not the best. It was easy to see that the task labeled "Rein in project team" should really be labeled "Partner with project team," and that the "Police/Enforcer" task could better be placed as an outcome of the "Partner" task.

Michael then turned to the Priorities column and made some adjustments. If he was really serious about partnering with the project team, he realized, he would have to increase the priority weighting of the communications tasks and decrease the weighting of the technical tasks. Initially it pained him to consider that the work he did for his profession should take a backseat to mere communications.

On reflection, though, he began to see that communicating more effectively would provide the tools that enabled him to do his accounting and finance work with greater efficiency. He also could see that communicating more effectively would ensure that his accounting and finance work produced greater effects and results for the company. With more confidence, he altered the priority weightings so that the accounting and communications tasks each accounted for half, or 50 percent, of his overall priority.

Michael finally turned to the Outcomes column. He attempted to take the goals that seemed implicit in the e-mail from corporate and convert them into clearer, more tangible outcomes. As he thought about it, some new outcomes became clear. For example, if one of his tasks was to collect data from the project team and he really followed the partnering goals, then he ought to consider collecting the data in ways that were efficient and easy for the project team. If one of his jobs was to write reports, then he should consider making the reports not only accurate and complete, but also fully understandable and useful to the project team members who read them.

Both of Michael's work spreadsheets, the traditional and partnering versions, follow.

The Finance Manager's Job: Traditional View		
Priority (100%)	**Tasks** Divide your job into seven to 10 task categories. Half will be technical/ quantitative; half will be more qualitative.	**Outcomes** For each task, note anticipated outcomes and results. Use numbers and timelines when possible.
20	Collect financial data.	• Meet reporting requirements. • Timely, accurate reporting. • Point out mistakes. • Catalog all activity.
20	Track project budgets.	• Identify problem areas. • Specify corrective action. • Report results.
20	Interpret data.	• Identify trend data. • Correctness of analysis. • Validity of response. • Finance manager peer review.
15	Prepare and write reports.	• Meet reporting requirements. • Informed decisions by senior management. • Comprehensive and well-documented.
10	Provide support when asked.	• Return calls quickly. • Open door; available.
5	Correct errors in reports.	• Provide backup. • Defend reasoning.
5	Rein in project team.	• Maintain project profitability. • Confront when necessary. • Be persistent in a professional way.
5	Police/Enforcer.	• Always do the right thing. • This is truly our role.

The Finance Manager's Job: Revised for Partnering		
Priority (100%)	**Tasks** Divide your job, into seven to 10 task categories. Half will be technical/ quantitative; half will be more qualitative.	**Outcomes** For each task, note anticipated outcomes and results. Use numbers and timelines when possible.
20	Collect financial data.	• Data presented should be user-friendly and valuable to customer. • Meet reporting requirements. • Timely, accurate reporting. • Devise ways to collect data that are efficient for project team.
20	Track project budgets.	• Identify problem areas and specify corrective action. • Identify key numbers project team should track.
20	Interpret data.	• Identify trend data. • Correctness of analysis. • Validity of response. • Finance manager peer review.
15	Prepare and write reports.	• Meet reporting requirements. • Informed decisions by senior management. • Provide analysis on managers' terms.
10	Initiate support.	• Reach out to project team. • Build relationships. • Return calls quickly.
10	Rein in project team.	• Police/Enforcer. • Maintain project profitability. • Confront when necessary. • Be persistent in a professional way. • Always do the right thing.
5	Correct errors in reports.	• Provide backup. • Defend reasoning.

Partnering Process Tool 2:
The Information Needs Spreadsheet

"Why didn't you send me the report?"

"I didn't know you needed it."

Information needs resemble the RFI example at the beginning of this chapter. They seem small and mundane, but when they are not working well, they can cause serious problems for the partnering. Like RFIs, information needs can be difficult to clarify and discuss. Also like RFIs, when information needs are addressed effectively, they generate valuable, positive results for the partnership.

When people start taking on tasks that involve partnering work, they often need new information, data, reports, schedules, and plans. New information needs become especially clear after people have clarified new roles and responsibilities. Often, it's necessary to have new information in order to address the new tasks.

It's not so much that this information itself is new, but that the people who develop and send it must now also send it to a new group of people in the partnering group. For example, in a customer partnering situation between a software service provider and its telephone company client, it might be useful for the service provider to know about the large projects and deadlines, the project status and timelines, and the reporting requirements and cycles on which the customer group is working. Conversely, customers might do well to have information about the number of software staff assigned to their project, the staff's schedule and work obligations, and the staff's status on other current work.

All this may seem straightforward enough, but it is problematic on both sides of the information exchange. People who are sending information don't necessarily know who in the new partnering group need it, and so are likely to overlook important recipients. People on the receiving end don't necessarily know what information is available, so they don't always ask for it.

And finally, people on both sides of a partnering arrangement may not be readily aware that the arrangement calls for new kinds of information—records, data, documentation—that are important for partnering success, but need to be created. Using the software service provider example again, that situation calls for a baseline of customer satisfaction survey data. It will take both the service provider and the telephone company working together to determine what questions to ask on the survey, whom to survey, and how to interpret the results.

Partnering groups can use a simple spreadsheet form to clarify who needs what information from whom when (see following sample). Despite the simplicity of the spreadsheet, it is worth pointing out that discussing and completing it may well involve some fireworks. Even in positive, trusting circumstances, people can bristle when asked to share information with new people. One can anticipate hearing the question, "Why do *you* need *that*?" when discussing new information needs. Of course, it's important to persevere and work on transferring the information, because the information makes it possible to do the partnering work.

Sample Partnering Information Needs Spreadsheet				
Person	**Company**	**Task**	**Info Need**	**Info Source**
John	Software Co.	Make software company staff accessible to provide quick response to customer company requests and questions.	Customer company employee work, project, and scheduling status.	Mary: Customer company scheduling coordinator.
Mary	Telephone company.	Coordinate with service provider to provide maximum resources for telephone company employees.	Software company staffing and schedule information.	John: Software company partnering manager.

Partnering groups can complete Information Needs Spreadsheets such as this one beginning with a blank sheet and taking a few minutes to review each participant's information needs. The group fills in the sheet as the information needs become clear and identifies people who will meet the needs as the discussion progresses.

In the Sample Partnering Information Needs Spreadsheet, people in the partnering group list the names of the key people in each organization in the first column, Person. They list which company the person works for in the second column. They list the task the person is trying to carry out in the third column, and the information they need in the fourth column. In the final column, they list the person who agrees to provide the information.

Partnering Process Tool 3: RFIs

We described the Request For Information (RFI) process architects and contractors use at the beginning of this chapter in order to illustrate the important part that processes play in enabling partnering to achieve the full measure of its potential success. In this section we explore the RFI process in greater detail because it provides the outlines for handling an issue that arises in many partnering situations: what to do when (usually not because it's anyone's fault) the original terms of the partnering arrangement change as the arrangement moves from planning to implementation.

The need for an RFI process is built on two assumptions: first, that no matter how good a job people do in planning partnering, new and unforeseen factors will arise, and second, that the group will devise a more intelligent way to handle these changes if it addresses them before they build up. Some old-school contractors like to contend that RFIs should never be necessary if the architects do their job. But the vast majority of people in the industry acknowledge that it is never possible, during design, to be able to fully anticipate all the things that might occur in the field to make it impossible for contractors to build the design.

Partnering situations that can benefit from developing an RFI process of their own feature any ones that involve a "handoff" (that is, a sequence of work in which one group hands off the task to the group it is partnering with so that the second group can add its own efforts). This can occur in Departments at War and Quiet Standoff, as well as in many Mergers and Acquisitions.

In all these cases, the RFI process resembles that in construction. People in the group agree on:

❐ The content of an RFI form.

❐ Protocol for filling the form out: Who should complete it under what circumstances, and with what goals and expectations.

❐ Protocol for tracking and addressing the completed forms: Who will log them and report the results when and to whom.

In many partnering situations, as in construction, keeping track of RFIs over time is a small task that contributes in large ways to overall partnering success.

Planning Partnering Meetings

The length of the meeting increases in direct proportion to the square of the number of people present and awake.

—Anon

Keeping awake at meetings is the least of problems that people have with meetings. Many, many people have had bad experiences with meetings and group communications, so it can be troublesome that partnering of any kind usually implies a need for more meetings. In any kind of partnering, ongoing, regular meetings can:

- ❏ Monitor and track overall partnering progress.
- ❏ Provide a form for regularly exchanging information and getting work done.
- ❏ Solving specific partnering problems.
- ❏ Exploring partnering opportunities.

Whether because of many people's negative experiences with meetings or because of their inability to envision how meetings might contribute to partnering success, we seldom see groups of any kind using meetings in an optimal way. Most often, we see groups meeting either too often or too seldom, and attempting to use meetings to accomplish either too much or too little. And within those two dimensions, the majority of the partnering groups we have seen meet too seldom and attempt to accomplish too much.

Many partnering groups begin work on follow-up by trying to plan their meetings. We think it is more useful to explore the issues the group will need to address first, and then to discuss what type of meeting content and schedule can best address the issues. After a partnering group has clarified who has what roles and responsibilities and who needs what information when, then it can be very useful to discuss how meetings can help people meet their responsibilities and obtain the information they need.

It is important for partnering groups to devise an intelligent plan for their meetings because meetings can contribute a great deal to overall partnering success. At the same time, it can be difficult to know how often to meet. Many groups decide on a meeting schedule without much thought: "In our company, we manage most projects with weekly meetings, so that is what we will do on this one." This approach is often ineffective because the partnering meetings people are trying to plan can differ significantly from the kinds of meetings they are using as their baseline.

While it is not effective to outline a one-size-fits-all recipe for meetings, we can describe several guidelines for meetings that consistently increase meeting productivity:

1. *Plan the meeting agenda to meet the information needs of people in the group.* Topics on the agenda should provide people in the group with the information they need in order to do their jobs.

2. *Avoid "meeting as needed."* Some groups prefer to avoid scheduled meetings, opting to get together only when problems arise. This approach saves some up-front time but usually creates much larger costs in the long run. If groups meet only "as needed," then all meetings are reactive and problem-oriented. The group never has an opportunity to develop the possible synergies and positive aspects of partnering.

3. *Schedule meetings as you would schedule maintenance for your car.* The rule of thumb is to schedule meetings frequently enough to identify problems when they are small and easy to address.

4. *In partnering, meetings that are short and frequent are usually more productive than meetings that are long and infrequent.* When partnering groups encounter significant conflict in their regular, half-day monthly meetings, switching to hour-long weekly meetings usually improves matters. Partnering meetings are more like newspapers than annual reports. People need the information in the meeting so that they can make quick changes and repairs. Waiting a month to hold a formal project review, complete with printed reports and overhead slides, may be worthwhile for reporting to senior executives. However, it is usually more productive for partnering to work with numbers in draft form more frequently so that it is possible to make small repairs as the relationships evolve.

Core Case Organizations' Experience With Implementing Key Processes

PCA Architects

"I think the most powerful, consistent process we have to strengthen partnering is our proposal," notes Eric Brown, a principal of the firm. "Up until a few years ago, we either used informal ones, we all did them differently, or sometimes we just went ahead with a project with no proposal at all, just a discussion. It wasn't a good thing, but we did it then. Some firms still do it that way. This can be a very informal business.

"But we knew that a better proposal would improve client relations and strengthen partnering. So a few of us redrafted a form, and we all worked on revising it. At this point, it's very distinctive in our industry. It's distinctive because it's comprehensive. It describes the project, the goals, the outcomes. Then it describes the scope of services by phase, the key people on the job, the schedule, fee, and a very clear delineation of services that are included and excluded. Also, we cover what our expectations are for the client, what we need them to do, what information they need to provide. This process goes a long way to building a strong partnership over the life of the whole project."

Lee Kennedy Co., Inc. (Construction)

"One process that strengthens our partnering is the project management software we use," explains Project Manager Pamela Bailey. "The software provides a running log of RFIs—the architect's Requests For Information. Weekly, you go over the log. It becomes a part of every meeting.

"The process of doing this has just become part of the way we do business. Lots of people forget that there was a time, not so long ago, when this process did not exist. You had to do it manually, and it created lots of miscommunication and conflict. By using the process now, you keep the information in front of the whole team. Everybody can see just where things are. It's a lot easier to partner on the job when you have accurate information in front of you, it reduces problems and keeps everybody accountable."

Keyes North Atlantic (Electromechanical contractors)

"Processes for access are the most important processes for us when it comes to meaningful partnering," CEO Susan Keyes explains. "Access means that we always take everyone's calls, we try not to let calls go through to the answering machine. If they do, we return them quickly. Most of the time that's within a few minutes. Once in awhile, it's in a few hours. It seldom, if ever, gets delayed to the next day. Our people also give out their cell numbers.

"All this may sound like low-level, uninteresting issues. But for our business, it's really what partnering is all about. Most of our calls from clients have a time value. An answer means more to them right away than it does with a two-hour delay. For us, access processes are the ones that help us achieve the larger partnering goals."

Foliage Software

Semiconductor Division Manager Norm Delisle comments, "The process we use on strategic consulting projects helps to strengthen our work with Clarifying Goals and with Building Trust. We start with a formal assessment of the business situation and very rapidly develop a strategic plan. We do it very quickly—pull out all the stops.

"Usually, within two weeks, we have collected a wealth of data. We prepare a detailed report with our findings and very specific recommendations for moving forward, often 50 pages or more, and no boilerplate. It's always customized to the specific situation. We deliver the report and present it to senior management. This process helps to define the issues correctly, and it clearly demonstrates our value to the customer. So far, all our customers have been amazed at how much we've been able to accomplish in such a short period of time."

SEi Companies
(Mechanical, electrical, and plumbing engineers)

"The way we define our PM [project manager] role is the main process we have that helps us achieve our goals for partnering," points out firm principal Bob Flaherty. "In a lot of firms, including ones that many of us worked in before, the PM is an administrator, a paper-pusher. He takes notes, makes lists, keeps records.

"All those things are important, but it takes a much more proactive PM in order to have a real partnering relationship with clients. In order for partnering to succeed, the PM has to take the pulse of the project at every step. PMs have to know everything that's going on, and they have to take whatever action is necessary to make things work. They have to be fast on their feet. Most important, the PM must do a lot of communicating with the client. Lots of our clients are complicated organizations. The PM has to know what's going on with all the people in the client organization who are involved with the project. Our PMs call on the client even when there is no issue, just to stay in touch."

ADS Financial Services Solutions
(Systems integration and software consulting)

EVP Erik Golz believes "one of the processes that contributes most to effective partnering is the set of agreements we make with the other consulting organizations who partner with us when we work with clients. In this process, we agree up front to several items that, left undiscussed, could cause trouble later on.

"We agree not to 'throw each other under the bus' in front of the client. We agree that if we bring another organization in, they can't go after the work independently. We agree not to hire from each others' staff. In some ways, it's unfortunate to have to do this. In other ways, it's just realistic. I do know that, following these procedures, our partnerships with other consulting companies are very strong."

8

Raising the Bar: Developing Partnering Opportunities

Most partnering situations have untapped potential. Often, it seems so difficult just to get over the bar that people don't even consider raising the bar. Often, people focus so much on partnering problems that they neglect to fully develop the opportunities built into most partnering situations. This is the most creative, innovative aspect of partnering. This chapter illustrates three ways to raise the partnering bar: (1) achieving goals far beyond those originally set, (2) developing new services and products, and (3) expanding the partnering agenda to include social responsibility concerns.

Raising the Bar

We are more mindful of injuries than benefits.

—The Book of 1000 Proverbs

You've got to think about "big things" while you're doing small things, so that all the small things go in the right direction.

—Alvin Toffler

On a teambuilding retreat, two executives encounter a grizzly bear. One immediately crouches to retie his shoe laces and gets ready to sprint away. The other comments, "Don't you know it's impossible to outrun a grizzly?" Looking up, the first replies, "I'm not even thinking about outrunning the grizzly. I just want to stay ahead of you!"

—Anon

Most partnering situations have untapped potential. The first quote here attempts to explain the reason behind this phenomenon: people tend to focus more on injuries and problems than they do on benefits and opportunities. That is especially understandable in many partnering situations, where the problems can seem so complex and daunting that it would take a true Pollyanna to even consider the opportunities that might lie beyond them.

The second quote makes a case for the importance of looking beyond short-term problems. Of course, part of the reason for focusing on "big things" is that they are interesting. But more than that, focusing on the "big things" also often helps ensure that the smaller things go well.

The third quote illustrates the importance of this whole process of setting expectations. What people and organizations achieve is often determined by the challenges they face.

We feature this chapter in part because we want to provide you with some tools to access the positive side of partnering. More than that, though, we do aim to inspire. Partnering that aims only to achieve short-term goals and resolve immediate problems can focus on negativity, blame, and punishment. Did a person meet his obligations or not? If not, how should he be punished so that he does a better job next time?

Partnering that aims beyond simple financial goals usually comes with a more positive attitude and tone, a more supportive culture. It's a lot easier, not to mention more exciting, to be a part of a partnering project aiming to eradicate child labor as it outsources than it is to be a member of outsourcing that only cares about revenues, profits, and controls. It's more enjoyable to be part of a partnering that breaks new ground than it is to split hairs about meeting requirements.

This chapter differs from the preceding ones. The preceding chapters detailing the various parts of the Partnering Solution mostly contain instructions, descriptions of how readers can implement the parts in their own situations. This chapter also instructs, but relies more on case examples to make the point. As our goal in part is to inspire, case examples work more effectively than bulleted lists to achieve that goal.

In partnering, the "big things" that can result from Raising the Bar can take three different forms:

1. Achieving goals in the categories originally intended for the partnership, but at a level far exceeding what anyone could have hoped for.

2. Developing new services, processes, and functions that help achieve original partnering goals, but are well outside

the scope of what anyone could have asked for in the early stages of the partnering.

3. Expanding the scope of the partnering agenda to include items outside the scope of simple profit and loss. This can mean using the partnership to advance goals that involve social responsibility; community development; voluntarism; and supporting charities, foundations, or nonprofit organizations.

We describe each of these forms in detail in the sections that follow.

Case 1: Surpassing Original Goals

When the building site was still a cornfield and the building was still in the planning stages, the 30-month schedule for completing the building seemed challenging. It was a complex project, more complicated than anything anyone had built within a 50-mile radius of the rural campus. With all of its state-of-the-art technology and advanced systems and design, it would be essential not only for each subcontractor to know their own field thoroughly, it would also demand a level of coordination and communications that few people in the industry ever encounter.

The college facilities manager wanted to set the schedule at 36 months to make allowances for all the complexities, but senior administration was more interested in getting the building completed. Faculty and students needed the laboratory space, and everyone wanted to keep to an absolute minimum the inconvenience of a construction project in the middle of the busy campus.

The partnering group that met to kick off work on the project shared the planner's concerns. Although they agreed to the legal terms of the contract with the 36-month schedule, they made it clear to the college that meeting this deadline would require a major effort on their part. Reluctantly, they signed the original project Goals Statement committing to meet the 36-month schedule.

They were not so concerned with the new technology and systems. Each member of the team—architect, engineer, general contractors, electrical subcontractor, plumbing contractor, and on through each subcontractor—felt they were up to the task from a technical perspective. They were looking forward to the project as an opportunity to demonstrate some of the new capabilities they had acquired in recent years. What worried them more was the need for extensive coordination and communications. Mostly from bad experiences, they knew how other team members' lack of communications could slow down their own work.

At the first follow-up partnering meeting several months after the initial partnering workshop, team members were less concerned. They had been able to work well together. They had solved some problems no one had foreseen in the initial workshop. They were beginning to get the information they needed about one another's work, the information that enabled them to coordinate their own work. Most of them reported fewer coordination problems than usual, even though the job itself was complex.

The positive reactions continued and grew. At the second and third follow-up partnering meetings held six and nine months, respectively, into the project, team members reported very favorably on the project. People working on several projects at one time commented on how different—and more difficult—their other projects were. On this project, they were not just communicating, they were communicating *well*. They were not just on schedule, they were a little ahead.

It was at the fourth follow-up workshop, a little more than a year into the project, that the suggestion first surfaced. It wasn't clear who made the suggestion. But, characteristically, later on when people tried to recall who supplied the suggestion, most people simply said, "It came from the group." The suggestion was to explore formally cutting the schedule from 36 months to 30 months.

It was a radical suggestion. In an industry more familiar with cost and schedule overruns than with opportunities to reduce schedules, the suggestion was overwhelming. If the group could do it, it would save the college and all the companies involved in the partnering millions of dollars.

The suggestion came up too late in the meeting for the group to make a final decision. There was, however, enough time for all present to reach an agreement that it was a possibility, that they supported it, and that a small working group of four people (one each from the architecture firm, the college, the construction company, and the electrical subcontractor) would carry out the discussions in detail and report back at the next meeting.

Buoyed by the enthusiasm of the workshop, the four people met the following week and quickly hammered out the details of the reduced schedule. They communicated their results to the overall group by e-mail and received approval back in less than a week. By the time the group had its next partnering meeting, they had already approved the schedule change in principal. It took just a few hours to work out some details, but enough time was left to make it possible to hold a celebratory dinner.

Case 2: Developing New Services

In this case, an electrical, heating, and alarm contractor develops a new service for one of its larger clients. The client, a local college, grows rapidly and increases its needs for service work. But the college does not hire the staff to provide the backup and accounting to keep track of the service work. The contractor steps into this vacuum to provide not only the electrical, heating, and alarm services, but also to develop a sophisticated accounting system for the college facilities department.

"It all started with a problem," Stanley McConnell, a service manager for Keyes North Atlantic, recalls. "The problem was the invoices. We had over 800 of them each year. For us, that was a lot. For the college, it was a nightmare.

"Our client, the college facilities department, was just not equipped to deal with the growth the college experienced. There was a period of time there, back in the mid-90s, when the college went from 60 buildings to 90. They were growing, expanding, building, adding on."

Susan Keyes, the company's CEO, adds, "Because the college took a conservative approach in its growth, they did not want to add staff in the service departments. That was understandable, but it left the facilities department with a high volume of work and not enough record-keeping and documentation to know how it was spending its money."

McConnell continues, "The real problem area was the alarms. In an office building, you might get one alarm call a month. But in a dormitory, the call rate is much higher. Kids burn things in their microwaves, that sets the alarms off. Then there's the celebrations after the big hockey games and the big football games when somebody inevitably feels like setting an alarm off adds to the festivities. We found one smoke detector full of shaving cream. It took us two and a half hours to clean it out. With 300 rooms in each dormitory, the number of alarm calls was substantial.

"The facilities department needed to know what the volume of calls was and what the costs were for each call, but they didn't have the resources to keep track of all that on their own. The situation was becoming more difficult because senior administration in the college was getting more and more concerned about rising costs. We had to be able to understand what they wanted and help train our immediate contact in the facilities department to be able to present it.

"We built the facilities department's record-keeping system over several years. We didn't really start out to do that, we were more just following one request at a time for specific pieces of information that the college senior administration was requesting. There was no plan, we had to piece things together.

"The typical phone call from the college went, 'I need to be able to understand what happened at an event last week, in order to justify the expense.'"

Susan Keyes continues, "Over the years, all those requests built up into an ongoing reporting system. Now we have cumulative records on all the buildings, along with all the services that have been provided to them.

"People who come to us from other companies tell me I'm crazy to have done all this extra work. But it's not our way to tell a customer, 'You have a problem,' and walk away. We just assume that if the customer has a problem, it's our job to figure out what we have to do to fix it."

"And it wasn't always perfect with the college, either," McConnell adds. "At one point when they were trying to save some money, they fired us. They thought our prices were too high. But it wasn't long at all—just six months—before they came back to us. They had found that they lost a lot of quality with the lower initial costs, and the quality was costing them in the long run. And then they found that they didn't even really save money with the initial costs.

"Since we've been back with them—it's been several years now—we've taken the report up a level. Instead of just doing it as a report manually, we built a database that tracks all the buildings. It's a great benefit for them; they know exactly how they are spending their money. And the historical data enables them to do some advanced projections for preventive maintenance and developing new systems. It's also good for us, it helps us deliver a higher quality of service for lower costs."

First Person:
Mark Stumer, Co-CEO, Mojo-Stumer Associates

Co-CEO of Mojo-Stumer Associates, a 20-year-old, 40-person architecture firm on Long Island, New York, Mark Stumer describes two new services the firm has developed in the course of its partnering with clients:

"One way we've raised the bar in our own practice: we've developed a way of working with clients who we think have worthy projects but don't always have money to fund them. We get involved from the very beginning, with the fund-raising effort.

"We did the marketing for the project, we even did the brochures the client used for their fund-raising. We wouldn't do this for clients we don't know. But for clients we know and partner with, it's a great way to go beyond our usual services.

"For the most part, it works well. We're members of the team with the client from the very beginning. We've done this now with two temple projects and one country club. They've all been successful in raising the funds.

"And this also got [us] involved with a second service: the printing and brochure business. We don't do a lot of this, just a few every year for key clients that wanted help and where we thought we could do an exceptionally good job. But it's helped raise the bar in our work with clients, having an additional service we can offer when it's a good fit."

Case 3: Reebok Outsources Its Soccer Ball Manufacturing, Eliminates Child Labor

Looking through the bins in any of the big sporting goods stores, the difference between the low- and high-end soccer balls is obvious even to a novice. The less expensive balls are molded and have the feel of a ball with lines notched in. Some of the mass-manufactured balls have panels glued on, which usually fall off after a few weeks of play.

The better balls are hand-stitched, better because they provide the player with a more sensitive feel and greater accuracy in shooting. The hand-stitched balls go where the player directs them, holding a straight line or curve as the kicker intended.

Until 1996, Pakistani child laborers and their families made many of these hand-stitched soccer balls in sweatshops or in their homes. The practice kept many children out of school, limiting their development and the opportunities available to them. In the sweatshops, labor practices were often brutal and exploitative.

Reebok's Actions

In 1996, Reebok crafted a new kind of outsourcing agreement with a Pakistani manufacturer. Reebok contracted with this manufacturer to produce all its soccer balls and build the manufacturer a new factory where all the balls were to be made. Having one factory gave Reebok the opportunity to inspect the manufacturing process to ensure that it did not involve child labor or any other exploitive process.

Shortly after Reebok announced its agreement, Nike followed suit. And shortly after that, the International Labor Rights Fund (ILRF) launched the "Foul Ball Campaign." Supported by politicians and policymakers, including Robert Reich, Tom Harkin, Christopher Smith, and Joseph Kennedy, the group mounted a massive publicity effort. The effort resulted in FIFA, the international soccer governance body, developing a Code of Labor Practice, which established standards for social responsibility in the manufacture of soccer balls all around the world. In other words, Reebok's actions started an effort that snowballed far beyond its own immediate concerns to affect the entire industry.

Reebok initially tried to use traditional auditing firms to check on the factories, but found their approaches ineffective in truly monitoring compliance with Reebok's human rights standards. Since then, the company has hired and trained a team of independent inspectors who monitor its factories all around the world. The company has a full-time director of its human rights program with a full-time supporting staff. In April 2004, Reebok became the first company to receive accreditation from the Fair Labor Association (FLA), a nonprofit organization that promotes adherence to international labor standards, when the FLA concluded that Reebok had met its obligations to independent and internal monitoring in the footwear factories the company uses.

Why Reebok Raised the Bar

Reebok's human rights vice president, Doug Cahn, acknowledges that supporting the human rights issues makes good business sense for the company. "At its most basic," he comments, "the business case for our work with human rights is our stakeholders, including our employees, the NGOs [Non-Governmental Organizations], and our customers. They insist on a human workplace, based on a credible set of standards."

In some ways it is possible to view Reebok's actions as preemptive, preventive damage control. If the company had not taken some kind of action against the child labor practices, there is a good chance it would have become a target of human rights campaigns. These would have damaged its reputation and affected its sales.

Yet it is also important to recognize that Reebok took the lead, moved first in the industry, and did more than it had to. Reebok did not have to force the hiring practices it did. The company did not have to develop a human rights agenda or take the extensive steps it took—building a factory and schools. A carefully documented case study of the changes, "Soccer Ball Production in Pakistan," notes that "for the well-known brands at the center of the child labor allegations, liability was not the critical determinant for action."

In trying to understand the motives for Reebok's actions, it is also essential to consider the company's history. Getting involved with human rights in manufacturing outsourcing was by no means the company's first foray into human rights issues. Reebok has a decades-long history of supporting human rights and social responsibility concerns:

- ❐ In 1986, the company withdrew from South Africa in support of the movement to end apartheid.

- ❐ In 1988, it created a human rights department, thought to be the first of its kind, and initiated a global Human Rights Award program that provides recognition and financial support for human rights efforts all around the world.

- ❐ In 1992, Reebok collaborated with Peter Gabriel and the Lawyers Committee For Human Rights to found WITNESS, a project that places video, fax, and computers in the hands of human rights activists worldwide.

In other words, Reebok's raising the bar in its manufacturing outsourcing had deep roots in the company's culture, history, and traditions. It was not a snap decision at all. Doug Cahn notes, "It was more of an evolutionary process. We supported human rights with the award programs, and that caused us to look at our own internal processes. How could we get involved in manufacturing that used child labor in one country at the same time we were giving human rights awards for another? We had to be true to our own values."

It is also important to note that Reebok's CEO Paul Fireman played an instrumental role in the company's support of human rights issues from the outset. He personally drove the company's initial involvement with Amnesty International. He personally was the only corporate representative on the National Welcoming Committee for Nelson Mandela upon Mandela's release from prison.

Doug Cahn explains, "We didn't do it because we had to. We did it because we wanted to. Fireman wanted to change the industry. We developed the supply chain management systems related to human rights to follow suit."

Implications of Reebok's Experience for Other Partnering Arrangements

Reebok's experience with the soccer ball manufacturers has direct implications for every organization that is involved with outsourcing partnering. Every outsourcing partnering relationship has the potential to address more than the bottom line, to develop human potential as well as to strengthen and bolster the bottom line.

It's true that Reebok's support of human rights helps the company's reputation, sales, revenues, and bottom line. But it's also true that the company has done far more than it has had to, that it has taken the lead in these issues instead of waiting to be dragged along by activists and government agencies.

Reebok's actions are especially noteworthy because they contrast so sharply with the "disposal mentality" other companies adopt in their handling of outsourcing partnering. By "disposal mentality," we mean that when many companies outsource a function, whether manufacturing, facilities, customer service, or support, they often walk away from it, leaving it understaffed, under-managed, underutilized, and underdeveloped.

Core Case Organizations' Experience With Raising the Bar

Lee Kennedy Co., Inc. (Construction)

"We actually give two awards internally to encourage people to raise the bar," Project Manager Pamela Bailey explains. "One goes to our field staff, the other goes to office staff. It all started with the field staff, which we call the 'Door Award,' and it traces back eight or nine years ago to a thing that Bob Hogan, one of our carpenters, did. As he was wrapping up a job, he heard that Boston Properties, one of our clients, had been getting complaints from one of their tenants about a door that didn't fit right.

"It wasn't our door, it wasn't our project, and Bob didn't ask permission from our offices to do it, he just went and spent some time, nearly a half day, making the door right. Boston Properties later asked him why he had worked so hard on something that wasn't even his problem. Bob replied that, as far as he was concerned, at the time he was working on the door, it was the most important project in the company."

Foliage Software

Co-CEO Tim Bowe comments, "We raise the bar as part of partnering in two ways. First, in a general way, we try to build Raising the Bar into everything we do. Whatever people ask us to do, we always try to deliver so that they are satisfied beyond expectations.

"Then, a more specific thing we've done to raise the bar a number of times has been to invest in our partnerships. We assign our staff to cover client projects that are not in our scope of work. Once we assigned two people for four months. We realized that our client did not have the staff or resources for work that their senior executives wanted, so we provided the staff ourselves. Once we assigned two people for four months. We didn't anticipate any new business would come out of this, it just seemed like the right thing to do."

SEi Companies
(Mechanical, electrical, and plumbing engineers)

"The way we raise the bar most often is with the timing and scheduling of our projects, and we've done this a number of times," explains firm principal Bob Flaherty. "Getting a project completed early has tremendous positive implications for most clients. We save money on the job, and they can get into the building sooner. In some cases, the company saves thousands of dollars for every day that the building is open sooner than planned.

"It takes real partnering to do this; both sides have to be getting along well in order for this to happen. The real key is that we go out of our way to have excellent communications at the beginning of the project. We do everything we can to avoid using formal channels for making changes because the informal route is much quicker. If you're there and available and you have to make a change on the project, it's just replacing a piece of pipe. If you wait two weeks, it's the same pipe, but now there's a pile of paperwork on the process, too. It's the paperwork that costs, even more than the work of the job."

PCA Architects

CEO David Chilinski comments, "The 'wow factor' is one way we raise the bar. We love to get that kind of response when people walk into their new space, it's what keeps us up at night. The way that we get the 'wow factor' so often is that I tell our people on every project, 'This is going to be our best project ever.' They tease me about it, but it's true. It's the way I really feel and it's what we really try to do.

"The other way we raise the bar is that we regularly try to get involved with projects that have some kind of social component," principal David Galler adds. "Now, for example, we're doing an intergenerational community of foster families and seniors. It's an opportunity to do something we've never done before; it's energizing. The project brings together senior citizens and foster families in one community, benefits both, and gets great social results. They're paying us a fee, but we're also investing lots of our own time because it's socially important."

ADS Financial Services Solutions
(Systems integration and software consulting)

EVP Erik Golz explains, "Raising the Bar is actually inherent to our business. When people come to us, it's not like when they are building a building, working on a tangible project. With us, they're coming to us most of the time because they are trying to raise the bar themselves, trying to make some kind of improvement in their business and processes. So we begin all our projects with this Raising-the-Bar kind of mentality.

"We are just completing a very good example of Raising the Bar. We worked with one bank that was attempting to acquire two others, initiate an IPO, and integrate their internal systems all within a very compressed time period. It's the kind of thing that had never been done before. There was some kind of blind faith (and trust) going on. We all jumped off together holding hands, and it worked."

Keyes North Atlantic
(Electromechanical contractors)

"What raising the bar is really about," contends Brad Keyes, the company's director of business development, "is challenging the customer, making sure that the customer knows what all the possibilities are. Sometimes this means not giving customers the first thing they say they want. Sometimes it's important to recognize that they don't know what they want. In fact, they can't know what they want at times because they don't know enough about what's possible.

"It's our responsibility to do this; it's not really an option. It's a funny kind of service because it doesn't always fit the model of 'customer service,' but I think that model can be too customer-centric. In a real partnership, both people take responsibility and both people do the best they can. Real partnerships are two-way streets. Ideally, both sides challenge each other, bring out the best in each other."

9

Partner, Heal Thyself: Addressing Key Internal Issues Essential for External Partnering

> Partnering initially focuses on external relationships between two organizations or departments. Yet internal issues often determine the success of external partnering. In this chapter, we examine the most important internal issues that arise and map out ways to address them. It's not necessary for organizations or departments to be perfect internally in order to partner externally. But it is important to address these issues.

External/Internal

We have met the enemy and he is us.

—Pogo

Much partnering success depends not on the relationship between two organizations, on what is going on outside the organizations, but, rather, partnering success depends in large part on what is going on *inside* the organizations.

Partner, Heal Thyself Case Illustration

A large corporate client once sponsored partnering work with one of its software service providers. The corporate client wanted the service provider to step up and improve its communications with the corporation. The corporate client liked the software service provider's technical know-how and attitude, but the client was frustrated by the service provider's slowness in responding to questions and requests.

To address this issue, we gathered a large group to work in particular on clarifying goals and mapping out processes that would ensure quicker response from the service provider to the customer. As we traced the progress of several different types of documents through the approval process, a surprise emerged that embarrassed the corporation. We discovered that the roadblocks in communications were not in the software company at all, but rather in the corporation itself. Tracing the path of actual documents, it became clear that three people in particular—including one person instrumental in initiating the partnering work—were the real culprits in slowing down communications and approvals.

When two organizations develop plans and commitments, they assume that they and their counterparts will be able to make good on those plans and commitments. However, this is not always the case. It's not that organizations attempt to mislead each other. It's more that they themselves don't know their own shortcomings. Returning to their organization after a partnering workshop, some groups have been unpleasantly surprised by their own organization's inability to deliver on the commitments they have made.

These issues should not be surprising. Partnering makes some extreme demands on the organizations and departments trying to work together. Operating alone, they may be able to stumble along for years, dragged down a bit by their internal problems, but not undone by them. But partnering bubbles and surfaces what may have seemed like minor internal problems, because the external partnering arrangement depends on several key internal issues working very well.

First Person:
A Client's Opinion About the Importance of Internal Issues

Frank Mahoney is the director of special projects at Northeastern University. As the university's point person for a number of construction projects, he has some clear ideas about what it takes for a service provider to work as an effective partner with the university. He comments on his experience working with PCA Architects on several projects, including a major dining hall renovation and a dormitory:

"Working with us as a real partner, PCA has been good in that they are in it for the long run. They understand that you have to take the bad with the good in the interest of having a long-term relationship. They also have the ability to work with us to find a middle ground between our budget constraints and their desire to build the best building possible at whatever cost. And they are very skilled at working with student involvement and teams. Having 300 students review a design can be a tough audience!

"But what makes all that work internally in their organization is, they have their act together. Most of the time I can work any issues out directly with their project manager. But when I can't, and I have to go directly to one of the owners, they're okay with that. I have to have access to everybody in their firm, and they understand that, and they make it happen. It's clear that they work together effectively internally: they communicate with each other and they get along with each other. That makes them effective partners as a whole organization, not just as individual players on the project."

5 Key Internal Issues

It is not necessary for an organization to be perfect in order to partner with other organizations. It is necessary for organizations that want to partner to handle five internal issues with particular competence: Performance Management, Internal Communications, Internal Conflicts, Unclear Lines of Authority, and Senior Management Leadership.

1. *Performance Management.* Many organizations fail to effectively manage the performance of their employees. They may use a formal mechanism of annual performance appraisals, but their system overall fails to bring individual employee performance into full alignment to support organization goals. If organizations cannot manage employee performance, they will struggle with partnering because partnering often involves changing employee job priorities. What may look like a partnering problem here—employees failing to take action on partnering goals—is really an internal organization problem, the organization's failure to manage employee performance not only in partnering, but in any significant way.

2. *Internal Communications.* Many organizations and departments themselves suffer from the Babel Problem, containing departments and groups that do not effectively share information with each other. When these organizations attempt to partner with other organizations, they often find that their internal groups that are responsible for providing information needed for the partnering cannot or will not provide it.

3. *Internal Conflicts.* Organizations that are trying to partner may also themselves be subject to their own Departments at War. It's not rare at all to have organizations at war with themselves develop partnering relationships with other organizations that also turn into pitched battles. Of course, organizations that are divided and conflicted internally often struggle when they try to partner externally with others.

4. *Unclear Lines of Authority.* People working in partnering groups sometimes make plans and commitments involving actions they anticipate they will be able to take in their own organizations. They are surprised when they discover that these actions offend people in their own organization and surface lines of authority previously hidden from view.

5. *Senior Management Leadership.* Sometimes the people who forge partnering relationships, usually people placed high enough to be considered leaders, do not lead effectively in their own organizations. Some people perform much more effectively outside their own organization than they do in it. When this occurs, it can be very difficult to resolve because it may entail making changes with the very person who initiated the partnering arrangement.

All of these key internal issues are important, but we devote the lion's share of this chapter to Performance Management because we think it is the most important item on the list. Without it, effective long-term partnering is next to impossible. With it, partnering can quickly reach new levels of performance and innovation. By providing a mechanism to alter employees' everyday job performances and priorities, effective Performance Management provides the foundation for addressing the other four internal issues of Internal Communications, Internal Conflict, Unclear Lines of Authority, and Senior Management Leadership.

Internal Performance Management Provides a Foundation for Partnering

This is an internal organization process that is important to "get right" in order for external partnering with other organizations to take place, but it is often a substantial problem. Many organizations struggle with Performance Management (that is, their ability to manage employee performance such that it truly reflects organizational goals). Consequently, they may have some kind of system in place for addressing this, which is usually an annual performance appraisal combined with employees' general efforts to do what they think their jobs are.

But in many cases, annual appraisals not only fail to align individual effort with organizational goals, they also cause a raft of problems on their own. People giving the appraisals seldom have data to back up their assessments going back for a full year. They may even be assigned to appraise employees they don't know very well. They often have to use paperwork and forms that do not bear immediate relevance for a person's job performance. And they frequently fail to use the appraisal experience as an opportunity to engage employees in career and professional development.

In the end, then, the annual appraisal process often fails to appraise fairly or to plan effectively. Most of the time it results in both the people appraising and the people being appraised justifying their positions and blaming each other for the problems. This is tragic, as it is often the annual appraisal system itself that is the real problem, not the people who are struggling to make it work.

All this is especially relevant for partnering because partnering often results in individuals needing to change their jobs. Usually this does not involve a complete, dramatic change in tasks and responsibilities, but rather a simpler adding or taking away of several specific tasks. Most often, partnering results in many employees needing to add tasks that make it possible for the partnering to work. These tasks often involve collecting new information, sharing it with the partnering organization, communicating with the partnering organization, and meeting with the partnering organization. Though these tasks are often seemingly small, they can, in all fairness, involve significant changes in a person's orientation to his or her work.

The annual appraisal process often fails to provide the infrastructure of an organization to reinforce the commitments the organization has made externally in its partnering with other organizations.

Case 1: The Annual Appraisal Problem

To say that Charles Hudson was curious about his performance appraisal did not begin to do justice to the anxiety and frustration he was feeling. It had been a full year since his last appraisal, but so much had occurred that it felt more like two or three years than one. First came the new CEO, usually not an issue. Charles had outlasted six of them in his 22-year career with Missouri Edison (ME), and noticed little change in the process.

This CEO was different, though, a troublemaker from outside the industry. Only an outsider could have had the silly notions that this one had. He reorganized the company so that the service departments, such as

Charles's real estate department, had more accountability to the business units instead of just to the company's chief engineer. Maybe that could work in companies where the business units had some faint idea about what the real estate departments did for them, but it could never work in ME. How could ME's business units assess and contract with the real estate department when they didn't fully understand what it did?

Like it or not, Charles's job began to change. For the first time in his career, Charles received directives about communicating more with the customer, satisfying the customer, and adding value. Nearly all of these memos had the word "partnering" in them. With the new focus on the business units, Charles was supposed to be partnering more—whatever that meant.

Whatever "partnering" did mean, Charles had a feeling he would find out soon—during the performance appraisal. Carl Polstan, his boss, had been trying to keep Charles on track during all the changes, offering occasional praise and more constructive criticism as Charles struggled to build partnering into his job. But Carl was part of the old system, too, so it was a little like the blind leading the blind.

Charles entered Carl's office. "Make yourself at home," Carl tried to be warm. Charles pulled a chair up to the small round table in the corner. "Go ahead," Carl advised, "take a look at the form." Charles slid the performance appraisal form over and squinted at it. Another new form? This made six, as they seemed to change with each new CEO. This form was the most confusing so far. It took Charles a good three or four minutes to find his overall rating for the year: "Acceptable."

With color instantly rising in his neck and face, Charles scarcely could hear Carl, "Now, now old man, I hope you won't take this one personally. It's just that, well, things change around here and there's been some talk from other places that you are not following the partnering line. Don't worry, it's not like you're being fired or anything, you'll just get a smaller bonus. And that's not much of an issue anyway, since all the bonuses are kind of small this year. And besides, it's only for now. If you put your heart into it, I'll bet you can turn this thing around with no problem so that things will be very different when we meet again next year."

From Annual Appraisal to Quarterly Performance Management

The previous little drama illustrates the major aspects of annual performance appraisals that make it difficult for organizations to implement partnering:

❏ *Formal feedback is too infrequent to drive change.* Carl gave some informal feedback to Charles during the year, but without a more formal conversation, Charles never fully understood the extent of the changes in his job.

❏ *Partnering tasks are unclear.* Often based on communications, the new partnering tasks Charles is supposed to carry out are not clearly defined, do not have clear outcomes, and do not readily fit in Charles's existing job description.

❏ *The conversation focuses more on justifying than on planning and problem-solving.* With a full year's worth of performance hanging in the balance, the one-hour conversation is too pressured to carry thoughtful conversation and effective problem-solving. Charles and Carl will have to meet "outside the box" on their own, if they do at all, to attempt to repair the damage.

❏ *The conversation is not an effective vehicle to plan the future.* Trying to make sense of a disappointing appraisal alone would make it difficult to plan. On top of that, there is the simple element of time. How can anyone make sensible plans for the next 12 months when it is highly likely that major changes will occur and unravel even the most thoughtful planning efforts?

While these problems with annual appraisals may seem clear, a solution often eludes organizations. Though fully aware of the shortcomings and problems built into the annual appraisal system, they live with it because they are unaware of any alternatives.

Quarterly discussions get the job of performance management done much more effectively than annual appraisals. For partnering, quarterly discussions are especially effective in providing a system to reinforce the changes people need to make in their jobs in order to take on new partnering tasks. Most people who have not experienced them react with disbelief to the thought of quarterly discussions. "You mean, the answer to this problem is to live this nightmare four times a year instead of one?"

Without directly experiencing the quarterly discussions, and with a track record of unpleasant experiences, it can be difficult to imagine that quarterly discussions work. Because they are held quarterly, the discussions follow an agenda that differs significantly from annual appraisals.

While the focus of annual appraisals is, as the label suggests, to appraise, the focus of quarterly discussions is to manage performance.

Well suited for partnering situations, the agenda for quarterly discussions addresses five points:

1. Discussing feedback, both positive and negative on the past three months. Making action plans to address any problems.

2. Linking the performance level to pay.

3. Asking the employee what he or she wants to improve on or get better at in the coming three months.

4. Writing clear job goals for the coming three months. This may take the form of the Goal-Based Work Plan described in Chapter 7. Or people can write five to seven goals reflecting a mix of tasks and roles. (The most useful goals meet the criteria of ASMART acronym. They are Agreed upon, Specific, Measurable, Attainable stretch, Results-oriented, and Time-bound.) Whether they use the Goal-Based Work Plan or five to seven ASMART goals, this is the mechanism for highlighting partnering tasks.

5. An unstructured "open door" time. During this time, either the employee or the manager may address items that are not directly related to job performance, but which they want to discuss.

Most people who consider this agenda say that it differs significantly from the annual appraisals they are used to. Quarterly performance discussions that use this agenda produce important results. Quarterly discussions:

❏ *Link feedback to action rather than to appraisal.* Because the discussions are quarterly, the focus is on using the performance feedback to make changes in the next quarter rather than justifying performance over the past year.

❏ *Provide a clear spotlight on new partnering tasks.* In planning the next quarter, manager and employee can discuss not only the new partnering tasks themselves, but also how they fit in the person's overall job.

❏ *Engage the employee in the process rather than have the employee be a "subject" of an appraisal.* It's much easier for people to buy into and take responsibility for job criteria they have been able to participate in developing.

❐ *Are less adversarial and more collaborative than annual appraisals.* Considering what annual appraisals attempt to do, it's no wonder that so many of them turn nasty and become adversarial. They are trying to accomplish so much in so little time and with such limited data. Quarterly discussions are less adversarial, and this is particularly important for partnering. It's much easier to participate in partnering externally when an organization has a harmonious environment internally.

Readers who still find it difficult to imagine how quarterly performance discussions would work might consider the way schools handle children's report cards. Most schools provide report cards four times each year. We often ask clients how they would react if their children's schools proposed to switch from this quarterly system to "one really big" report card given annually each June. Like companies that use annual appraisals, the school might explain that children will continue to receive feedback every day, and that teachers would contact parents if there was a real need or problem.

Even with this, our clients immediately reply that the annual approach would be unacceptable. They point out that the quarterly report cards provide opportunities for children to get a more comprehensive overall picture of their performance. And the quarterly approach builds in more of an opportunity for children to make changes and improvements in a more positive way.

If annual feedback is not acceptable for children in elementary school, why do adults accept it as standard practice for their own organizations and careers?

From Annual Appraisals to Quarterly Discussions: An Internal Process Essential to Support Partnering	
What's Wrong With Annual Appraisals	**How Quarterly Discussions Work**
◆ Too infrequent to track and monitor changes. ◆ Too infrequent to introduce new partnering tasks. ◆ Conversation focuses on justifying. ◆ Employee participates passively as "subject" or "victim." ◆ Inevitably adversarial.	◆ Link feedback to action rather than just judgment or appraisal. ◆ Provide a clear spotlight on partnering tasks. ◆ Engage the employee as collaborator rather than as "subject" or "victim." ◆ Conversation focuses on planning. ◆ Are more positive and less adversarial than annual discussions.

Case 2: Quarterly Performance Discussions

To say that Charles Hudson was curious about his performance discussion captured most of what he was feeling just before the discussion. It had been three months since his last discussion, so not too much time had passed. Charles thought three months was just enough time to enable him to have made some changes, but not so long that he was in an information vacuum about how he was doing.

Charles's job began to change when the new CEO came on board. For the first time in his career, Charles received directives about communicating more with the customer, satisfying the customer, and adding value. Nearly all of these memos had the word "partnering" in them. With the new focus on the business units, Charles was supposed to be partnering more—whatever that meant.

Charles began to find out more clearly what "partnering" meant, as the new CEO also instituted quarterly performance discussions. When he first heard about this idea, Charles was stunned. What possible good could come from having those meaningless discussions four times instead of one? Charles's boss, Carl Polstan, was skeptical about the quarterly discussions also. But both Charles and Carl tried the discussions with the agenda their human resources manager suggested.

Though it took a little getting used to, both Charles and Carl were pleased with the quarterly discussions. In the very first one, Carl praised Charles for the effort he put into handling the technical aspects of his job, the new building systems he had researched, and the extra effort he put into keeping the department on the leading edge of technology in the field. Even with all his experience, Charles was pleased to get the recognition. Sometimes he wondered if anyone noticed.

Carl also brought up the new tasks Charles was supposed to be taking on as part of his work in partnering with the business unit customers. He told Charles that he thought Charles could do a much better job communicating with the client, monitoring project budgets, and bringing some of the new recruits in the department up to speed on the new technologies. He told Charles that the company had communicated expectations in these areas more than six months ago, and Charles seemed to have neglected them.

Charles objected. As he saw it, the customers didn't know enough about what he did to participate in the process, the project budgets were meaningless paperwork, and the new recruits were lazy. Carl listened without agreeing or disagreeing. He reminded Charles, calmly but steadily, that this was the way the company was going. Charles was about to object with the line "I was not hired to do this," but he stopped himself. Of course he hadn't been hired to do these things. What he was hired for 20 years ago was probably irrelevant now.

What really got Charles's attention was the bottom line: he would not be receiving the traditional bonus in the coming quarter. Carl apologized for it, hemmed and hawed, but still held his ground. "I'm sorry it has to be this way, but it really does. This is what the company wants, and in the end, once I've calmed down myself, I have to agree with them. The senior managers have been telling us this for months. They're entitled to pay for what they get."

Charles fumed silently. In his entire career with ME, this was the first time he had ever heard of anyone not getting his or her bonus. And now he himself was the one not getting it. His first thought was that he would be the brunt of all sorts of gossip and speculation among his peers. (Although the company mandated that all salary-related discussions were to be strictly confidential, somehow the grapevine consistently produced accurate, highly personal information for anyone who cared to listen to it.)

Carl interrupted Charles's mood, "Why don't you and I try to figure out some ways that you can involve the customer that will satisfy both them and you also? It doesn't have to be either one or the other."

Begrudgingly at first, Charles began to work with Carl. Once he accepted the fact that he really had to do it, he found that it was easy to come up with ideas for addressing Carl's criticisms. He had little trouble thinking of ways to involve the client and communicate more with them. There were three or four logical stop points in every project when it would be easy to meet briefly with the client and get some input. There were also regular project meetings that the client could attend. Similarly, Charles found himself able to quickly outline how he might be able to improve his ability in managing project budgets and how he could find some time to mentor some of the younger ME staff.

Charles and Carl drove their discussions a little further, delineating ASMART goals Charles felt comfortable he could achieve in the next quarter:

❑ Earn customer satisfaction ratings on surveys at a level of 20 percent Excellent, 60 percent Good, 20 percent Average, and no serious complaints.

❑ Participate in discussion of job priorities with four major business unit customers. Adjust job priorities accordingly.

❑ Manage budgets to be aware of all conditions and encounter no surprises. Increase project profitability by a factor of 20 percent. Manage budgets to withstand peer audit.

❏ Take on one junior staff member in mentoring work. Move
that person to be one level closer to being able to take over
Charles's job.

❏ As a team member, make sure that all other team
members know enough about Charles's work to avoid any
duplicated effort and to identify possible collaborations.

Addressing the topic of what Charles wanted to improve on, he and
Carl discussed training that interested Carl. He knew that he needed
business-skills training as well as some work with improving his mentoring
skills. What excited him more, though, was his interest in the new technologies the business units were exploring on their own. Carl and he worked
up a brief plan to involve Charles in the technical training the business
units were scheduled to work with in the coming year. That would both
place Charles into more partnering communications with the client and
enable him to pick up more of the technical skills that energized him.

Finally, reaching the "open door" topic on the agenda, Charles re-
laxed. "You know, I came in here fully prepared to tell you off. But somehow, the way the discussion went took the wind out of my sails. I can't say
that you've completely won me over. I can't say that I fully buy into that
partnering concept. But I will give it a shot."

The Issue of Pay

As the previous case profile illustrates, what the organization reinforces in what it pays employees for is an essential part of performance
management. Unfortunately, few organizations do a good job in this area.
Many organizations give all employees blanket raises or decreases, simply
following the rise and fall of the economy. It's difficult for organizations
to link pay to individual effort. They worry about offending people who
don't receive the bonuses they think they have earned.

Several times a month, we ask groups of people in seminars and consulting projects about their organization's pay practices—usually, 3,000 to
4,000 people annually, over the past 10 years. When we ask about pay
practices, people say, "Well, we have an annual appraisal process." But
when we ask if the pay process is effective in holding people accountable
and in reinforcing the company's goals, the clear majority of people in
all kinds of organizations respond in the negative. Their organizations
do not hold people appropriately accountable or reinforce the
organization's goals.

This problem area, the failure to link pay practices with organizational
goals, is a huge problem for partnering. It is also difficult to get people to

change their job priorities to include new partnering tasks if an organization's pay practices don't reinforce the changes. All the memos from corporate, the slide shows, the formal announcements, and meaningful discussions don't have as much impact on employees as the criteria for deciding what goes in their paychecks.

Agenda for Effective Quarterly Performance Discussions

1. Discuss feedback, both positive and negative, on the past three months. Make action plans to address any problems.
2. Link the performance level to pay.
3. Ask the employee what he or she wants to improve on or get better at in the coming three months.
4. Write clear job goals for the coming three months. Use ASMART goals format and/or Goal-Based Work Plan.
5. Unstructured "open door" time.

After Performance Management: Addressing the Other Internal Issues

What's an organization to do? How good does an organization have to be internally in order to partner externally with other organizations? It's obvious if an organization has problems in Internal Communications, Internal Conflicts, Unclear Lines of Authority, or Senior Management Leadership, those problems will undermine the organization's ability to partner externally with other organizations.

But what is an organization to do? Is it necessary to be perfect in all these areas? If it is, then many organizations will turn away from attempting to partner. They know that their internal problems are too severe.

The answer to the "how good is good enough for partnering" question is simple, but in most cases it has ramifications. Organizations that want to partner externally don't have to be perfect internally, but they have to be "good enough" to effectively follow through on the commitments they make in their partnering agreements. In most cases, this means both that partnering is possible and that it will take some internal work in order to make the partnering effective.

In the four areas noted earlier in this chapter (Internal Communications, Internal Conflicts, Unclear Lines of Authority, and Senior Management Leadership) the work to be done follows the criteria outlined in the following sections:

Internal Communications

No organization has perfect internal communications, and perfect internal communications are not necessary for external partnering. What is necessary is that both organizations in the partnership develop an ability both to share existing information with their partner and to develop and coordinate new forms of information necessary to track and monitor the performance of the partnership. Sharing existing information across organizational lines with the partnering organization may sound simple, but it often is not because some people resist doing it. "Yes, I know we are partnering with them, but does that really mean we need to share our xyz (salary, project profitability, schedule, customer satisfaction, and so on) information?"

Developing and sharing new information is even more complex because it often asks people to report in some way on their own progress. People often resist doing this because it spotlights any performance problems they may be having. People also often resist doing this, even when the information they are being asked to report is simple, because they find the act of reporting it annoying. Every organization that asks its staff to submit weekly time sheets struggles at least at some times with this simple request. The same struggle emerges when partnering arrangements ask people to file any kind of new report on their work.

Whatever the struggles for improving internal communications are, it's usually possible to solve them in two ways. First, partnering organizations can clearly make new information-sharing tasks part of people's jobs by using the quarterly performance management tasks outlined on page 166. Second, it's often useful for partnering groups to designate one or two people in the group to take responsibility for coordinating all the new information-collecting and -reporting tasks necessary for the partnership to be effective.

Internal Conflicts and Unclear Lines of Authority

Some internal conflicts may surface in organizations before they attempt to partner, but the issues that most concern partnering are the conflicts and lack of clarity that arise later on. Conflicts before partnering are not so difficult because they usually sort themselves out before the partnering begins. People in an organization may well differ, and differ with some emotion, in their opinions about whether the organization should partner with others. But it's unusual for people to get involved in partnering without some mandate from their own organization that the partnering effort is acceptable.

The larger issue is about what the organization is able to do to follow up on the goals, processes, and procedures that partnering groups develop. People usually describe these issues either as "Internal Conflicts" or as "Unclear Lines of Authority." In these cases, two processes usually resolve any problems: performance management that clears up the new tasks people need to take on as part of the partnering work; and internal partnering, following much the same set of steps as the partnering between organizations.

For example, a partnering arrangement between a design department and an accounting department produces an agreement that the accounting department will produce integrated reporting of both its accounts payable and its accounts receivable for the designers. Upon returning to the accounting department, people at the partnering workshop encounter a conflict between the accounts payable and the accounts receivable groups. Their longstanding tradition of Departments at War makes it difficult for them to deliver the coordinated report the partnering group promised. Department management addresses the problem in part by clarifying that this is a part of their job, and holds them accountable for it with their pay. Going a step further, the department embarks on its own internal partnering.

Senior Management Leadership

Occasionally, ineffective senior management and leadership are the internal issues that stop an organization from implementing partnering plans and promises. Senior management problems can undermine partnering in especially serious ways, because it may be the senior managers who themselves initiated the partnering who are most criticized in their own organizations.

Fortunately, the Partnering Solution process itself seems to address most senior management and leadership problems, though not always in a way that is graceful for the leader. As the partnering groups form, they dilute the power and influence of individual leaders. Groups, not individual leaders, write partnering Goals Statements. Groups implement partnering processes. Groups of individuals learn to work with each other. Especially when meetings are facilitated effectively, the power and influence of any one individual is limited and redirected to the partnering group.

Thus, individuals are seldom placed in a position where they have to exert a lot of leadership in their own organizations. When individual leaders do come back to their organizations with leadership approaches and communications that may undermine partnering, the rest of the partnering group is likely to challenge them. Well-facilitated meetings, and the Partnering Solution overall, "level the playing field." No one individual is intrinsically worth more or less than any other. The partnering group uses its peer power and pressure to govern itself and maintain its own equilibrium.

First Person: Internal Processes That Reinforce External Partnering

Mark Stumer, co-CEO of Mojo-Stumer Associates, a 40-person architecture firm based on Long Island, New York, comments, "We actually have two internal processes that reinforce our partnering efforts with clients. We didn't intentionally develop them that way, but they amount to a combination of a carrot and a stick, a reward and a reinforcer.

"The carrot we have is what we call the 'In-House Consultant.' That's a bonus we give to four or five employees about every two weeks. It's usually $100 or $200 each time. We give it for going above and beyond in working with clients. Not just for doing their job anyway, but for really going beyond the job.

"We have examples of that all the time. Last week one of our people drove a client home after a meeting. He didn't have to do it, and it took him out of his way. He just went ahead and did it. Another project manager forgot some fabric samples. The client said it wasn't a problem, but our project manager still made the trip all the way back to our office and then back into the city. The client was delighted. Another one of our people bought a client a birthday gift with his own money. All these are little things, but we think they add up.

"Then on the reinforcement side, we have an internal process we think is very important. We require all our project managers to keep a phone log, to record every contact they make with clients. Some people may think this is a bit much, not the right kind of thing to ask professionals to do. But for our client base, it's extremely important.

"This is New York. Our clients are very demanding people. We get calls every week, complaints from clients that their project manager hasn't kept in touch. By having the phone logs, we are able to get back to them and remind them of calls our people made that they forgot.

"So the phone log supports partnering, it strengthens our relationships with clients. It helps our people get back to the client, it supports our people. And it reminds the client of the good work our people are doing."

Core Case Organizations' Experience With Internal Processes

PCA Architects

"We actually do the quarterly performance discussions," principal Eric Brown explains, "and they really do help to keep us focused on partnering. It was a big change for us, since we really didn't even do much with annual appraisals before.

"But the quarterly discussions work great. They are not adversarial, both our managers and our staff like them. They force us to pay attention to our staff's professional development needs, and that contributes to partnering. And they are extremely effective in surfacing and addressing any problems that come up with staff behavior. Seeing how well the quarterly discussions work, I can't imagine how any organization could do a good job reinforcing partnering behaviors without them."

Foliage Software

"To reinforce our external work with partnering, we've become a completely different organization internally over the past few years," reflects co-CEO Ron Rubbico. "We used to be organized horizontally, with all the technical staff in a large group. But we realized, in order to really partner with our customers, we had to reorganize into divisions that reflect our four different customer bases: financial services, semiconductors, aerospace, and medical. The new organization gives our customers much more specialized knowledge of their issues.

"We also had to retrain our technical staff to pay much more attention to business issues, not just technical ones. We used to think of ourselves only as excellent technologists. Now we also think of ourselves as being able to solve business problems. It's a big leap, but our staff welcomed it. There was some reticence at first, but they've come to embrace the change in focus."

SEi Companies
(Mechanical, electrical, and plumbing engineers)

Principal Bob Flaherty points out, "Our CEO has developed an absolutely brilliant set of formulas that make it sure that we pay people to reflect our partnering orientation. He's presented these at seminars at Harvard and had people tell him he is a genius. The formulas deliver on the premise that we believe in partnering; they carry our partnering philosophy into the everyday operations of the firm.

"But I don't think that's what really makes the difference. I think the pay-for-partnering performance approach is solid, sure. But I don't think most of us sit here and say, 'I'm making the extra call to the client because I'm getting paid for it.' I think we make the extra call because we believe it's the right thing to do. I think the real thing we've done internally to help us deliver on our goals for partnering externally is to hire people who have that orientation in the first place. We're very careful about who we hire. Their support of a partnering orientation is as important as their technical engineering skills."

ADS Financial Services Solutions (Systems integration and software consulting)

"It's our project management office, our PMO, that provides the internal mechanism that helps us achieve our external partnering goals," EVP Erik Golz notes. "The PMO is an internal group, like an audit team, that rides herd over all our projects. The group conducts a weekly internal review of each project. If you have that accountability on projects, it keeps 'surprises' from happening.

"The PMO can be tough. The members don't care how hard it may be for you to get the reports ready, they come after you. It's not so much that they are difficult people, it's more that they are slaves to the process. They believe, we all believe, that it's crucial for us internally to have this kind of discipline in order to partner effectively with our clients."

Lee Kennedy Co., Inc. (Construction)

"Training we've done internally has helped us deliver on our partnering goals," comments company president, Lee Michael Kennedy. "We did communications skills training—learning how to communicate effectively in one-on-one situations, delivering bad news; communicating in small groups, learning how to get your point across while also empathizing with others; also how to speak in front of large groups. In the beginning, people were nervous, reluctant. But at the end, people felt better about themselves.

"It all helps with partnering because so much of partnering involves communicating. Any way we can improve our communications skills has got to help our ability to partner with our customers. Ninety-nine percent of what we're doing is solving peoples' issues—their issues and challenges. Part of it all is being a good listener. That's what this training is about."

Keyes North Atlantic (Electromechanical contractors)

"The internal work that we do to support external partnering focuses on processes," CEO Susan Keyes comments. "We find that it's useful to develop internal processes that reflect our client's internal issues. For example, we have one very big client who operates on a long payment cycle. That has the potential to be damaging for our cash flow, but we have just developed our own processes so that we can absorb that issue.

"We also do training internally to support our external partnering. We provide lots of technical training. Because our field is always changing, there are always new products. We also have done communications training for our field staff. It's been effective, but in a funny way. I doubt that anyone who participated could remember the concepts, but they do remember the intention: that we make more of an effort to communicate effectively. I know that counts when they are talking with our customers."

10

Improving Meetings and Group Communications Skills

Much of the work of partnering gets done in meetings. This may initially trouble many people, because many people's experiences with meetings are frustrating. However, it is quite possible to substantially improve meeting effectiveness by following several relatively simple guidelines.

In this chapter, we describe the recurring, predictable problems meetings encounter and provide straightforward strategies and skills that consistently improve meetings of all types. Whether you work with the full Partnering Solution or not, you will find these strategies and skills helpful for understanding groups and running many kinds of meetings more effectively.

Improving Meetings Skills for Partnering

A meeting is a cul-de-sac down which ideas are lured and then quietly strangled.

—Sir Barnett Cocks

With all the negative experiences people have had in meetings, it can justifiably worry people that meetings figure so prominently in shaping overall partnering effectiveness. Yet it is important to recognize that it is quite possible to dramatically improve meeting effectiveness, and with relatively little effort.

Even with advanced electronic communications, video-conferencing technologies, and groupware software widely available, meetings remain essential for much of the most important work done in partnering. In particular, it seems that meetings are the most effective means for handling partnering tasks including:

- ❏ The initial partnering workshop.
- ❏ Follow-up partnering workshops.
- ❏ Small group work addressing action items between partnering workshops.
- ❏ Ongoing meetings between partners to track and monitor partnering performance.
- ❏ Ongoing meetings between partners to identify new opportunities and raise the bar.
- ❏ "Lessons learned" meetings.

The criticisms many people have of meetings are well-founded. We frequently hear about meetings of all kinds that are unproductive in achieving results, uncoordinated, wasteful, disorganized, and plain old boring. We often directly observe intelligent, well-trained managers running meetings with little or no real skill.

However, it is quite possible to substantially improve meeting effectiveness by following several relatively simple guidelines. In this chapter, we describe the recurring, predictable problems meetings encounter and provide simple guidelines for improving meeting effectiveness. We also describe specific agendas for several different types of partnering meetings so that all those meetings deliver the significant potential that all meetings have.

Understanding Group Communications: Potential and Problems

It's useful to begin improving meetings by trying to understand the built-in problems and potentials that all groups have. This in itself is a useful perspective to keep in mind for every partnering meeting: every time one convenes a group or calls a meeting, one faces built-in problems and potentials—recurring, predictable problems and potentials.

It is also always useful to keep in mind that people change their behavior in meetings. The same person who chatted with you amiably in the hallway a half hour before the meeting is likely to change when he or she sits in a meeting, surrounded by others in the group. (At least, the changes are somewhat predictable!)

The potentials that all groups have are powerful, providing a driving force for the increase in committees, task forces, and group work at all levels of organizations.

Groups: The Problem

"All those in favor say 'Aye.'"
"Aye."
"Aye."
"Aye."
"Aye."
"Aye."

❐ *Synergy.* Every group has the potential to perform at levels greater than the sum of its parts. This is the equivalent, for businesses, of a basketball team that passes well. The passing, the connections among the players, multiply their individual skills.

❐ *Positive individual impacts.* Every group also has the potential to improve every member, to bring each member at least up to the level of the highest player.

❐ *Motivation.* Groups have a strong potential to motivate their individual members, to provide positive encouragement, constructive criticism, and praise.

❐ *Diverse thinking.* Every group has the potential to bring diverse kinds of thinking to its work. This diversity can help it spot problems and explore opportunities more effectively than people working individually.

❑ *Link to the larger organization.* Even small organizations are often too large for people to bond with at a deep level. Groups of all kinds help their members forge a bond with the larger organization of which the groups are a part.

At the same time, groups also face a daunting list of predictable negative forces:

❑ *Negativity.* Some research strongly suggests that people in a group tend to be much more negative than people working individually.

❑ *Passivity.* People who take an active, positive stance can easily and quickly become passive in a group. (Anyone who has spoken to people individually before a meeting and then been disappointed by their passive response in the meeting is painfully aware of this problem.)

❑ *Individual focus.* Quite often, and even when the topic a group is addressing is "teamwork," individual members are thinking most about how the discussion affects them as individuals.

❑ *Groupthink.* Sometimes the problem with groups is not that they disagree too much, but that they agree too easily—to a solution that proves to be shortsighted and incorrect. (The researcher who coined the term *groupthink* based it on his studies of government and military groups who agreed to invade Cuba at the time of the missile crisis. Their quick agreement and neglect of data that could have helped them led the United States to the brink of a nuclear disaster.)

❑ *Vocal minority.* Groups tend to be led by a minority that is vocal, but not necessarily representative, of the overall group.

❑ *Ethical dark side.* Groups have extreme power to influence individual behavior, and not always in support of ethically positive choices. Some of the most chilling cases of bad ethics are stories of a group's power to get individuals to conform.

All of both the positive and negative tendencies of groups are possible in every partnering group and meeting. The chief implication for partnering of the positive and negative tendencies of groups is that it is extremely important for people trying to partner to facilitate meetings with a high level of skill. With skills, partnering groups and the meetings they hold can be extraordinarily productive. Without skills, partnering groups and meetings may not only be unproductive, they may actively cause problems.

First Person: Improving Meetings and Group Communications— A Partner's Perspective

Jeanne Vanecko is president of Vanecko, Ltd. Architecture and Design, a six-person architecture and design firm based in Charlestown, Massachusetts. She describes how partnering involves meetings, and what it takes to communicate at high levels of effectiveness in the meetings.

She uses a partnering approach in much of her work, but notes, "The partnering model produces excellent results but it's not right for everybody. We tried to involve a famous local designer in one of our projects, and we explained how our partnering approach works. He agreed to everything, but didn't do any of it in communications and meetings.

"By contrast, Keyes North Atlantic understands partnering and the company is very effective at it. We work with Brad Keyes a lot. He's very good at listening, but that's just part of it. He's also very participative and active. He brings ideas to the table in addition to listening.

"Brad has this great integrative skill for communicating in meetings. He may come in with a solution, but he modifies that based on listening to the whole team. *That* makes the whole team more effective.

"Their whole firm is wonderful at problem-solving in the field. That's how so much of this business works. No matter how detailed the drawings are, you have to be fast on your feet, working with small groups in the field to solve problems to get all the pieces to fit together. The group has to be able to come up with solutions on the fly."

Partnering Meetings Without and With Skills

To provide a more accurate sense of how unproductive typical group discussions are and how productive they can be, we provide two brief case examples and an explanation of the skills used to make the improvements. For both cases, we use the partnering agenda item of Taking Stock.

The Discussion: Beginning

Fourteen people are supposed to be attending this partnering meeting between the college dining managers and Dineco, the service provider firm that provides the meals and hospitality services. The college has been registering complaints, and Dineco has tried to respond, but neither organization is pleased with the overall results. The college would like Dineco to do better, and Dineco would like to make improvements that will help, but different people in the college tell them different, and often conflicting, things.

Once everyone has arrived, Mary Moore, Dineco's account manager for the college, kicks the meeting off: "I guess we all know why we're here. There have been some problems expressed and some attempts made to resolve them. I think we are seeing some progress, but neither side is really completely pleased with the results so far. Now, we all know what the agenda is, because I sent it out last week. Why don't we begin with that Taking Stock piece and an open discussion."

Discussion 1: Unfacilitated

"So let's keep it open," Mary continued. "Why don't you just speak up when you're comfortable, say anything that comes to mind. Just what are your concerns about all this?"

A long moment or two of silence passed while the group sat frozen in place. Finally, George Plante, one of Dineco's account managers spoke up, "All right, I'll go first if everyone else is uncomfortable. Somebody's got to get this thing rolling.

"My concern," he continued, "and I don't quite know how to put this, is that we can't seem to satisfy you people. You've made some complaints, and that's fine. But we've tried to respond, and we can't seem to get a straight answer from you. It's as if the only time you talk to each other is at these meetings. Different people on your side tell us different things." George tried to sound apologetic and respectful, the college was a big account and he did not want to lose it. He paused, "Does anybody else want to say anything here? I'm kind of out on a..."

Before George could finish, Mary interrupted. "I know, I know, you've said this before. But we just can't make sense of that kind of criticism. We're communicating with each other all the time. We meet with each other as a group every week. We agree to the basic principles of this thing months ago. I really think the problem here is that you're not trying hard enough." Mary did not try to sound apologetic. There were plenty of service providers out there. It was time to get Dineco to do the job they were contracted for.

"Come on staff," Mary chided her managers. "Feel free to disagree with me, say what you really think. This is an open meeting, after all." She really did hope that, if they did disagree, they would feel comfortable saying so. She was more interested in solving the problem than protecting her ego.

"No, boss, you're right about this one," Jim Laker agreed. Jim was the manager of dining services, a good manager with more than 20 years' experience at the college. The others said nothing, but Mary thought they looked positive. None of them disagreed, anyway.

"Well, if none of them will speak up, I guess it's back to me," George stood up. He wondered a little why his own staff wasn't backing him up, but continued. After all, somebody had to come to Dineco's defense. "I just happen to have brought along a small stack," he waved a sheaf of papers at the group, "of information requests the college has filed in the past two months. When you take a few minutes to go through these, you'll see…"

Again, Mary interrupted him, "Does this mean you've actually been counting these things, keeping some kind of records to cover yourself? So, I guess all those things my staff has been telling me about a 'lack of trust' really are true…."

The Problems and the Skills

As the discussion continues following this pattern for another half hour, several important statistics emerge:

1. Of the 14 people present at the meeting, only six participate: Mary, Jim, George, and three middle managers from Dineco.
2. Of those six, George and Mary do most of the talking.
3. Most of the discussion consists of "point-counterpoint," accusations and defenses, with no real in-depth exploration of the issues.

This kind of discussion, all too familiar to many people who spend a lot of time in meetings, illustrates the predictable problems of groups: a vocal minority dominates, most of the discussion is negative and critical, and most of the group is passive.

Making just two small changes in the way the discussion is set up would produce significant, almost incredible improvements. (We are very confident about this claim because we frequently do this as a learning exercise in our seminars. We run a typical meeting for five to 10 minutes, make the following suggestions for changes, then watch and listen as participants express amazement.) The two changes are first, changing the wording of the question, and second, reorganizing the large group into several smaller groups.

It's interesting just to think about the question the facilitator asks the group. In our seminar exercise, few people recall the exact wording of the question. That seems to be how people think about questions in their regular meetings as well, which is to say that they do not think about them. People think about the slides they are going to show, the points they are going to make, and the agenda items they are going to address.

But people seldom think about the questions they are going to ask, and that's a pity because groups answer whatever question they are asked. They take the question at face value and give it their best shot. If a leader asks a group, "What are your concerns?" the group will answer with a lengthy list of concerns. If the leader asks, "What problems do you have with this?" the group will list their problems.

Taking this point along with the point that groups tend to gravitate to negativity in their discussions, it is essential to ask all group questions in a (+) and (−) form. In other words, instead of asking, "What are your concerns about the partnering arrangement?" the facilitator should ask, "What three aspects of the partnering arrangement are working well, and what three aspects of the partnering arrangement most need improvement?"

In a partnering workshop discussing a new project, the question is worded, "What three major aspects of the project do you think will work well, and what three major aspects of the project do you think may be problematic?" In a meeting where the facilitator knows the two partnering groups have a history of mutual frustration and distrust, it's important to use that information and ask, "What three things does the other group do that frustrate you most, and what three things do you do that you know frustrates them most?" This question surfaces the information, disarms and loosens up the group, and gets everyone in the room laughing.

After rephrasing the question, the second change the facilitator must make is to divide the large group into several smaller subgroups. Three or four people in a subgroup is productive. Two is okay, if necessary. At five, the group begins to lose a person. The facilitator forms these subgroups with a purpose, not just on a whim. In the Taking Stock case example on pages 70–72, the facilitator might divide the group of 14 into four groups, with several people from each organization in each group. Or the facilitator might choose to create four groups, all comprised of members of the same organization only. The facilitator would choose the mixed group approach if it seemed that people are open and comfortable enough with one another to speak openly in the small group.

To get a sense of how these two changes impact the group discussion, we can return to the case sample discussion and start it again from the point at which Mary asks the group the discussion question. In the new version of the case that follows, Mary asks a different question.

Discussion 2: Facilitated and Productive

"So let's keep it open," Mary continued. "Why don't you just speak up when you're comfortable, say anything that comes to mind. Just what are your concerns about all this?"

"Actually, wait a second, before you answer that question, let me change it a little. What I really want to ask is a more specific question: What three major aspects of our partnering do you think are working well, and what three major aspects of our partnering need to be improved?"

"Before we dive into this," Mary continued, "maybe it would be useful for you to write down a few of your own thoughts on this question." To Mary's surprise, no one objected to this suggestion, and several people reached for notepaper and pencil.

After a few minutes, once Mary could see that most people had a few items written down, she spoke again, "In order to make this discussion organized and make sure all of you really have a chance to voice your opinions, I want to organize you into four smaller groups. I thought ahead of time about how to structure these groups so that each one will have a good mix of people from both organizations. Here's my list."

She read the list hesitantly, wondering if anyone in the group would protest to being moved around. No one protested, but several people seemed confused.

"What?" George Plante asked, scratching his head. "Where do I go? Who do I sit with?"

Jim Laker also stared blankly, "What are we supposed to do? What question are we trying to answer?"

Though she was surprised that apparently neither George nor Jim had paid attention to her directions, Mary patiently repeated them.

"Small groups?" George asked as he moved. "Why are we doing that? That's the kind of thing we do at church meetings. How will we hear everybody's opinions if we're all split up like that?"

Mary replied, "Oh, I'll bring you back together for that. But first, it's very important that everybody has a chance to speak. If we stay in one big group, that will take much too long. Breaking up like this for a few minutes is just a more efficient way to have the discussion."

"Okay, if you say so," George replied, shaking his head and settling into his group.

Choosing the person in each group who was lowest in the formal hierarchy of the organizations, Mary assigned a person in each group to take the notes for that group. She asked them to take the notes on flip chart pages she had taped in the four corners of the room. She had them divide each chart into three columns. The first column was headed "Working Well," the second, "Needs Improvement," and the third, "Questions or Suggestions."

Mary asked the note-taker in each group to be sure to get one or two items in each column from each person in the group. She repeated that request several times, observing that it seemed to address peoples' concerns about what they were supposed to do.

As the four groups milled quietly around the flip charts, Mary's stomach plummeted. She worried that they might all just stand there, perhaps for hours, saying nothing.

Then one of the note-takers, an hourly employee from the college, quietly asked his group, "Well, what do we think? Can I get one or two positives from each of us? What aspects of our partnering do we think are working well?"

One of his counterparts from the college, another hourly worker replied, "Well I'm not so sure about the partnering side of it, but I can tell you that the actual food that you people prepare is better than anything the college has ever seen."

"Really?" a Dineco manager in the group replied. "That's great to hear. I was worried that all we were going to hear today was complaints. As long as we're on a positive roll here, I'd like to say that, as far as colleges go, you people aren't nearly as disorganized as some of the other ones I've worked with. And at least when you are disorganized, you're polite with us about it."

"So shall I list 'Polite' in the 'Working Well' column?" the note-taker asked, the group nodding affirmatively.

As she continued to listen to this group, Mary realized that the other three groups had also all started. Pausing to look around the room, she noticed that every person, all 14 of them, was actively involved in the discussions. As she continued to watch, she also noticed that, unlike in the unstructured discussion, no one dominated in this one, and, equally, no one dropped out. Watching the groups all list items in the "Working

Well" column, she also realized that they all had some positive things to say.

Continuing to observe, Mary reflected that the groups were getting a lot done in a brief period of time. Within 20 minutes, each group had completed its chart and was beginning to look at the other groups' charts. Mary began to bring the groups together to report to the whole group on what they had discussed.

Unfacilitated vs. Facilitated

What really differs between the unfacilitated and facilitated versions of the meeting? It's worth noting that the differences occur in three areas: who participates, the tone of their participation, and the results of their participation.

☐ *Who participates.* In the unfacilitated meeting, a vocal minority dominates. Most people are passive, and some do not participate at all. In the facilitated meeting, everyone participates about equally. No one dominates and no one drops out.

☐ *Tone of participation.* In the unfacilitated meeting, most of the discussion is negative, critical, and focused on blame. In the facilitated meeting, the discussion is more balanced and focuses on plans and actions.

☐ *Results of participation.* In the unfacilitated meeting, the outcomes and results are "venting" lists of complaints. In the facilitated meeting, the results are more productive for solving problems and taking action.

Unfacilitated vs. Facilitated: A Tale of Two Meetings	
Unfacilitated, "Open," Unstructured	**Facilitated, Structured, Small Groups**
◆ Vocal minority dominates. ◆ Most people are passive. ◆ Some do not participate at all. ◆ Discussion is mostly negative and critical. ◆ Disorganized. ◆ Focused on blaming others. ◆ Chaotic and unproductive.	◆ No one dominates. ◆ Everyone participates comfortably. ◆ No one drops out. ◆ Discussion is balanced, pros and cons. ◆ Organized. ◆ Focused on action. ◆ Productive.

A Note on Using Flip Charts

Group discussions are almost always more productive when the group uses a flip chart to record its notes. Flip charts contribute to group discussions in several important ways:

❏ *Making the collective wisdom available for each individual.* Even after just five or 10 minutes of discussion, most groups have generated a wealth of ideas. Listing those ideas on a flip chart page makes them all accessible to all the members of the group.

❏ *Action bias.* Many groups complain that they seem to have effective discussions, but often fail to convert their insights into clear action steps. Groups can successfully address this issue by dividing a flip chart into two columns at the beginning of their meetings. They head the left column "Agenda Topics" and the right column "Action Items: What, Who, When." Throughout the discussion of each agenda item, the chart reminds the group to move toward outlining an action item specific enough to assign it to an individual and commit to a completion date.

❏ *Less repetition.* Seeing what the group has already covered, individuals are less likely to repeat.

❏ *Synthesis.* Reviewing a whole list of what a group has discussed, individuals can assemble strings of items into coherent combinations of ideas.

❏ *Visibility.* Working in small groups, people can glance at the charts of the other groups to keep up to date with what the other groups are addressing.

❏ *Portability.* Unlike whiteboards and electronic bulletin boards, low-tech flip charts can be easily moved from one place to another and folded and unfolded for easy viewing and review.

❏ *Note-taking and meeting minutes.* Flip charts offer an efficient tool for keeping the notes and minutes of a meeting. When the meeting has ended, the facilitator can have the charts reduced to 8 1/2 × 11 standard size paper for minimal cost at many commercial copy centers.

Frequently Asked Questions About Facilitation: Can I Really Do This?

Whenever we demonstrate the facilitation skills in seminars, people have the same reactions and ask the same questions. They always express amazement that the small changes in the group, changing the question and reorganizing the larger group into subgroups, have such dramatic effects.

Despite the power of what they've seen and their own comfort with the effectiveness of the skills, though, people also usually worry when they imagine using the skills with their own group. They ask questions such as these (read on for answers):

- ❐ Can I really do this with my own group?
- ❐ How will they react?
- ❐ What if they refuse to do the things I am asking—the subgroups and all that?
- ❐ Am I supposed to run every meeting like this? Surely, this method is not appropriate in some cases, for certain kinds of meetings?

Can I really do this with my own group? Of course you can. Just because groups have been working a particular way for some time, that doesn't mean that they can't make changes.

How will they react? A seminar participant who tried the facilitated approach in a weekly partnering meeting that had been going on regularly left us a voice mail noting, "They just about fainted. 'You want us to do *what?*' they kept asking. But they did it, and I am even now, four days after the meeting, still getting e-mails telling me it was the best meeting we ever had. We had people participating who hadn't said anything in months, and others who usually dominate the meeting keeping quiet."

What if they refuse? In 20 years of running meetings this way with thousands of different kinds of groups, none has yet refused. This is not to say that it's impossible that it could happen, just that it hasn't occurred so far. I believe one reason groups go along when we run meetings this way in part is because they expect us, as facilitators, to do things differently than they are used to. I also believe groups follow our requests because we make them respectfully, and because we explain that they are not tricks or gimmicks, but a necessity. We have a limited amount of time and a number of people who should participate. In order to have everyone contribute, it's necessary for at least part of the meeting for the large group to work in smaller subgroups.

Is it necessary to run all meetings this way? Experiencing a well-facilitated meeting can shake peoples' foundations of expectations for meetings—in a good way. Surely there is still a need to bring a whole group together to make announcements, or to have a status meeting. We hold beliefs in this area that some people may consider radical, but we think they are essential for partnering success. We believe that the only circumstance in which it's all right to have a meeting where one or two people announce (or worse, read—or worst of all, read bulleted items on a PowerPoint slide) to a group is if the group is illiterate. On the other hand, we do believe that it is often important to meet to discuss what has been read. In partnering, people need meetings not to announce, but to discuss. We detail how this principle applies to specific types of meetings in the following sections.

Discussion Agenda 1: Getting Input

The Taking Stock discussion described on pages 70–72 fits this category. The purpose of this type of discussion is not to solve a problem or take action (yet), but, more simply, to get input from the group. This kind of meeting follows this sequence:

"Getting Input" Discussion	
Topic	**Format**
Leader describes the issues.	Leader addresses whole group. (5 minutes)
Small group discussion. Each subgroup lists three columns: Major Positive Aspects of the Topic, Major Negative Aspects of the Topic, and Questions/ Suggestions (for example, major aspects of partnering working well and major aspects of partnering needing improvement).	Leader divides group into subgroups of three to five people. Each group lists one or two items per column for each person in the group. Leader/note-taker for each group is person with lowest title or experience. (15–20 mintes)
Whole group synthesis.	Representative from each subgroup describes one or two key points the group addressed in each column. The representative does *not* read all the group's items. (10–20 minutes)

Discussion Agenda 2: Solving Problems

This is the facet of group communications that truly taps into the "wisdom of the group" and has the potential to produce highly creative, innovative solutions. Beyond simply getting input from a group, it is also possible to use facilitation to have a group solve a problem. Partnering groups typically engage in this kind of problem-solving well into their meetings, after they have identified issues, written goals, and worked with personalities. As with the Getting Input discussion, it is necessary to carefully plot the question put to the group and divide the group into subgroups in order for it to perform at optimal levels. Using this format, it is quite possible for groups to devise solutions far beyond the imagination of any individual in the crowd.

"Solving Problems" Discussion	
Topic	**Format**
Leader describes the issues.	Leader addresses the whole group. (5 minutes)
Small group discussion. Each subgroup lists three columns: Aspects of the Problem, Possible Actions, and Specifics to Try.	Leader divides group into subgroups of three to five people. Each group lists one to two items per column for each person in the group. Leader/note-taker for each group is person with lowest title or least experience. (10–15 minutes per column, 30–45 minutes total)
Whole group synthesis.	Representative from each subgroup describes two or three of the Specifics to Try the group concluded with. The representative does not read all the group's items. (10–20 minutes)
Clarify action plans.	The overall group chooses several of the Specifics to Try and discusses them in detail.

In this discussion, the headings of the three columns are especially important: Aspects of the Problem, Possible Actions, and Specifics to Try (under this heading, the group lists Who, What, When). Part of what is significant about these headings is some words they do not include: define or solve. The groups do not attempt to "define" a problem because many problems that partnering groups face do not really have a definition. Rather, they have multiple facets and aspects.

Similarly, the groups do not try to solve the problem because, working within the confines of a discussion, they can't. The best they can do is to come up with specific things to try. It's only after they try the actions that they will know if they have solved the problem.

So the focus is not on forcing a definition or a solution, but rather on defining action steps that will, as the group tries them, demonstrate what works.

Discussion Agenda 3: Status Reporting

"Status Reporting" meetings are useful in many kinds of ongoing partnering. These meetings should consist of two parts, but many groups leave out one of the parts, with the productivity of their meetings suffering as a result. Most groups cover the first part of the meeting effectively, with each group member updating the overall group on his or her progress and issues during the past week. The part of the discussion that groups often omit is the discussion of each individual's plans for the coming week based on what the person heard from the other members of the group.

Effective facilitation can substantially improve Status Reporting meetings. In an unfacilitated meeting, people typically "go around the table" one at a time, describing their previous week. This may sound easy enough, but, often, the group does not listen while the person is talking. And if there are a lot of people in the group, it can take a long time to get all the way around. Some people under-report what they've done, thinking it may not be interesting enough. Others over-report, droning on endlessly.

"Status Reporting" Discussion	
Topic	**Format**
People report on their activities of the past week, answering the question, "What are three things you've been working on that are most likely to impact other members of this group?"	Instead of sitting in a large group, people can start in organized subgroups immediately. The subgroups are chosen to put together people who especially need to exchange information. (15–20 minutes)
Subgroups report their three main exchanges to the overall group or people "go around the table" reporting on their actions individually.	Whole group is intact.
People answer the question, "Now that I've heard everyone's update, here are my plans for the coming week and here are the three most likely ways I will need to work together with others in this group."	The group can be reorganized again into smaller groups to discuss in detail how their plans reflect what they've heard.

11

Improving One-on-One Partnering Communications Skills

One-on-one conversations are the DNA of partnering between organizations and departments. As with group communications, predictable problems arise in one-on-one communications, and a set of straightforward skills improves communications effectiveness. In this chapter, we map out the predictable problems and describe the skills.

How One-on-One Communications Affect Overall Partnering Success

I wish people who have trouble communicating would just shut up.
—Tom Lehrer

When most people think of partnering, they think of strategies and goals, not conversations. Yet it is often the everyday, grassroots conversations between the people involved in the different organizations and alliances that most determine partnering success. When mergers come undone, producers lose clients, or outsourcing breaks down, a weak strategy didn't cause the problem. Often, what causes partnering breakdown is ineffective communications among individuals.

On the opportunity side, the issue is equally pointed. The difference between a moderately successful partnership and one that breaks new ground is seldom in the cleverness of the partnering agreement. Most often, what separates average from excellent partnering is the ability of the people to hold productive discussions.

It's useful to think of one-on-one situations in six different ways:

1. *DNA.* Just as the DNA in a person's fingernails carries the genetic code for the whole person, the one-on-one situations in a partnership carry the genetic code for the overall partnering relationship.

2. *Leverage point.* One-on-one situations reflect what's going on in a partnership, and they provide a point of entry and leverage to make changes and improvements in the overall relationship as well.

3. *Shock absorbers.* One-on-one situations "where the rubber meets the road" have the potential to absorb the bluntness of ineffective, unwieldy partnering policy, and somehow make it work.

4. *Real point of power.* Just as the efficacy of criminal law is determined not by the letter of the law but the tone of enforcement, what happens at the grassroots levels among lower-level supervisors and employees often creates the real policies that provide lasting shape for partnering.

5. *Skills base.* Much of what occurs in one-on-one situations depends on the participants' communications skills. The "skills" label is important because it implies that improvement is possible—if people strengthen their skills.

6. *Theory roots.* This book can apply communications skills, but it does not need to invent them. Established literature, theory, and research provide an excellent foundation for understanding the problems and strategies of effective communications in collaborative one-on-one situations.

Typical One-on-One Situations in Different Partnering Arrangements

How do one-on-one conversations shape overall partnering effectiveness? The following table describes typical, pivotal one-on-one situations that contribute to the overall success of partnering in a wide range of situations.

How Overall Partnering Success Plays Out in One-On-One Situations	
Type of Partnering	**Pivotal One-on-One Situations**
Customer Satisfaction	◆ Help-desk calls. ◆ Customer service conversations. ◆ Responding to suggestions and complaints.
Merger/Acquisition	◆ Choosing processes and methods to use. ◆ Planning for sharing work. ◆ Collaborating on tasks.
Strategic Alliance	◆ Dividing tasks and responsibilities. ◆ Deciding which organization does what. ◆ "It's not my job" arguments at low levels.
Preferred Vendor	◆ Addressing customer concerns about unwieldy processes. ◆ Vendor unwelcome sales efforts.
Project/Multiple Companies	◆ Choosing processes and methods. ◆ Attempts by any one company to "steal" sales from others.
Outsourcing	◆ How customer can manage and influence service provider. ◆ Service provider response to complaints.
Internal Customer (accounting, IT, human resources, facilities, training)	◆ Addressing customer complaints. ◆ Educating the customer. ◆ Increasing value-added service.
"Departments at War" (turf wars, conflict over resources, overlapping responsibilities)	◆ Differences of opinion about methods, processes, or decisions among staff from warring departments.
Advisory Departments—have responsibility but limited authority (statistics dept.)	◆ Advisory staff conversations trying to exert influence with others over whom they have limited authority.
Monitoring Departments (audit, quality assurance)	◆ "Enforcement" conversations between monitoring department and those monitored by them.
Handoffs (between multiple shifts or between departments working in sequences)	◆ Specific content of the conversations that occur before, during, or afte handoffs in the organization.
Multiple Departments Working Together (all the departments involved in getting a software product out and updated)	◆ Choosing processes and methods. ◆ Attempts by any one company to "steal" sales from others.

Using a Personal Case to Improve One-on-One Skills

Personal Cases where people write about real one-on-one situations can be especially effective tools to build one-on-one skills. Because people write the cases themselves, the cases are highly relevant for their work. Because the cases are real, it is easy for people to apply the skills they learn in working with them when the situations occur again.

A Personal Case is a brief, two-page document that a person writes to describe a real one-on-one situation that did not go as well as he or she would have liked. It's usually most productive to write about situations that involve small conflicts and differences of opinion rather than focusing on large conflicts that occur rarely.

One page of the Personal Case outlines several aspects of the background of the situation. It's often effective to write this page as brief bulleted lists under these headings:

❐ *The Situation:* A one-sentence description of the situation.

❐ *What's at Stake:* Why the situation is important in the writer's work.

❐ *Relevant History:* Past events that shape the writer's assumptions and strategies in the current situation.

❐ *Assumptions:* Key assumptions the writer was making about the situation or the other person.

❐ *Strategies:* Key strategies the writer was following during the situation.

On the second page of the case, the writer reconstructs, as best as he or she can recall, a few minutes of the actual conversation. Usually it's most productive to focus on the first few minutes of the conversation, but it may also be useful to focus on a point in the conversation where the tone changed or something surprising or unpleasant occurred.

The writer begins by drawing a line down the middle of the page. On the left side, using a form similar to that of a play, the case writer writes a few lines of the dialog. On the right side of the page, the writer notes what he or she was thinking or feeling, but did not say in the conversation. The writer notes these comments both on his or her own spoken words and on the words spoken by the other person.

Working with the case in seminars, we follow the same five steps that we take in this chapter:

1. Analyze the case, examining what did not work and trying to understand why. We use the framework of Model I/Model II to explore the writer's strategies and develop a clear Model II approach.
2. Use I-Messages to replace key writer's lines that did not work so well.
3. Use Active Listening to replace other key lines.
4. In the seminar, practice the replacement lines with others to test how they will work.
5. Plan in detail how the writer can try the skills in a future situation.

The "Convince Him to Do the Right Thing" Case

We use the "Convince Him to Do the Right Thing" case in this chapter because it is a pivotal one-on-one situation in many partnering arrangements. A person in one organization or department must influence a person in another organization or department. In many partnering situations—outsourcing, mergers, alliances, internal service, and so on—this often occurs where there are only general, often vague guidelines about the extent to which the person hearing the advice must follow it. In other words, the success of the person making the point has more to do with communications skills than with any formal power the people have.

The particular case we use involves a statistician pointing out problems to a clinician in a pharmaceutical company. This is a situation that could occur in Case 4 "Quiet Standoff," described in Chapter 3. The clinician is managing the research project, the statistician is in an advisory role. The statistician presents concerns about the clinician's research plans.

The clinician is not compelled to follow the statistician's advice. The statistician's advice is costly and inconvenient. If the clinician follows it, it will cost his project thousands of dollars in increased direct costs and several months' delay. However, if the statistician is correct and the clinician does not follow his advice, it could cost the clinician much more than the increased project costs. The project would have to be redone, and the huge costs attendant to that could cause the company to cancel it.

We like this kind of case because it is quiet, subtle, and recurring. It's a quiet failure, not a noisy conflict. Loud arguments are certainly interesting, but in real partnering they tend to occur much less often than quieter disagreements.

"Convince Him to Do the Right Thing": A Statistician's Personal Case

Taken from a "Quiet Standoff" partnering arrangement, but this kind of conversation exists in numerous partnering situations—outsourcing, alliances, mergers, service departments, and so on—whenever one person tries to influence another and the formal hierarchy and structure provides no clear rule for the discussion.

The Situation

Statistician Dilbert (me) is trying to point out problems with research plans developed by my partner clinician, Malcolm.

What's at Stake

If Malcolm doesn't respond to my concerns, it's likely that he will go on to develop the research project in a flawed way. Months from now, the FDA will reject the project. If it doesn't, flaws in the research methodology may well be responsible for new users of the drug developing harmful, possibly lethal side effects. The following is written from Dilbert's point of view.

Relevant History

Though I have not worked with Malcolm before, I've worked with numerous others like him. Often, it has not gone well. Even though I have had the right answers, they have chosen to ignore my concerns.

My Assumptions

- ❐ The company wants us to "partner" and work together effectively.
- ❐ Malcolm doesn't want to hear what I have to say.
- ❐ He's right; my recommendations probably will cost him money and time.
- ❐ He thinks I am being overly cautious.

My Strategies for the Conversation

- ❐ Be objective; point out the problems with the research in the way he has done it so far.
- ❐ Convince Malcolm to adopt the more rigorous statistical standards I am suggesting.

- ❏ Remind Malcolm that the last time he led a project, it got in trouble as a result of his pushing too far, too fast.
- ❏ Be logical and calm; no need for emotion here.
- ❏ Be sympathetic, but overcome his resistance with facts.

The Dialog	My Thoughts and Feelings
M: So, how was your weekend?	How can you be sociable at a time like this?
D: Okay, I guess.	Try to be social and polite at least, don't upset him.
M: So what can I do for you? I know you sent me a memo, but I didn't really understand it.	Not understand it? I'll bet he didn't even look at it.
D: I actually thought it was kind of clear.	Try to be polite.
M: Whatever. In any case, what is it?	Whatever?
D: Well, for one thing, just something small. I don't think you transposed the numbers accurately from page four of the report to the final pages.	Start out small and simple, build up to the big problem.
M: Really? What page is that? Are you sure? Wait a second while I find my copy. Did I send that to you last week? Where did I put that?(A few moments pass while M shuffles papers.)	He is so disorganized.
D: (Hesitantly) And then there's the bigger problem of your sample size.	Here comes the real trouble. I hope I can convince him that I am right.

Chart continued on following page.

M: (Drops the papers, looks up, challenging) Oh no, you're not going to pull that one on me. We covered that much earlier in the project. I worked hard with Cecil, your predecessor, and we agreed to the sample size of 20 that we used. You're not going to dredge that one up again, are you?	For a smooth guy, he can become hostile pretty quickly. Doesn't he know how much trouble he can get into if he doesn't listen to me?
D: I'm just doing my job. The sample size you specified was acceptable for a preliminary study. However, since then you changed project goals to aim for more extensive results. Because of that, a sample size of at least 100 is now mandatory.	Doesn't he remember that he changed the goals? He must know that a change like that requires the sample size to change.
M: Mandatory by whose definition?	He's angry now, and nasty.
D: It's the generally accepted industry norm at this point.	You should really know this. Why do I have to be the one to tell you?
M: What do you know about what's generally accepted? Just how much experience do you have, anyway? Have you ever worked on anything like this before?	Now I am feeling attacked.
D: Well, not exactly like this, but I have worked on many similar studies.	Defend myself.
M: So is this like grad school for you?	Ouch.

Analyzing the Case: Transaction Analysis

What could Dilbert have done differently? A first step in improving one-on-one skills is to improve one's understanding of what went wrong in a conversation. The concepts and language of Transaction Analysis provide a simple but valuable set of tools for this kind of understanding. We believe we have developed a unique way of using Transaction Analysis as a tool for building skills in one-on-one collaborative communications.

In Transaction Analysis, everything a person says can fit into one of three categories: Parent, Adult, or Child. In an effective collaborative dialog, both people stay in Adult and produce optimal results in terms of both the content of their solution and their commitment to carrying it out. The "Convince Him to Do the Right Thing" case initially seems Adult in that both people are somewhat calm, polite, and logical. There is some disagreement, but no out-and-out violence.

But a deeper look at the meanings of Parent, Adult, and Child makes it clear that the conversation is not in the Adult at all:

❑ **Parent.** When people are in the Parent role, they devote most of their effort to trying to exert control. In "Convince Him...," both Dilbert and Malcolm have their moments in Parent, and the case ends with Malcolm in Parent. Parent control can take the form of Critical Parent, which includes threats, pronouncements, allegations, accusations, and other mostly negative messages. Typical Critical Parent statements include:

   ♦ "What do you know about that?"
   ♦ "You'd better stop doing that."
   ♦ "You always make that same mistake."
   ♦ "That's unacceptable."
   ♦ "Why did you..."(most "why" questions are accusations in thin disguise).

Alternatively, a person can function as Nurturing Parent. In this instance, the person exerts control in warmer, friendlier tones, though control is still the dominant theme. In the case, Dilbert functions as Nurturing Parent early on, when he worries, "Don't upset him." Other classic Nurturing Parent lines include:

   ♦ "Are we having a problem?"
   ♦ "What's gotten into you? You never used to act like this."

❑ **Adult.** Dilbert and Malcolm actually spend little time in the Adult role. When a person is in the Adult role, he or she is primarily focused on solving the problem at hand, focusing little, if at all, on controlling anyone or on dodging responsibility. Conversations that stay anchored with both people in the Adult role often produce solutions that neither person thought of before the conversation. After an Adult conversation, both people are confident that the other will fulfill the promises he or she has made. We describe typical Adult lines in detail in the following section I-Messages and Active Listening.

❑ **Child.** Malcolm and Dilbert each take some time in the Child role, Malcolm at the beginning of the conversation and Dilbert at the end. When people are in the Child role, they focus on dodging responsibility. Sometimes that dodging is out in the open, in the form of the Free Child. More often, the dodging sounds like whining, in the form of the Adapted Child. Typical Adapted Child lines include:

♦ "I'm just doing my job."
♦ "Why are you picking on me?"
♦ "It's not my fault."
♦ "It's not my job."

So, overall, little conversation in the case occurs in the Adult. Beyond the labels of Parent, Adult, and Child, Transaction Analysis features several other concepts that can lead to a deeper understanding of the problems and provide the first steps to improving the situation the next time it occurs:

❑ The Adult role provides a useful, working definition of collaboration that is valuable in a wide range of partnering situations.

❑ Most people are in the Adult role most of the time. (People who are not are interesting and troublesome, but not the norm.) However, most people also have moments and situations outside the Adult role every day.

❑ Communicating in the Adult mode can be difficult and elusive when people are discussing awkward topics. Many conversations that initially may seem successful ("That wasn't bad, we didn't have an argument") can actually mask Parent-Child dialogs.

❑ Each conversation sets the stage for the next conversation. When a conversation ends in a Parent-Child dynamic, it becomes more likely that the next conversation between the same people will also move toward Parent-Child.

❑ Each person reinforces the other. It's difficult enough when a person participates in a conversation outside the Adult role, but it's even more unfortunate—and almost inevitable—that once one person falls out of the Adult role, he or she will drag the other person along.

Most importantly, effective partnering depends on the ability of people at all levels to communicate in the Adult role.

Analyzing the Case: Model I and Model II Framework

Chris Argyris and Donald Schon's framework of Model I and Model II provides a second useful framework for understanding one-on-one situations that are pivotal for partnering success. Model I and Model II are useful because they explore the meaning of collaborative communications in depth.

Argyris and Schon believe that, in awkward situations, many people fall into a Model I communications style that includes owning and controlling the task alone, trying to win at the other person's expense, and either advocating strongly for one position or inquiring to a point that one has no position at all. Model I produces limited learning and is not effective in situations that are intended to be collaborative.

By contrast, Model II focuses on sharing the control of the situation with the other person, aiming to win along with the other person and both advocating for one's point of view while also inquiring into the other person's. By not focusing on a win-at-all-expense approach, Model II has the potential to redefine problems and produce innovative and useful new solutions.

In the "Convince Him to Do the Right Thing" case, Dilbert operates in a Model I way:

- ❐ He owns and controls the task, defining the situation alone. He does not get input from Malcolm as to what could be occurring in the situation.
- ❐ He focuses on winning alone.
- ❐ He advocates for his own position without inquiring at all into the relevance of the points Malcolm is trying to make.
- ❐ He flip-flops to inquiring with no advocating when Malcolm begins to attack him.
- ❐ Focusing on winning, he never tries to work with Malcolm in exploring how, together, they can address the problem of the need for a larger sample size.

If he took more of a Model II approach, Dilbert would:

- ❐ Begin the meeting by clearly telling Malcolm what he wanted to get out of the meeting, asking Malcolm what he wanted to get out of the meeting, and then working to address both of their concerns.

❏ Replace the words "convince" and "overcome" in his strategy for the conversation with words such as "present," "test," and "explore alternatives."

❏ Both advocate for his own position and inquire into the validity of Malcolm's concerns.

❏ Work to achieve solutions that benefit both himself and Malcolm.

Core Concepts of Argyris and Schon's Model I and Model II Framework	
Model I	**Model II**
◆ Own and control the task unilaterally. ◆ Make assumptions. ◆ Protect self unilaterally. ◆ Protect others unilaterally. ◆ Win; don't lose. ◆ Keep feelings out of it. ◆ Either advocate or inquire. ◆ Single-loop learning.	◆ Share control of the task and agenda. ◆ Test assumptions. ◆ Make self vulnerable. ◆ Share protection with others. ◆ Work to achieve win-win. ◆ Use feelings as data. ◆ Advocate and inquire. ◆ Double-loop learning.

Analyzing the Case:
Using the Guiding Concept of Congruence

The concept of Congruence provides a third approach to understanding what occurs in one-on-one conversations. Writing the case with the dialog on one side and the writer's thoughts and feelings on the other also makes it possible to use the issue of Congruence as a tool to understand and improve the dialog.

When people are not congruent, when they withhold their deeper thoughts and feelings, they make it impossible to address those real concerns, and so limit their own effectiveness. When people do not surface and address their deeper thoughts and feelings, they engage in a kind of conflict avoidance. The conversation they have may be calm and unemotional, but it falls short in the sense that it fails to address key issues, much less resolve them.

In the "Convince Him to Do the Right Thing" case, Dilbert's genuine worries and concerns are buried on the right side of the page in thoughts and feelings that are largely unexpressed. Instead of expressing those concerns, Dilbert vacillates between treading very lightly in the conversation ("start easy with a small disagreement") and self-defense in response to Malcolm's attacks.

The concept of Congruence leads to a general action item based on the case: to close, as much as possible, the gap between the left side of the page and the right—to have what Dilbert says more accurately reflect what he thinks and feels.

Communications Skill for Partnering: I-Messages

The concepts of Transaction Analysis, Model I and Model II, and Congruence are tools to analyze what happens in a conversation, but they are not skills. They do not provide direct, specific instruction about what to do to make sure that a conversation is effective.

I-Messages and Active Listening are two classic communications skills that were developed for a wide variety of situations, but which provide special value for pivotal partnering situations. I-Messages are ways of structuring difficult or awkward information, critical feedback, and advice. Active Listening is a method for working to ensure that one understands the other person and works with his or her ideas. Both I-Messages and Active Listening improve the odds that the other person will respond in the Adult role. Both skills help a person move from Model I to Model II, and help the person to be more congruent in the conversation.

In the "Convince Him to Do the Right Thing" case, there are several opportunities to improve the dialog by replacing what Dilbert said with an I-Message (see chart on page 210).

Using I-Messages in the "Convince Him to Do the Right Thing" Case		
When the Issue Occurs	**Dilbert's Original Line**	**I-Message Replacement**
At the beginning of the case.	Okay, I guess.	Actually, I'm pretty concerned. I sent you an e-mail about increasing the sample size for our project. I've seen the FDA reject projects similar to this one four times in the past year due to this problem. If we don't make some changes, I'm worried that they will reject us, too.
In the middle of the case.	I'm just doing my job.	I'm surprised that you would bring that up. As best I can remember, you initiated the change in goals two months ago. I assumed that, with your experience, you would have encountered the necessity to increase sample size in situations such as this one.
At the end of the case.	Well, not exactly like this.	I'm feeling kind of put on the spot here, having to defend myself. I'm worried that if we focus on this kind of conversation, we'll never discuss the best ways to address the sample size problem.

How the I-Message Links With the Analysis

The I-Message approach addresses all three approaches of analyzing the case. For example, to use the I-Message at the beginning of the case:

Actually, I'm pretty concerned. I sent you an e-mail about increasing the sample size for our project. I've seen the FDA reject projects similar to this one four times in the past year due to this problem. If we don't make some changes, I'm worried that they will reject us, too.

In Transaction Analysis, this I-Message is clearly anchored in the Adult role. Dilbert is focusing on the problem and the solution. He is not trying to control Malcolm, nor is he trying to dodge responsibility for the issues.

The I-Message also provides a simple framework to help Dilbert work towards a Model II approach. He is not controlling the agenda for the meeting or trying to control Malcolm. He is not trying to convince, not trying to win. He is advocating his position but not setting up the situation as a win-lose.

With the I-Message, Dilbert is congruent. What he is saying much more closely reflects what he really thinks and feels than does his original opening line.

Communications Skill for Partnering: Active Listening

Active Listening provides a second useful one-on-one communications skill that contributes to overall partnering success. Active Listening works in tandem with I-Messages. Most people say that it is more difficult for them to learn to use Active Listening than I-Messages. They say the difficulty is not so much that the skill is technically difficult, but that it requires one to actually listen and work to understand what the other person is trying to say.

In the "Convince Him..." case, Dilbert could have used Active Listening to improve the dialog in a number of situations. The following table tracks what Malcolm said and how Dilbert responded in the original case, then lists an Active Listening line Dilbert might have used and anticipates how Malcolm would likely respond to it.

How Active Listening Could Have Improved the "Convince Him to Do the Right Thing" Case			
What Malcolm Said	What Dilbert Originally Replied	Active Listening Dilbert Could Use	How Malcolm Might Respond
So, what can I do for you? I know you sent me a memo, but I didn't really understand it.	I actually thought it was pretty clear.	That must have been annoying for you.	To be honest, it completely baffled me.
Oh no, you're not going to pull that one on me.... You're not going to dredge that one up again, are you?	I'm just doing my job.	You sound angry.	Of course I'm angry. I spent a lot of time with all this, and what you're suggesting would cost the project and my career.
Have you ever worked on anything like this before?	Well, not exactly....	You really think I don't have the right experience.	Well—you probably do, but what you're suggesting will be extremely difficult for me.

In all three situations, the Active Listening line has several important effects, all of them helping to keep the conversation in an Adult role and move toward a Model II orientation.

❏ Intentionally working to understand the other person's point of view helps keep Dilbert out of Parent and keeps him from trying to control Malcolm.

❏ Active Listening slows the conversation down. This in itself can be helpful in that it creates a space where thought can occur. Rapid-fire dialog may occasionally be witty, but fast dialog is more often a sign that people are speaking reflexively without much thinking.

❏ Active Listening breaks destructive patterns of conversation. Malcolm could respond to the Active Listening lines the same way he responded to Dilbert's original lines, but he would really have to work more at being in Child or Parent. An Active Listening line does nothing to trigger or reinforce Parent or Child.

❏ Active Listening often surfaces the underlying feeling and emotion in a conversation, making it easier to discuss and manage. The outbursts that Malcolm uses make it difficult to understand what is really driving him.

First Person:
Linking Communications Skills to Partnering Goals and Leadership

How do the skills in this chapter relate to larger partnering strategies and goals? Jim Martin, CIO for TRO/The Ritchie Organization, describes his experience. Jim has worked on refining his communications skills in the Leaders Circle, a year-long leadership development program. TRO/The Ritchie Organization is a 200-plus person architecture firm with offices in Newton, Massachusetts; Birmingham, Alabama; Sarasota, Florida; and Memphis, Tennessee.

"IT management is change management by necessity. There's a lot of inherent mistrust in changing technology for technology's sake. A lot of work needs to be done communicating the necessities of implementing a new technology with the people who are going to be affected by it. Good technologies can fail if you don't partner effectively with those who will have to adopt it.

"Effective communication is critical for the successful development and implementation of any technology change in an organization of any size. Oftentimes, technology changes also necessitate changing business processes, trying to fit a new piece of software (technology) into an existing business structure, or changing an established process to compensate for changes made due to improvements in existing technology.

"Working with individuals to identify opportunities where technology may help a business process is one of the main functions of my position. We're trying to tie what we know together so all the people in the firm can use it. It's a risk because we have to put our limited resources where it will have the most impact, we have to elicit the information we need and make sure we're solving their actual problem, not the problem we think they have.

"Successfully managing this kind of change takes a lot of communications. Strong one-on-one and group communication skills help keep the interactions focused, and allow for the level of trust necessary to have a successful process. It takes a strong leader to keep the partnering process moving in a positive direction. That's the key, though: the leader is leading the PROCESS, not the discussion.

"Trying to improve my own communications skills, I've found the easiest things to improve are those that I can choose to do myself. The only thing between you and change is resolve. I've tried to work at being more open and genuine in conversations, looking at both sides of an issue, empathizing with all parties to understand their position, and recognizing that people think differently—and that's a good thing.

"What's been more challenging in trying to improve my own skills has been focusing on the goals and outcomes, not the path you take to get there. It's also been difficult to get past what people are saying to try and understand what they mean, what they feel. Hardest of all has been putting aside my own expectations and plumbing the conversation itself for the best solution.

"Working at all this, I think I've changed my attitude. I've made myself more vulnerable. I try to speak my mind (respectfully) and close the gap between what I say and what I'm thinking.

"This has not been easy, but it's produced positive results, increasing my effectiveness as CIO and for my personal interactions. I have more confidence in dealing with people and a greater understanding of how I affect the directions of the interactions I have with them. It takes a lot of the stress out of one-on-one communication and makes the entire change process more satisfying in the long run."

In Summary: The Consultant's Lament

If I'm the expert, why aren't you listening to me? This is the lament of many people in consulting roles.

Much of the success of partnering in any situation depends on the one-on-one communications skills of people at all levels. Many partnering arrangements involve pivotal one-on-one situations in which individuals negotiate how processes and information are going to be handled.

Increasing the success of one-on-one partnering conversations involves abandoning the all-too-familiar notion that consulting means getting other people to take one's advice. Successful partnering depends on all partners' abilities to engage in real dialog; to not only provide advice, but also to work with their partners' ideas and focus on developing optimal solutions.

12

Partnering Leadership: Translating Partnering Initiatives Into Individual Actions

If it's to be, it's up to me.

—Motivational slogan of karate academy

How can people who participate in partnering demonstrate leadership? What is the nature of individual leadership in a partnering arrangement?

It's important to understand the answers to these questions because, in the end, productive partnering depends on individual action. It's people who Take Stock, Build Trust, Clarify Goals, Implement Key Processes, and Raise the Bar. It's people who determine partnering success.

Partnering raises problems for individual action, though. For many people, the meaning of the two words "leader" and "partner" are in direct conflict with each other. In this traditional view, leaders are anything but team members. Rather, they are the ones who direct the team. And team members in this view are not leaders, but followers; sheep awaiting a shepherd to provide direction and order.

We observe this dilemma taking place in many partnering situations. People who are strong, effective leaders seem at a loss in partnering situations. Sometimes they retreat into uncharacteristic passivity, waiting for others to take charge and tell them what to do. At other times, they try to take over themselves, usually on behalf of scoring gains for their own organization at the expense of their partner.

We address this dilemma in this chapter by:

❏ Pointing out the traps and problems with the leadership roles that people often identify with partnering.

❏ Drawing on five core concepts in leadership theory that provide special value for partnering.

❏ Examining methods for leadership training and development that are particularly useful for partnering.

❏ Profiling several first-person accounts of people who have extensive experience combining both partnering and leadership.

Grassroots Definitions of Partnering Leadership

Coffee breaks in partnering meetings provide a candid window into the ways people think about leadership in partnering and the ways that thinking obstructs productive partnering. Chatting about people who are providing leadership (usually standing with others from their own organization), people often describe with some enthusiasm members of their own group who take various leadership roles.

Many of the leadership roles that people describe in these situations involve leadership for one part of the partnership, not for the partnering arrangement overall:

❏ *Used car dealer.* This type of leader negotiates cleverly and succeeds in winning more than a fair share of gains for one organization.

❏ *Problem finder.* This leader can always be relied on to find some kind of problem with ideas, goals, proposals, and suggestions the other organization makes. Part of this leader's skill involves being able to make small problems seem large.

❏ *Obstacle.* This person leads primarily by resisting. He or she resists suggestions offered by the other organization. The group admires this leader for his or her sheer stubbornness, not for the solutions he or she offers.

❏ *Troop master/Spokesperson.* This person leads by speaking on behalf of his or her entire group. Though efficient, this approach renders passive many people at all levels who should be involved in partnering. This leader draws his or her power from others who become more passive when they should be participating more actively.

❒ *Falsely humble servant.* This leader brings partnering to a halt as he or she begs off taking responsibility action until checking back with their larger organization.

Some of the leadership roles that people describe are not so short-sighted, though. These roles provide the outlines of a useful definition of partnering leadership:

❒ *Initiator.* This leader not only finds problems, he or she also offers solutions.

❒ *Mediator.* This leader does not just voice concerns and complaints, but also takes responsibility and action to define middle-ground courses of action.

❒ *Whole group spokesperson.* This leader tries to summarize the views of the entire group, not just his or her side.

❒ *Inclusive winner.* This leader tries to achieve wins for the whole partnering group, not for one partner at the expense of the other.

❒ *Facilitator.* This kind of leader works to break down the walls between the different sides of the partnering group, getting people to work across their base organizational lines in a variety of ways.

Grassroots Partnering Leadership Roles	
Individual Focus	**Partnership Focus**
◆ Used car salesman.	◆ Inclusive winner.
◆ Problem finder.	◆ Initiator.
◆ Obstacle.	◆ Mediator.
◆ Spokesperson.	◆ Whole group spokesperson.
◆ Falsely humble servant.	◆ Empowered.

> **First Person: Partnering Leadership in Action**
> **From a Client's Perspective**
>
> Lisa Chapnick is director of facilities at Simmons College in Boston's Back Bay. Working with Lee Kennedy Co. to construct several new buildings on the urban campus, Ms. Chapnick explains her view of the relationship between partnering and leadership:
>
> "You can't have partnering without leadership. You can talk about teamwork and collaboration and collegiality, but somebody has to set the tone and create the culture to make those things happen. That's what Lee Michael Kennedy, their president, does. He's got great people working at the company, and they would be great anywhere they work. They're all highly skilled at what they do.
>
> "But what Lee Michael does to add to that skill level, he is the one who creates the values, the culture, the expectations. Our college is mostly a women's college, over 80 percent women. That's our heritage and our special focus. Lee Kennedy workers have been on campus now for three years, working on various projects at all levels, typical construction workers. We've never had a complaint from any of our women about any of their men.
>
> "In fact, I see them walking around the campus. They act like they live here. If there's litter on the sidewalk, I've seen them bend down to pick it up. That's what partnering leadership creates."

Leadership Theory: Dead Ends for Partnering

Some of the most popular writing and theory about leadership is also some of the most destructive for partnering. More specifically, four aspects of leadership theory are dead ends, or worse, for leadership in partnering situations: trait theory, the Great Man theory, sports leadership metaphors, and individual focus.

Trait Theory

It's time to bury the trait theories of leadership once and for all. They make for endless speculation and cocktail party chatter, but they predict little in the real world and are completely off base when it comes to partnering. Trait theories of leadership were popular before World War II. They held that the way to predict and discover effective leaders was by their physical traits—for example, height, weight, eye color, and that all-time favorite: skull shape. Although the experience of the military in World War II thoroughly disproved and discredited these theories, people even now persist in using traits ("She just doesn't look like a leader") to describe effective leadership. This approach poses tremendous difficulties because it shifts focus away from outcomes and behaviors, which are much more productive areas for inquiry and discussion.

Great Man Theory

The shelves at Barnes & Noble and Borders are packed with books about great leaders. Yes, that's the Great Man theory because nearly all of these books are about men. There's nothing wrong with these books as sources of inspiration and motivation; however, they have little to offer for people involved in partnering because they tend to glorify people who demonstrate an autocratic, one-way, win-at-the-expense-of-others-losing kind of leadership style.

Sports Leadership Metaphors

These extend the Great Man book approach, but they are usually a little more entertaining because of the sports angle. The message of these books for partnering is not a good one. They seem to say that groups and teams need an all-powerful, intelligent coach to provide guidance, direction, and, often, a kick in the pants. ("Thanks Coach, I needed that.") There's no place in these books for groups and teams that have wisdom, nor for a leadership style that collaborates with the team as a full and equal partner.

Individual Focus

This is the problem with nearly all of the leadership books and theories: they treat individuals as if they are leading in isolation. In these works, groups and teams are something to overcome, to provide direction for, to spoonfeed. Teams and groups have limited, if any, intelligence. Leaders are set apart, isolated, locked in struggle with recalcitrant, unappreciative groups.

It's not that these theories have no value; they can be quite useful for people in some situations. It's just that they offer little guidance (and sometimes, problematic advice) for people working in partnering situations.

Leadership Theory: More Useful for Partnering

Fortunately, some leadership theory is quite useful for partnering. Four different leadership approaches have special value for partnering situations:

Behavioral Theory

The approach that usurped trait theory some years ago, behavioral theory offers three core concepts that are valuable for partnering. First, behavioral theory contends that it is necessary to focus on leaders' behaviors rather than their traits to understand the nature of effective leadership. Second, it identifies one kind of important leadership behavior as "initiating structure"—that is, knowing how to invent a process to get something done that has never been done before. This ability is often important in partnering situations that require an ability to invent new processes. Third, behavioral theory stresses the need for effective leaders to demonstrate "consideration," also an essential behavior in partnering that always depends on productive human relationships.

Contingency Theory/Situational Leadership

Initially outlined in the 1980s and still widely used, contingency theory or situational leadership focuses on the need for leaders to develop a wide repertoire of approaches to various situations, and to address each situation based on its own contingencies, or requirements. This perspective is useful in partnering situations that often pose novel challenges to people who have a limited repertoire of situations they may have worked in previously in their own organizations.

Transactional/Transformational Leadership

James MacGregor Burns articulated the notion that leaders both transact and transform, and in the process are themselves transformed, in his Pulitzer Prize–winning book *Leadership* published in 1978. This book is important for partnering because both the concept of effective transactions and of transformation are valuable in partnering situations. Transactions are important because partnering often requires that people in both organizations be able to structure fair deals, trades, transactions, and negotiations with each other. Transformation is important because it is a potential that many partnering arrangements can aspire to if they are aware of it. (For more details on this issue, see Chapter 8 on "Raising the Bar.")

Level 5 Leadership

Jim Collins's 2001 book, *Good to Great*, offers especially useful insight into leadership for partnering. Drawing on extensive research, Collins identifies the key elements that move companies from good to great with sustained business success. He has determined that the single most important element of a company's ability to make the leap is what he calls "Level 5" leadership. Level 5 leadership poses an excellent model of leadership for partnering situations. It is a combination of a unique, counterintuitive quality of humility and unwavering perseverance. Typically not people who look or sound like the classic "Great Man" leaders, Level 5s are selfless, "servant" leaders.

Leadership Theories and Partnering	
Dead End Theories	**More Relevant for Partnering**
• Trait theory. • Great Man theory. • Sports leadership metaphors. • Individual focus.	• Behavioral theory. • Contingency theory/Situational leadership. • Transactional/Transformational leadership. • Level 5 leadership.

First Person:
Chief Operating Officer, Architecture Firm

Now in his mid-40s, Mark Jussaume, P.E., COO of TRO/The Ritchie Organization, has worked extensively with leadership in his firm and his own professional development. Trained as an engineer, he has participated in a year-long leadership training program and led leadership training efforts in his organization. He comments:

"Leadership in a partnering environment is enhanced by a sense of shared mission. As partners, we work together to leverage our individual leadership strengths. We hold each other accountable for our mutual success as a team. With a strong team of partners, we are able to bring out the best in each other.

"Trust is an essential component to great teamwork. You need to feel confident that you can rely on your partner to be open and honest. In my experience, the willingness to make yourself vulnerable is necessary to achieve high levels of individual and team performance. Vulnerability can only occur in high-trust environments.

"Diverse leadership working together towards a common mission is very powerful. In our firm, we have experienced the energy a cohesive team can generate when there is a real sense of mission and shared values.

"What all this implies for leadership competencies is, you have to be self-aware. You have to have great communications skills and the ability to empower and inspire others. That's many skills coming together. You have to have an ability to bring out the best in your partners. Ideally, the entire team is better because you're around them.

"You can't develop these kinds of competencies with traditional training. You have to 'work on your own elephant,' not just professional development, but also personal development—body, mind, and spirit. It crosses all boundaries. As you grow and evolve as a person and a professional, you gain the ability to inspire and lead those around you. You have to go there first. Conversely, if you're weak, those around you are negatively impacted."

Leadership Training for Partnering: The Content

The steps of the Partnering Solution themselves provide an excellent outline for the content of leadership training that is effective in partnering situations. Each step that organizations follow for partnering has a parallel that is useful for leadership training and development:

- ❏ *Taking Stock/Increasing self-awareness.* Just as Taking Stock of organizational issues provides useful information for partnering, Taking Stock of individual performance provides a solid foundation for improving leadership performance. Where surveys such as client satisfaction surveys provide the data for partnering, 360-degree leadership surveys and personality profiles provide the data for leadership development. Especially valuable are 360-degree communications effectiveness surveys. For these, program participants give survey forms to eight to 12 key people they work with, a mix of clients, peers, bosses, and subordinates. An independent third party, such as a human resources manager or external consultant, collects and tabulates the surveys and provides the participants with a confidential, aggregate summary of the results.

- ❏ *Defining vision and goals.* Just as partnering arrangements benefit from developing a written Goals Statement, people working on their leadership development benefit from developing personal and professional written goals. An extensive and growing bank of data in human resources documents the powerful impacts that writing and using a Personal Vision Statement has for leadership development and job satisfaction. The Goal-Based Work Plan we mentioned in Chapter 7 on Implementing Key Processes provides another useful form for clarifying individual goals. The Work Plan focuses more on goals for a person's current job. Both the Personal Vision Statement and Goal-Based Work Plan are especially relevant for partnering, as they make it possible for participants to integrate specific new partnering tasks with their overall goals and direction.

❐ *Improving skills.* Few people are as skilled at communicating what they do as they are at doing it. Many partnering situations suffer because the people involved possess limited skills at collaborating and facilitating. Several core communications skills build leadership effectiveness in partnering: one-on-one collaboration and negotiations, group facilitation skills, and presentation skills. Many of these skills are not intuitive; it really does take some conscious work to develop the skill. On the other hand, none of these skills is unattainable. With a little work, it's quite possible to increase one's proficiency in any of these areas.

❐ *Improving processes and procedures.* Just as quarterly performance discussions help organizations build the internal infrastructure to achieve external partnering goals, they also help people increase their individual leadership effectiveness. The other kinds of processes that enhance leadership for most people involved in partnering are processes that involve holding meetings. Figuring when to convene meetings, whom to involve, and what to cover in meeting agendas results in processes for meetings that improve leadership performance for partnering.

❐ *Raising the Bar.* As with partnering, it is essential for leadership development to place this item on the agenda from the outset. A strong, ongoing drive for continuous improvement underlies leadership behavior for all kinds of partnering situations.

As with the Partnering Solution, this approach to leadership also posits that leadership training should involve all five kinds of learning and that work in any one area should complement, reinforce, and advance work in the other four. For example, when leaders improve their awareness of how they affect others, it spurs them to develop more targeted goals for how they communicate. Formulating goals creates a need for skills. Building skills improves leaders' level of performance, changes their effect on others, and encourages individuals to formulate goals at a higher level.

Leadership Training for Partnering: Process

The problem with available leadership training and partnering is not so much the content of the training, but rather the format (that is, the way the program is designed and delivered).

If you hold a position of even moderate responsibility in nearly any organization, the odds are that you regularly receive a barrage of direct-mail that advertises leadership training. Whether you are an architect, accountant, dentist, exterminator, or truck driver, the odds are that the professional society you belong to also wants to provide you with leadership training.

The content of much of this leadership training is at least partially relevant for partnering. Most leadership training programs include work with personal goals, self-awareness, and improving communications skills. As the organizational world evolves to include more partnering situations, leadership training also increasingly includes case material relevant for partnering.

The format of most leadership is what's problematic for partnering, and it's problematic in two ways. First, the format of most leadership training is a one-time "intensive" seminar, workshop, or retreat. Second, most leadership training targets groups of people in the same business or industry. The format used to deliver it does not work well at all on two counts.

The one-time seminar approach, efficient for sponsors and participants, is easy to schedule and administer. It's relatively easy for sponsors and participants to find a one-time block to insert in a schedule of ongoing work. The one-time approach can also seem appealing from a learning perspective, as it offers a potential for depth and intensity.

However, the one-time approach has limited effectiveness for leadership training, and especially for leadership training that is relevant for partnering. The problem with the one-time approach to training is that it places the application and implementation of new skills and insights outside the immediate realm of the training program, leaving them more to fate and luck. This may be all right for training that involves acquiring an insight, and where applying that insight is simple, but with training that involves people changing their habits, communications style, or job priorities, acquiring the insight is just the beginning of learning the skill.

For the kind of learning that goes along with leadership and communications skills, a format of several sessions is almost always more effective. That way, program participants can apply the skills and insights between sessions and discuss their experiences in the sessions. In addition, applying and refining the skills is built into the training instead of left as an afterthought. This approach is especially relevant for partnering leadership, where so much of what's difficult is not in the communications skills themselves, but in applying the skills in everyday partnering situations.

Finally, the format of leadership training that brings 20 people of any one profession or trade together builds in serious limitations. Working with others in one's profession or trade may be useful when one is young, inexperienced, and lacking in understanding about one's own business roots. However, for most people, at mid-career and afterwards, it's important to consider one's peers as not only the people in one's profession or trade, but also one's clients.

Too often, leadership training aimed at one profession includes a great deal of complaining about the other people the profession works with. Not only is this not fair (the people being complained about are not present or able to defend themselves), it is also not productive. Often, the people being complained about possess insights that could be very valuable for the people doing the complaining.

In partnering leadership in particular, it is important to pursue leadership training not isolated from, but in collaboration with, one's partners. It's not so necessary to pursue leadership training with the actual people one is partnering with, though that is an excellent and productive possibility. It is important that one at least pursue leadership training with people who share the experiences, priorities, understanding, and biases of the people one is trying to partner with.

These two principles of training design—spreading training out over time and working with mixed groups—fly in the face of much of the training industry. The industry features many, many programs that are designed as one-time sessions for people in the same business. And, of course, these programs do have value. Many executives credit such training with making significant contributions to their understanding and performance.

For partnering, however, it is often worth considering leadership training that is spread over more time, that actually builds work with skill application into the program instead of leaving it to chance, and that involves people across partnership lines instead of engaging only one side of the partnership equation.

First Person:
Partnering Leadership Training and Development

Reginald "Buzz" Stapczynski is town manager for the Town of Andover, Massachusetts. Andover is a large (31,000 population) town whose residents are higher income, well-educated, and demanding in their expectations for the professionalism of their town government offices. Buzz initiated an innovative and somewhat risky approach to leadership development for the senior managers of the 14 major departments in the town offices.

"I wanted to both provide leadership development for them, and I wanted to do something that would strengthen their partnering with each other. The classic thing that happens in town government is that one department doesn't talk to the others, and I wanted to make sure that doesn't happen here.

"At the time I put the program together, several years ago, the managers already were getting along pretty well and they had a high level of trust. I wanted to take things up a level. How they partner with each other matters a lot. It's true that they are independent departments, but the departments depend on each other. For example, the police department depends on public works for information about street closings. The fire department inspects the plant and facilities departments. No department operates in a vacuum, and there are plenty of opportunities for new ways to communicate, too.

"Because the group got along well, I took a risk with the design for our leadership training. In every session, we put one or two members of the group under the spotlight. We had them get in-depth feedback and commentary from all the other members of the group. We began each session by having one or two departments present their department's 'business case' and then get in-depth feedback from all the other members of the group.

"We did 360-degree surveys of all the participants, and used that data in our discussions. We also included work with a leadership skill in each session, such as listening or group facilitation skills. We stretched the program out over 10 months, running a half-day session each month so that people could apply the skills and we could track progress between sessions.

"Going into it I had some level of trepidation, not knowing if people's feelings might get hurt. I think some of them may have been a little concerned, too. But they all rose to the occasion, and the program was a big success. I went first. I had them all give me feedback to try and set a tone and reduce the anxiety. After that, people looked forward to the sessions. They were hungry for them.

"The program definitely opened up some communications that weren't there before. Several departments that had a little friction between them surfaced their issues and resolved them. Several others that were already working well found new ways to share information. People welcomed each other's input. Everyone did a good job of raising the key issues, but also maintaining respect for one another. Overall, it was a great combination of both improving our leadership skills and strengthening partnering between the departments."

13

Death by Outsourcing: The Partnering Mystery Case

> *There will be time to murder and create.*
>
> —T.S. Eliot

Some of the management books that have had the most impact are written as novels or fables. Hersey and Blanchard's *One Minute Manager* tells the story of a harried executive who learns to become a better motivator. Eli Goldratt's classic *The Goal* uses a simple, soap opera–like tale to provide excellent instruction about the details of quality improvement.

We expand on this tradition with "Death by Outsourcing." Like most management fables, it's pretty poor fiction—maybe even intentionally so. But by portraying partnering in this way, we can answer many of the everyday questions people have about partnering in an entertaining way.

Scene of the Crime

"Serves him right."

Did somebody actually say that? Ron Riggio can't believe what he is hearing. Here is poor Malcolm Klebanoff, lying lifeless on the Techsol company parking lot pavement, and someone in the group comments, "Serves him right." Looking up from his position kneeling at Malcolm's side, Ron squints, trying to pierce the darkness to determine which person in the small group had made the comment. He can't tell much of anything. The seven or eight people stand almost still, anonymous in the night, rocking slightly to the left and right in the cold.

It was true that Malcolm, Ron's boss and marketing vice president of Magna Software, was obnoxious. Ron's peers disliked and distrusted him, and their subordinates feared him. Employees in companies throughout the region despised Malcolm because Magna had put so many of them out of work with Malcolm's ideas and sales skills. Malcolm had developed a package of IT services that companies loved because it enabled them to wash their hands of the troublesome IT function once and for all. Malcolm's efforts had brought millions of dollars of service work and revenues to Magna, but at a cost of hundreds of technology jobs in local companies.

Ron didn't know for sure, but he thought he had heard somewhere that even Malcolm's family disliked him. His wife had divorced him long ago, and none of his three children were on speaking terms with him. Malcolm seldom commented on his family situation, but he seemed to enjoy his solitude, focusing on his work with almost superhuman efforts.

Yes, Malcolm was a tough case, but Ron still thought that this kind of violence was uncalled for. And such a grisly way to go. When he could stand to really look at Malcolm, which was only a little, Ron couldn't make out many details. What he could discern in the dark was disturbing evidence of a struggle. Malcolm's blazer and pants were mussed and pulled asunder, his usually tame hair tangled in knots.

Searching for answers, Ron squints again, trying to focus on Malcolm's face in the dark. He becomes aware of the siren sounds of police cars in the distance, then closer.

From Witness to Suspect

"Another win. How does he do it?" Carol Adelman asks Ron as the customer group applauds Malcolm, marking another new contract for Magna.

But as Ron tries to answer, Carol somehow changes. Her sharp features soften and fill out. Her pale face reddens. Her long brown hair, showing more gray, is now all gray. No, wait, she is balding. No, wait. It's not a she at all. It's a he.

"There you go, big guy," the morphing face soothes, looking and sounding more like a police officer. "You'll be okay. Just don't go under on us again, we've already lost enough people for one day."

Trying to shake the bite of the smelling salts, Ron sits slowly. He clearly was not in the conference room where Malcolm had presented Magna's plan to the pleased Techsol group. That was quite a win for Magna, a big contract for interesting work.

With increasing awareness of the ground underneath and the darkness around him, the chain of events replay themselves in Ron's mind. The good feelings after the presentation, the excitement of a new project Ron would manage himself. The walk to his car to call Diane and share his excitement. The confusion that Malcolm's car should still be in the lot after Malcolm's usual brisk departure. The sickening feeling of the soft mass tripping his step in the shadows of Malcolm's Jaguar. The discovery the mass was Malcolm. The group of people in the dark. The silver clouds.

"Are we losing you again?" the police officer queried gently. "It's a lot to take, this kind of thing. We do this for a living, see it all the time. But it can still be pretty disturbing."

The officer's voice clearing the fog from his brain, Ron sat up straighter and looked around. With the patrol cars' lights glaring, he could see that Malcolm had been taken away. Just a few feet to his right, another officer sketched Malcolm's profile on the Techsol pavement with a large piece of chalk.

Where was the group? The seven or eight people? Where was Carol? Who had said, "Serves him right"? Had Ron imagined all that? Or just some of it? Or not?

"I'll be okay, I think," Ron reassured the police officer.

"I hope so. I feel badly for you, I know it's rough." The officer broke eye contact with Ron for a moment, then resumed his gaze, now less comforting. "But I also have to tell you right away. We are going to have to treat you as both a witness and a possible suspect, too. You were the only person present when we arrived at the scene of the crime.

We're not taking you in, at least not yet. But we will be keeping our eye on you."

In Deeper

"Tell it again," Carol egged Ron on, "and don't be so fast when you get to the part about the expression on Malcolm's face."

"There never was a part about the expression on Malcolm's face," Ron replied, "only the part you made up. Did anybody ever tell you that you have a sick mind?"

"Of course they have," Carol smiled, trying to look demure. "And most of them know I like it that way. And seriously, don't you have mixed feelings about what happened to Malcolm, just a little?"

"Of course I do, how could I not?" Ron answered. "Malcolm could really be a tough case. Customers loved him, but just about everybody here hated him. He wouldn't give anyone here the time of day, much less do any of the motivating or mentoring he should have been doing.

"And he was spiteful," Ron continued. "Last month I had to go to his house to pick up some materials for a presentation, and I ended up having to separate him from his next-door neighbor. They were just about to come to blows. Malcolm didn't like the loud music that his neighbor played sometimes at night, so he let his grass grow really long. It looked like a meadow."

"Why would he do that?" Carol wondered.

"His neighbor was trying to sell his house, and Malcolm thought the long grass would make it harder for him to find a buyer. Months had gone by with the house on the market, and the neighbor was pretty ticked off. It took some of my best moves to get them apart—they were both pretty upset. I was pretty upset myself. It's quite a thing to get between two people and physically push them apart. I felt pretty brave about doing that, and it mussed me up a little. Things came flying out of my pockets, their pockets, too. There was stuff all over the lawn by the time we were through."

"Wow, big boy. I didn't know you had it in you," Carol couldn't help herself. She excused herself to get another up of coffee. "But I'll be right back, I also want to talk to you about the client."

Ron passed on Carol's offer for more coffee, he had had more than his quota already. The morning was going much better than he had anticipated. He had driven home slowly after his exchange with the police officer and told the whole story to Diane, at least as much as he could remember. Though he worried that he would be unable to sleep, he nodded off quickly and remained asleep until the alarm jolted him awake.

He worried his way through breakfast. What would people at the office say? How would they approach him? What did they already know? What did they think they knew that he would have to correct? What would they do to handle the formalities of Malcolm's funeral? What would happen to the job Malcolm had just won? Would Ron stay on as project chief?

And just how serious was the police officer's threat that Ron was a suspect? This was just too far-fetched for Ron to consider seriously. Besides, he really was worried about how to keep the company going, how to handle the project, and what to say to the people with whom he worked. With Malcolm gone, people would be looking to Ron to take on more of a leadership role. After all, he had the technical experience, and he had something that Malcolm was never able to attain in spite of all the work he had brought to the company: people liked Ron.

Ron's fears about having to do a lot of talking about the situation melted as the morning wore on. He called a quick meeting shortly after he arrived and tried to fill the group in on the basics—what he knew and what he guessed. He left out the part about the police suspecting him.

Only Carol displayed more curiosity than the others, and that was understandable, to a point. After all, she had been at the evening presentation the night before also. It could have been she who discovered Malcolm if she had been the one to leave earlier.

"So let's get back to the client," Ron began as Carol returned. "They like our work well enough, but they are a complicated company. I can't tell who the customer really is. It seemed like there were four or five different departments giving us orders, and they disagreed with each other a lot."

"There are seven different departments, actually," Carol pointed out, smiling.

"Does this confusion make you happy?" Ron pressed. "It could cause us a lot of trouble. You know how it goes when different people in the client organization give us different orders. I know it should be simple, but lots of times I actually wonder who the client is."

Noticing Carol's smile, Ron stopped. "Now what?"

Carol hesitated. "Nothing. Well, maybe. I have an idea. Maybe it's a little crazy. Jerry is always telling me about the partnering work they do on the construction projects he works on to get the different contractors and subcontractors onto the same page."

Jerry was Carol's husband. Not really a friend of his, but Ron knew Jerry well enough to have a few laughs with him when the group got together with their families. Thoughtful, soft-spoken, quietly funny, Jerry constantly broke Ron's image of what a construction worker should be.

Carol continued, "I tease him about it a lot. You know, teambuilding for contractors. Hugs for steelworkers and all that."

"And?" Ron queried. "That's interesting, but…."

"I know, but what does it have to do with us, right? Well, maybe it's worth trying out some of those construction partnering things with our Techsol project."

"What kind of crackpot idea…" Ron began, but stopped when the phone rang. He picked it up, nodded, nodded again. Looked down. Closed his eyes, nodded again.

Carol thought she heard him mutter, "The murder weapon?" Then he hung up. She waited for him to speak, a good, full minute while he composed himself.

"It's worse," he announced. "That was the police. They confirmed the murder weapon. Don't laugh, it's the stylus from a PDA."

Carol tried to hold it back, but the laugh escaped. Loud.

"There's more," Ron continued. "Not just any PDA. *My* PDA."

Construction Partnering

"You really want to hear about this?" Jerry asked, incredulous.

"I really do," Ron reassured. And he really did. After a full day of grief, fear, anxiety, tension, and melodrama, Ron wanted to hear about anything that might take his mind of Malcolm's case. He was happy to have a few minutes in the conference room with a human being from the normal world outside. The possibility, however slim, that what Jerry had to say might actually help his job made it even more compelling.

"Okay, then. We have a few minutes before Carol finishes her last few calls," Jerry began. "A big thing that's happened in my industry is that this very structured form of teambuilding, we call it construction partnering, has become a standard approach when we run our projects."

"Did you really say…" Ron tried to interject.

"Yes," Jerry interrupted. "Teambuilding. Every project is a team. I know, I know, it seems unlikely—construction workers doing teambuilding. Sometimes I can't believe it either. But we do it because it works. We fought it the first few years, but then our bosses had a series of cost-benefit studies done. They showed so clearly that the partnering work consistently produces results that we made it a standard practice for ourselves."

"So what is it? What do you actually do for this teambuilding, partnering, or whatever it is?" Ron asked.

"It's actually pretty simple," Jerry replied. "We have a big meeting at the beginning of the project. Lots of people are there from every company working on the job: architects, engineers, plumbers, electricians, site people, representatives from the client organization. It can be more than 20 people, sometimes more than 40 if the job is complicated.

"We hold a workshop, usually a day long, maybe a half day for a simple job, and we work on four things. First, we discuss what we each think about how the job is going to go—problems, easy tasks, that kind of thing. Then we write a Goals Statement for the project, and we sign the statement. Then we work on some of the nitty-gritty procedures that make the job work. You know, change orders, conflict processes, that kind of thing. Then we play around with one of the personality profiles that we use in our management training."

"I'm sorry, I must be slow," Ron muttered. "Unless I'm missing something, I don't see how this is any different than the hundreds of teambuilding activities the big companies hold all the time. Those are fun, but they hardly ever actually accomplish anything."

Jerry paused, "I've been on a few of those teambuilding things. Ropes courses, trust walks, deep discussions. This is different, and it should be. Don't forget, it was 25 years ago. They take an engineer's approach to teambuilding. The meeting has four parts: Taking Stock, Clarifying Goals, Piloting Processes, and Building Trust."

"That does sound like an engineer created it—very clear, step-by-step," Ron commented. "But how does it actually get anything done, how does it produce results?"

"Good question," Jerry observed. "Because in my business, we are obsessed with results. If it doesn't make a real difference, we aren't going to waste our time with it. I think one reason is because we are doing it ourselves. Nobody from the outside is cramming answers or requirements down our throats. Another reason it works is because it's the right set of topics. Those four things are topics we always say, on every job, we should do. And the last reason why I think it works is because it doesn't really focus on the meeting you're in, it focuses on the next meeting. All the time we are in the meeting, the leader keeps reminding us that we will be meeting in about a month to check on how all of our decisions and plans are working."

Carol tapped lightly on the conference room door and entered. "Hope I'm not interrupting anything here, with all this brain power concentrated in this small room."

Ron was about to tell her that she was, in fact, interrupting some important things, but Jerry broke in. "Naw, honey, we're just about finished. I've told him most of what I know about construction partnering. Besides, we've got dinner reservations. What I can do, though, is get you some of the material and books I have on all this. You can probably find your own with them, they're pretty detailed."

"So what do you think?" Carol asked Ron. "Am I crazy, or does it seem like this might be a good approach to working with our new client?"

Ron couldn't walk away from the set-up, "Yes to both."

"Hey Ron," Jerry called over his shoulder as he started to walk away with Carol. "It's too bad, all that's happened with Malcolm and everything."

"Yes, it is. Thanks for the empathy," Ron acknowledged.

"But," Jerry continued, "in some ways, you've got to agree, with all the trouble he caused, it kind of served him right."

Homework

Three piles of papers and books surrounded Ron's home computer, one each on Techsol, construction partnering, and Malcolm's case. Unable to eat much dinner, he had helped Diane clean up and began to check on his teen daughters' homework. The two girls chased him away quickly, though. They reminded him that, even though he had once taken the same subjects they had now, the methods he had learned were "hopelessly out of date." Susan, the younger of the two, tried to encourage him, "We love you dad, but you have to recognize that when it comes to our schoolwork, you're just a dinosaur."

So Ron brought a cup of tea up to his home office and tried to organize his papers and his thoughts. Though some people did best working on one task at a time, Ron preferred the three-pile approach. He found that, working on one task, he could often make connections to two or three very different items. Ron recalled that this approach drove his own father to distraction. "You'll never amount to anything if you keep this up!" the old man had warned.

Ron reached for Malcolm's case pile first. He read over the short, subdued clipping from the suburban newspaper based in the town where the customer's office was located. The writer must have been trained in how to write about upsetting events in a calming way. He leafed through some of Malcolm's own job notes, finding them cryptic and undecipherable.

Then Ron started making his own list of all the companies Malcolm had sold projects to in the past few years, companies that had laid people off when they outsourced their IT work to Magna. The list grew to 14 in just a few minutes, then Ron lost momentum. He knew there were a few more, but he couldn't recall the names. He went back and started estimating the number of people put out of work at each job. The total grew quickly, past one and up to several thousand.

As far as Ron was concerned, all those people who had been put out of a job by Malcolm's efforts were possible suspects. It could be a senior executive who lost a high-paying job and had lots of financial pressures, maybe somebody who actually saw Malcolm in action at one of his presentations. That personal contact with Malcolm's arrogance could have been the thing that pushed the culprit over the edge. But then, maybe it could be a lower-level programmer analyst who had just plain reached the end of his rope.

Though he shuddered to admit it, Ron also realized that any number of Magna employees themselves might be guilty. It wasn't just that no one liked him, but so many people had good reasons to hate him. He had stalled, even ruined a number of careers at Magna.

With all these suspects around, why did the police have to settle on Ron? He certainly had his own issues with Malcolm, but violence was not his way. After all, Ron reminded himself, he was the peacemaker. He shuddered again, realizing that whoever killed Malcolm might now be setting his sights on Ron himself. After all, he would be carrying out many of the tasks Malcolm had left behind.

The Techsol pile was not very encouraging either. Magna's work plan listed a series of smart, possibly brilliant solutions to problems Techsol had been struggling with for years. And Magna's solutions were inexpensive, too. The disturbing papers in the pile were from past jobs. In those records, Ron began to see what a difficult customer Techsol could be. He found memos between Techsol department chiefs debating how to direct previous projects, e-mails reflecting internal battles, and notes addressing stalled decisions. It seemed that nearly every paper Ron looked at had the words "communications problems," "internal politics," or "silo organization" embedded in the text.

Unable to tell if it was his desperation or the quality of the ideas that was driving him, Ron found himself agreeing with all the steps in the construction partnering material, linking virtually each item to the Techsol project. Within a half hour, he had composed a draft agenda for a partnering workshop between key project staff at Magna and Techsol, 12 people in all.

A Facilitator and a Detective

As he worked at them over the following week, Ron found the two tasks of planning the partnering meeting and trying to find Malcolm's killer to be equally frustrating. For starters, Techsol's senior manager's reaction to Ron's proposal to have a partnering meeting was disappointing.

"A what?" their finance director asked. "I thought you people were the experts, that you've done this kind of work before. The kind of meeting you're suggesting is very expensive. You're asking us to take what will amount to hundreds of billable hours during a very busy season."

Techsol's chief operating officer also did not help Ron's cause. "It's a cute idea. You know we love the whole concept of partnering around here. But I don't see why such a detailed workshop is really necessary. We've never had to do it before. Can't you just do the standard kind of start-up meeting other companies do? You know, show a few slides, tell people how happy you are to work with them, that kind of thing?"

Cute?! Maybe the fact that you've had the troubles you've had with previous jobs should suggest that you do this one differently, Ron thought, but stopped himself from saying.

Anyway, Techsol's senior managers eventually did come around to agreeing to have the partnering meeting. It just took longer than Ron had anticipated.

Work on Malcolm's case was also more difficult than he anticipated. Ron was able, fairly easily, to identify all the companies Malcolm had signed up as customers in the past two years. But it was proving to be much more difficult to fill out the two lists Ron was convinced would lead him to the killer: one list of the people who had attended Malcolm's presentations and another of the people in customer companies who were experiencing extreme financial pressures.

The companies were able and willing to supply the lists of people who attended the meetings. This was helpful, and it led Ron to several individuals he recalled having had a strong reaction to Malcolm during the presentations. Managers from three companies in particular stood out in his mind, all senior level people whom Malcolm embarrassed in front of their peers at the meetings with an offhand comment or joke. While all this seemed like some progress, the companies were either unable or unwilling to share information about who on their staff was under the gun financially.

More disturbing than all this was Ron himself. He could not figure out the PDA stylus. The police showed him his prints all over the stylus and, sure enough, it did look exactly like the one he used. How did it land on the parking lot? Did someone else pocket it and switch it for a duplicate? Or did Ron somehow commit the murder himself and then block it from his own memory? After all, Malcolm did have the ability to get him pretty worked up.

The Partnering Meeting

By the time Ron led the actual partnering meeting on the following Monday, he was feeling much better. He was grateful to have the meeting to take his time off the case. He had done all the homework he could think of to make the meeting successful—interviewing all the participants and collecting their thoughts in questionnaires. He had also quickly put together a survey of the larger group of customers in the Techsol organization.

The survey results were encouraging, suggesting that the larger group was not as upset as the meeting participants had portrayed. The survey showed that there were clearly some issues to address, but that those issues were pretty specific and focused on Magna's communications, not their technical ability. From the outset, Ron had the hunch that simply getting procedures to work that Magna had "on the shelf" for years would resolve most of the issues.

Carol helped Ron lead the meeting, which Ron liked, then disliked, then liked again. He liked having the extra set of eyes and ears. He initially disliked Carol insisting that he organize people into small groups to do all the partnering work, that he have people sign the Goals Statement, and that he work in the meeting with the Myers-Briggs personality profile both Magna and Techsol also used for their own management training.

"Jerry says if you're going to go through all this, you really need to do it right," Carol pointed out. By the time the meeting ended, Ron had to agree that Carol and Jerry were right, but it was still hard to do. He had read all the information on facilitation skills, so he knew it was important to set up the room so that people would sit at small tables.

Still, when it came time to ask the participants to change seats (between the work on Taking Stock and the work with Building Trust), Ron got cold feet. If Carol hadn't been there, glaring at him, he wasn't sure what he would have done. And ditto with having people really work with the personality profiles and asking people to sign the Goals Statement after they drafted it. He knew they were the right things to do, but it took Carol's glare to propel him into action.

The group's positive response to the Myers-Briggs pleased Ron. A few of them resisted using it. "We already had this in management training," Magna's purchasing manager whined. But the more technical people liked it. It didn't surprise Ron that they enjoyed talking about themselves. "Oh, I keep lists for everything!" one of their technical specialists exclaimed at one point, as if it were the most interesting personality quirk on the planet.

It did surprise Ron both that people said so much about themselves and that people in the group seemed so interested in each other. For a group of people that were supposed to be cold and impersonal, they definitely had a human side. As several of them—the list-makers—compiled a detailed list of the lists they make, Ron reflected that their human side was a quirky one.

Ron also found the group's overall Myers-Briggs information valuable. Every person in the group except one, Magna's human resources manager, was introverted. Ron had kind of expected that, but the high introversion scores and complete absence of anyone on the project team in that category prodded Ron to work extra hard on initiating communications processes that would provide adequate information over the life of the project.

Knowing the group's strong introversion bias had helped Ron avert a disaster, he thought. During the Taking Stock discussions, the group had pointed out how complicated the project was and how much coordination it would require. Yet later in the day, when they were discussing how often they needed to meet, the group seemed set to agree on a monthly meeting schedule and then, only if it was really needed. At that point Ron reminded them of both their introvert bias and of their previous discussion about the complexity of the project. Before he could finish asking them if they really thought monthly meetings would get the job done, most of them had started laughing.

"You're right, you're right," the technical specialist admitted. We really do need to meet more often. It looks like the introverts have been 'outed' this time. At least, can we keep the meetings short?" The group then agreed on weekly meetings.

However many points Carol had on him, Ron also knew he held one big edge on her in the brainstorming topic he had insisted in tackling towards the end of the workshop. Ron had had the idea that, working with Techsol staff, it might be possible to come up with some new project types that could save some of their jobs. He hadn't wanted to be in the position of putting people out of work, and a part of him thought that some possibilities existed. He knew that Techsol managers and Magna staff each saw part of the opportunities, and wondered if putting them together could create some sparks. He also knew it was risky because he didn't want to raise false hopes.

But the session went very well, producing four different ideas for special projects that had a strong likelihood for keeping Techsol employees busy for at least a few months more. With this initial success, Ron was hopeful that the joint group would be able to further develop new ideas.

Even the skeptical Techsol senior management group gave in, praising Ron for his efforts by the time the workshop was over. "I never could have guessed that a meeting like this could be so productive," their human resources manager reflected. "No disrespect intended, but I get the sense that your recently departed boss would not have done anything like this. I know it sounds incredible, but I've actually heard some people say that what happened served him right."

Ron twitched at this comment. He also found himself reacting badly in general to the human resources manager. She was so energetic, so enthusiastic, so…extraverted. He wondered if, as a long shot, maybe *she* was the killer? After all, she did have the motive of wanting to keep more people employed at Magna. It would be difficult for her to play that cheerleader human resources role if there were fewer people left to cheer her.

Trying to maintain his objectivity, Ron mumbled a few nice things about Malcolm, but guessed he didn't sound very convincing. As he and Carol read through the feedback forms people completed at the end of the workshop, Ron tried to savor the workshop's success. It was clear that he had succeeded in addressing Techsol's interests and putting solidly into place the procedures it would take to partner with this interesting but disorganized client. Ron was also pleased with the progress one agenda item had made: by using these procedures, it would be possible for Techsol to keep most of their employees.

But it was difficult to fully enjoy the workshop when Malcolm's case still awaited him. He wondered how much longer he would be able to put off the police.

Wrap Up

Ron didn't have to wonder long. The police were waiting in the parking lot, and they had company with them. At first Ron couldn't recognize the person, but then it began to dawn on him. It was Malcolm's neighbor, the one Ron had separated from Malcolm in the squabble over the lawn. The neighbor was scowling.

"Does this look familiar to you?" the policeman asked, holding up Ron's PDA stylus.

Before Ron could answer, the policeman continued. "It's yours. I know, I know, they all look alike to me, too.

"We picked it up when we picked him up. And we picked him up when he was snooping around Malcolm's lawn. He seemed, you know, maybe just a little too happy about a lawn."

The lawn. Now it flashed back to Ron. The squabble with the neighbor. The odds and ends from all their pockets strewn over the lawn. In his haste to get going, Ron and the neighbor must have inadvertently switched PDA styli.

Ron looked at the neighbor again. Was this really someone capable of committing a murder with a PDA stylus?

Interrupting Ron's thoughts, the neighbor called out, "What are you looking at? Are you really surprised that it was me? After all…"

"I know," now it was Ron who interrupted. "He had it coming."

14

Planning Your Own Partnering

Most readers probably already have a situation in mind for applying Partnering Solution strategies and skills. If you do not, don't worry. In this chapter, we provide guidelines to help you identify situations where the Partnering Solution can help—situations in the organizations you work in, belong to, and work with. We also provide checklists and clear instructions for developing straightforward, simple plans to carry the Partnering Solution through from early discussions to full implementation.

Planning for Action

In preparing for battle I have always found that plans are useless but planning is indispensable.

—Dwight D. Eisenhower

Planning your own partnering is not only indispensable, it is an effective way to learn the principles in this book. Reading with your own situation in mind will provide a "reality hook" that makes the strategies, skills, and concepts come to life. Most readers probably already have a situation in mind, but if you do not, don't worry. We provide guidelines for helping you to identify situations in the following section.

In most situations, planning for partnering should focus on two meetings: an initial meeting and a follow-up meeting. People leave the initial meeting with increased understanding about the partnering situation, draft goals, pilot action items, and enriched mutual understanding and trust.

After the meeting, they work on the action items they developed in the meeting. Four to eight weeks later at the follow-up meeting, they refine the goals they formulated in their initial meeting, track the effectiveness of the action items they have been applying, and discuss the observations they've made using the insights of the personality profile.

These are more detailed steps involved in planning and leading the two meetings (initial and follow-up):

1. Feasibility (identifying partnering situations).
2. Pre-work and planning (first partnering meeting).
3. Holding the first meeting.
4. Evaluating the meeting.
5. Planning the follow-up meeting.
6. Working between sessions; planning the follow-up meeting.
7. Holding the follow-up meeting.
8. Evaluating the follow-up meeting.
9. Long-term planning.
10. Evaluating the overall process; planning next steps.

The sequence of two meetings usually provides a foundation of noticeable results. It also provides participants with enough first-hand experience with partnering so that they can effectively plan action steps that will enable their partnering to succeed over a longer term. They may decide to meet monthly, quarterly, or even less in order to sustain their progress. They may decide to start exploring opportunities as well as addressing problems.

Identifying Situations for Using the Partnering Solution

The cases in the previous chapters should help you identify a range of possible applications for the Partnering Solution. But identifying viable partnering applications in one's own organizations can be difficult. When one is in the midst of a situation, it's easy to lose perspective. We observe managers missing prime opportunities to use the Partnering Solution in their work. We also observe managers using the Partnering Solution in situations where it is destined to have little effect.

The following checklist is intended to further assist readers identify partnering situations in their own organizations. It may be useful to think about working with Partnering Solution methods when several of the following conditions exist between or within organizations:

❏ *Noticeable problems.* Clearly visible communications problems and their resulting costs are the leading indicator for many partnering applications. Examples of this include dissatisfied customer and Departments at War situations.

❏ *Unmet potential.* In some partnering situations, it's not so much that problems exist, but that the situation has much greater potential than is currently being achieved. Examples of this are some mergers and Quiet Standoff situations.

❏ *Focus on dividing.* Another indicator of a situation that can benefit from partnering work is one in which people focus more on how work is divided than on how the divisions are put back together.

❏ *Complexity.* Sometimes complexity provides strong motivation for partnering. After all, partnering work can clarify and simplify tangled communications processes.

❏ *Incentive.* When communications problems actively cost one or both of the groups involved in partnering, or when improving communications would clearly benefit one or both of the groups, it raises the likelihood that partnering will succeed.

❏ *Strong participant or senior management interest.* Partnering can also be worth pursuing whenever participants in the situation themselves or senior management express a strong interest in making improvements.

Qualifiers and Prerequisites for Effective Partnering

Beyond factors that indicate the partnering work may produce worthwhile results, it is also useful to consider factors that are necessary in order for partnering to succeed. If any of these factors are not addressed, it can be difficult to achieve meaningful results.

❏ *Adequate empowerment.* In their enthusiasm, partnering groups occasionally attempt to take action in areas in which they do not have sufficient formal authority. It is important that partnering groups have adequate power and authority to act on the decisions they reach and the plans they make.

❏ *Technical competence.* Partnering can improve communications, trust, and procedures, but it cannot do much if any of the parties lack the basic technical skills of the field. Working on partnering usually reveals that customers would register higher levels of satisfaction if service providers improve communications. Occasionally, though, customers also complain that service providers lack technical skills. In those cases, service providers can respond by providing increased technical training or bringing in more experienced staff.

❏ *Senior management support.* Senior managers seldom need to be actively involved in partnering work at a detailed level. However, it is often essential that senior managers communicate their support for a partnering effort and that they participate in at least a brief part of partnering meetings.

❏ *Group acceptance.* Partnering groups can be skeptical, reluctant, frustrated, and cynical, and partnering work can still succeed. But if partnering groups are actively dead set against trying to make improvements, partnering efforts are likely to fail. Senior managers can force a meeting, but they can't force groups to own the results.

Identifying Situations to Apply the Partnering Solution	
Identifying Factors	**Qualifiers/Prerequisites**
• Noticeable problems. • Unmet potential. • Focus on dividing. • Complexity. • Incentive. • Strong participant or senior management interest.	• Adequate empowerment. • Technical competence. • Senior management support. • Group acceptance.

First Person:
Starting Small—A Good Way to Build Confidence

If the thought of trying the Partnering Solution in any kind of organization without getting some other kind of experience with it is intimidating to you, you might take the approach of one of the participants in one of our Leaders Circle leadership development programs. To build comfort and skill with the Partnering Solution process, George tried it in a discussion with Tim, his 13-year-old son, about how the two of them work together on his son's homework. A good sport, Tim agreed to go along with his dad's little experiment.

George and Tim followed most of the partnering agenda, leaving out only the personality profiles. They had a Taking Stock discussion, worked on Clarifying Goals, signed the Goals Statement, and developed key processes to enhance the quality of their discussion. (Note the key process: "No swearing.")

Now several months since their initial discussion, George reports that the partnering discussion agreement did not solve everything, but that it did have lasting results in improving the tone and quality of his communications with Tim. George also reports that the discussion did give him the experience and confidence he needed to try it out in several group situations in the office.

The results of George and Tim's Taking Stock, Clarifying Goals, and Implementing Key Processes discussions follow, unedited:

Taking Stock	
What Works Well	**What Does Not Work Well**
Quiet space to work in.	Yelling.
End up understanding the material better.	Working too late at night. Feeling like we are in a hurry.
Being "in the zone."	Sometimes takes too long.
Doing many problems together (practice).	Not showing all steps.
Practice problems.	Not following step-by-step instructions.
Everyone feels good when you are doing well.	Being lazy.
Everyone feels great when you do well on tests.	Taking too much of Mom/Dad's time.
	Relying too much on Mom/Dad for help.

Clarifying Goals

1. Reduce the amount of yelling by 75 percent when helping with/discussing homework.
2. Finish math homework in two hours or less and finish by 8 p.m.
3. Show all steps on all homework and double/sanity check all work.
4. Spend at least half an hour "in the zone" whenever doing math homework.
5. All end-of-term grades are a B+ (88) or better.

Key Processes

- No swearing.
- Dad to keep an eye on things for at least two problems to make sure they are being done correctly.
- Each person can call two 30-second time-outs per night. No talking by the other person during the time-out.
- Tim to do a study/review session with either Mom or Dad the night before any test or quiz.
- On math homework:

  Step #1: Copy the problem from the book onto the homework paper.

  Step #2: Show **ALL** steps.

  Step #3: Write neatly and keep organized.

Developing a Brief, Overall Partnering Plan

Once one has identified a situation that can benefit from partnering work, it is useful to develop a brief but comprehensive overall partnering plan. This plan uses the framework of Issues, Outcomes, Work Plan, Who, and Where to produce a simple understanding of the partnering work. Developing this type of plan is useful to continue to test the potential value of partnering work as well as to share the idea with others.

The table on page 250 illustrates one sample of a brief, overall partnering plan. To explain the column headings:

❑ *Issues.* This is usually the "leading edge" of the partnering work: the issues, and often the complaints, people are raising. These are the initial, leading reasons or triggers for the partnering work. In some ways these are problems; in some ways these are symptoms. In any case, it is helpful here not to work too hard at getting the wording right but rather to use the same language that people are using in the field.

❑ *Outcomes.* This is the most important column on the plan, and it requires more thinking than the first column. This is an important column because the clearer groups can be about the outcomes they want the partnering to achieve, the more likely it is that they can accomplish them. Also, it is important to discuss outcomes in order to anticipate and resolve potential differences participants might have in this area. Even with plenty of thinking, expect to revise this column over time as more people have an opportunity to work at defining what they would like the partnering work to accomplish. It is very important, from the outset, to try and specify what the partnering work is trying to achieve. Partnering itself is intangible. The more clearly it is possible to define outcomes, the easier it is to achieve them.

❑ *Work Plan.* This provides an initial overall outline of planning and meetings. It is very useful from the outset to show people in the partnering group this overall plan because it enables them to better anticipate what the partnering work can accomplish. It also enables them to set their own expectations about how much effort the partnering work will take and what it is likely to produce.

❑ *Who.* Surprisingly, deciding "who" should attend partnering can often be quite difficult. Determining who should attend a partnering meeting is not simply a matter of filling chairs. The attendance list must include people who know enough about all the different levels of partnering activity to devise intelligent plans. It also must include people placed highly enough in the organizations to ensure that any decisions made or work plan can be carried out after the meeting. A "vertical cross-section" often provides a productive mix. In other words, it's usually useful to involve some people placed high enough in the organizations to have the authority to act on partnering decisions. It's also usually important to involve people placed low enough in the organization to have first-hand, grassroots insight into the issues the partnering meeting is attempting to address.

❑ *Where.* Even this aspect of partnering can influence partnering results. Some organizations use off-site retreat facilities for meetings such as these. They believe that going off-site enables groups to get away from mundane distractions at work and focus on the more large-scale issues the meeting is addressing. However, we often achieve better results by holding partnering meetings on-site in the organizations involved in the partnering work. In particular, we find that meeting on-site sometimes makes it easier and more natural for participants to make connections between the work they do in the meeting and the more difficult work they will do later, on-site, to apply meeting plans in their everyday work.

Sample Customer Satisfaction Initial Partnering Plan				
(Used to clarify overall plan and provide basis for discussion and approval.)				
Issues	**Outcomes**	**Work Plan**	**Who**	**Where**
◆ Increasing number of customer complaints. ◆Customer organization need to reduce costs. ◆ Increasing frustration of service provider staff. ◆ Service provider staff complaints that customer company senior management reverses many agreements that their field staff make with the service provider.	◆Clarify components of customer satisfaction. ◆ Increase customer satisfaction. ◆Reduce customer costs. ◆ Reduce service provider staff. ◆Increase decision-making authority of customer organization field staff.	◆Interview participants to plan meetings and clarify their issues and concerns. ◆Two half-day partnering meetings separated by about a month. ◆Agenda for Meeting 1 is to review data, write clear goals, pilot three new communications processes and increase trust and understanding. ◆Agenda for Meeting 2 is to review progress on Meeting 1 action items and explore new opportunities.	◆A working group of 14 people total. ◆Seven people from each organization: a mix of senior, middle, and line staff. ◆Senior managers participate only enough to support the partnering effort.	◆Initial meeting at customer offices. ◆Follow-up meeting at service provider offices.

Pre-Work and Planning

Workshops and meetings of any kind are expensive. Not so much in the costs of the meeting room, food, or fee for a facilitator, but the most substantial cost for any meeting is usually the total salary time of the participants. Thus a four-hour meeting involving 14 people can easily represent thousands of dollars of participants' salaries.

Careful pre-work and planning can significantly improve the value of partnering meetings, ensuring that they are well worth the time that participants take. Depending on the particular project, several different types of pre-work can be worthwhile:

❐ *Obtaining participant input.* In almost every case, it is useful for the meeting leader to interview meeting participants before the meeting. These interviews serve the dual purpose of providing the leader with information about the participants' interests and enabling the participants to get to know the leader. In most cases, it is both efficient and effective to interview participants in small groups rather than individually. It is also possible in many cases to conduct interviews by phone. When it is not possible to interview either by telephone or in person, it can still be worthwhile to obtain participant input by e-mail. In interviews, we try to ask all respondents a core, short set of questions so that we can compare responses. We also ask a few open-ended questions to capture items that we may have otherwise missed. The core questions we ask are:

- What are the two or three most important aspects of the partnering that are working well?

- What are the two or three aspects of the partnering that most need improvement?

- What are two or three goals you would suggest as goals that the whole partnering group should support?

- What processes or procedures do you think need to be working very well in order for the partnering to succeed?

- What outcomes would you like to see result from this partnering effort?

- What comments or suggestions do you have regarding the draft Work Plan describing the partnering work?

❐ *Obtaining senior management input.* It is often also useful to obtain input from senior managers who have opinions about what the partnering work should accomplish or who must approve any recommendations coming from the partnering group. We usually ask senior managers the questions listed previously.

❐ *Obtaining stakeholder input.* Sometimes, organizations or departments working at partnering with each other also have an impact on other groups around them. Although these other groups may not participate in the partnering, it can be useful to obtain their input.

❐ *Assigning participant pre-work.* The partnering agenda asks participants deep questions. Most often, they produce more useful responses when they have been able to think about their responses before having to discuss them in a meeting. We usually ask participants to do three things before attending the first partnering meeting—put in writing their responses to several of the questions in the list on page 251 (no need to write in complete sentences, simple lists will do just fine); complete any personality profiles we may be using in the meeting; and look over the workbook section on partnering just to become familiar with the key concepts.

❐ *Summarizing participant input and returning the summary to participants.* If time allows, the meeting leader summarizes the interviews and/or e-mails received and sends the summary to participants before the meeting. This enables them to see where others stand on key issues before they even get to the meeting. If the facilitator is not able to do this, the first block of meeting time will go to participants just learning where their peers in the meeting stand. If the facilitator can get this information out, participants can take much less time just hearing each others' opinions and devote more time to working on what to do.

Meeting 1 Agenda

Even with all the pre-work and planning, it is useful to circulate the agenda to participants at least a week before the meeting so that they can better understand how the meeting works. It is also helpful to give copies out at the beginning of the meeting itself, quickly review the time frames, and then use the agenda to keep the meeting on track.

Our most productive partnering agendas have equally divided the time available for the meeting into four equal parts: Taking Stock, Building Trust, Clarifying Goals, and Implementing Key Processes. We usually prefer to follow this order, also. It's useful to begin with Taking Stock so that all the discussions can be based on input from the whole group.

We usually like to do the Building Trust piece next. (For more details on this work, see Chapter 5.) We find that working with the personality profiles early in the meeting addresses the interpersonal issues that provide a foundation for the more business-oriented meeting topics that follow. In addition, working with the personality profiles usually moves meeting participants to a more reflective, less blaming stance. Using the personality profiles, participants openly discuss the strengths and weaknesses someone with their personality is likely to bring to the partnering work.

In cases where trust and mutual understanding seemed high, though, we have ended with Building Trust to enable the group to focus on other agenda items that were more pressing for particular partnering work.

After exploring what's working well and what is not in Taking Stock and Building Trust with the personality profiles, it seems logical that the next item is to ask participants, "What goals do you think are important to agree on to guide your partnering with each other?" The work on goals sets the stage for work on processes, which are used to help the group achieve its goals.

If at all possible, it is most productive to address all four items equally in whatever amount of time is available. The four parts of the agenda play off and inform each other, and the interaction among the topics is lost if a group tackles one agenda item a week.

Thus, a typical half-day initial partnering meeting agenda is:

8 a.m.	Introductions, coffee.
8 a.m.	Taking Stock.
9:30 a.m.	Building Trust.
10:30 a.m.	Break.
10:45 a.m.	Clarifying Goals.
11:45 a.m.	Implementing Key Processes.
12:45 p.m.	Summarize action items.

If the meeting is a full-day program, the times should be adjusted accordingly.

Using a Meeting Process Outline

In some ways it is unfortunate that so much of the effectiveness of partnering overall depends on the effectiveness of partnering meetings. Many people dread meetings of all kinds, and with good reason: their experience with meetings has been awful. At best, they've been boring and productive. Worse, they may have been unfocused, chaotic, and conflicted. Please refer to Chapter 10 for information on improving group communications. The chapter details why group communications is often problematic and how to facilitate groups to ensure that discussions are productive.

The partnering meeting differs significantly from meetings most people are used to. It's not a presentation, a discussion, or a training program. The point of this meeting is to get work done, reach agreements, and plan and produce documents, not to listen to other people discuss their PowerPoint slides. The success of a partnering meeting hinges on the effective involvement of all participants. They will produce the work, the answers, the plans, and the methods. Thus the guidelines for running a great meeting involve making sure that the meeting manages participant involvement.

One tool that helps ensure meeting success is a process agenda that provides notes on how the partnering group will be configured for each of the agenda topics. A Process Agenda lists who sits with whom, what the small groups are discussing, and what the time frames are for the groups to complete their tasks.

Process Agenda for Initial Partnering Meeting		
Topic	**Discussion Topics**	**Groupings**
Taking Stock	◆ List the three main aspects of the partnering that are working well. ◆ List the three main aspects of the partnering that are not working well. ◆ List three outcomes you would like to get from this meeting.	◆ Groups of three to five people. ◆ People sit with peers from their own organizations so that they are comfortable.
Building Trust	◆ What are the most likely assets people of your personality profile bring to partnering relationships like ours?	◆ Groups of two to four people. ◆ People sit with others who have same or similar personality profiles.

Chart continues on next page.

Topic	Discussion Questions	Groupings
	◆ What are the most likely problems people of your personality profile bring to partnering relationships like ours?	
Clarifying Goals	◆ List three to five performance goals you think are important for the whole partnering group to support. ◆ List three to five communications goals you think are important for the whole partnering group to support.	◆ Groups of three to five people. ◆ People sit with their counterparts, similar levels, in the partner organization. These groups serve as "filters" to sift through ideas before bringing them to the overall group.
Implementing Key Processes	For the process you are working on, List: 1. The challenges and obstacles the process must overcome. 2. Possible ideas that might help. 3. Specific action plans for one or two of the ideas.	◆ Groups of five to seven people. ◆ People sit with others they will use the process with in their everyday work.

Meeting Tips

Beyond this process outline, several specific tips can help make an initial partnering meeting great:

❏ *Start early.* One of the best ways to kill the energy and motivation people bring to a partnering meeting is to wait until the meeting's formal start-up time to begin. That 15 or 20 minutes of people sitting around, checking their watches, flipping through newspapers while they wait for all participants to arrive have deadly effects on discussion for hours after. An even better way to ruin a meeting is to make the people who have arrived on time wait for stragglers. So, start the meeting a few minutes early. Never make people wait. You can create a strong, positive momentum that will carry through the whole meeting if you engage people immediately when they arrive.

❏ *Put people in small groups, and get them started working quickly.* Help people entering the meeting get connected with small groups of four or five people. Start the groups with the Taking Stock discussion, listing major issues that are working well, others that need to be improved, and what they would like to get out of the meeting. Flip charts and clusters of chairs around the room make this process go quickly and smoothly. Starting in this way makes it easy for people who come into the meeting to quickly and quietly join a small group engaged in a task. Starting in this way does imply that you choose a suitable agenda topic, something that does not require a quick decision by the entire group first thing in the meeting. Better topic choices are those, such as Taking Stock, that enable people to begin the meeting by informally discussing their opinions.

❏ *Start again, more formally, on time.* At or very near the formal starting time, start the meeting again. This is when all participants quickly introduce themselves and say something brief about what they would like the meeting to accomplish.

❏ *Move people according to the agenda topic they are working on.* Chapter 10, which discusses improving group communications skills, provides details on why and how to organize the meeting using lots of small group activities. The point to emphasize here is that there should be a logic behind every move, a reason that by putting person A with person B, the quality of the dialog and discussion will improve.

❏ *Stay with the balance on the agenda.* It is all too easy when discussions are going well to let them go on too long. The meeting will usually run better overall if you adhere to the original time allotments you specified, dividing the meeting time into four approximately equal parts.

❏ *Take the scheduled breaks.* Simple biology limits what people can accomplish at a lengthy meeting. They get tired, bored, distracted, and irritable. Trying to work through fatigue seldom produces results. Better to take the scheduled break, get some fresh air for a few minutes, and return to the meeting renewed and ready for action.

❏ *End early.* If at all possible, it helps to end a few minutes early. This creates a positive dynamic to set up the next meeting.

❏ *Evaluate the meeting in writing.* Use the sample survey form below.

Partnering Meeting Feedback Survey							
The Meeting	Strongly Agree	Agree	Slightly Agree	Slightly Disagree	Disagree	Strongly Disagree	Not Applicable
1. Was well-organized and planned.							
2. Stayed focused on key items.							
3. Followed the planned agenda.							
4. Discussion was evenly balanced among all participants.							
5. Environment was open for discussion.							
6. Materials contributed to the meeting's productivity.							
7. Accomplished useful work for the partnership.							
8. Produced specific action plans.							
9. Focused appropriately on follow-up after the meeting.							
10. Overall, was effective and worthwhile.							

11. The three best things about the meeting were:

12. The three things about the meeting that most need improvement are:

13. The three most important items to follow up on after the meeting are:

14. My three most important recommendations for the next meeting are:

Using Flip Charts as Collective Wisdom and Meeting Minutes

Flip charts can add to the productivity of partnering meetings in two important ways. First, they provide a tool to enhance group communications and problem-solving. Second, and more pragmatically, they can be used, as is, as minutes of the meeting.

As a group discussion tool, flip charts perform an influential summarizing function. As a group brainstorms an item and lists ideas, the flip chart provides a list of all the ideas for all participants. This makes it possible for all participants to use the ideas that all the other participants have contributed. Because of this, the flip chart contributes more positively to group discussion than a single note-taker can. With a note-taker, the only person in the group who has access to the whole group's thinking is the note-taker him- or herself.

One way to use flip charts for meeting minutes is through copying services. They usually have machines that reduce flip charts to 8 1/2 x 11–inch sheets. Reduced in size, flip-chart writing usually becomes darker and clearer. The reduction does not fix spelling mistakes, but it often does preserve the sentiment behind the writing. Also, using flip charts can increase participants' ownership and accountability for the items they discussed. Seeing one's own handwriting on the chart provides an excellent reminder that one needs to be taking action.

As an alternative to having the flip charts copied, it is also possible to take a digital photo of the charts and post the album to the Web on one of the photo posting services such as *www.Ofoto.com* or *www.shutterfly.com*. Participants download or order the photos at their own convenience.

Working on Follow-Through in the Partnering Meeting

At the beginning of most partnering meetings, when people are usually enthusiastic about the meeting, we like to tell groups that the meeting they are about to have doesn't matter. Yes, we acknowledge it will be stimulating and interesting. Yes, it will produce useful ideas and plans. However, what really matters is not the meeting itself, but rather what happens afterwards. In order for the initial meeting to succeed, it must do everything possible to ensure that participants follow up and act on their plans.

The most important thing that people can do in the meeting to ensure that follow-up will occur afterwards is to drive for a high level of specificity in all discussions. For example, it's not good enough for the group to agree, "We will work at improving communications." A more effective way to put it would be, "We will work at improving communications by holding weekly project meetings every Wednesday morning from 9 to 10 a.m. George will lead the meeting. The agenda will always cover these three items, and will always allow 15 minutes for open discussion."

During the meeting, it helps to ensure follow-through later by posting a flip chart page headed "Follow-Through Actions" in a prominent, visible spot. The chart is divided into three columns: What, Who, and When. Discussion on each partnering agenda topic ends with with five minutes devoted to carrying the major issues over to action items. Throughout the meeting, the group quickly reviews the action items to ensure that they understand and are comfortable with the expectations. Following is a list of typical follow-up action items that groups might address after each agenda item:

- ❏ *Taking Stock.* Meeting participants might decide that they need more data or more analysis in order to better understand partnering performance.

- ❏ *Building Trust.* Meeting participants might decide that they should sponsor some social or recreational activities to build the team. If they find the personality profiles useful, they might assign "homework" to the whole group that involves noting examples of themselves and others "acting in type," illustrating their personality types.

- ❏ *Clarifying Goals.* To follow up on an initial meeting, participants often find it useful to assign a small group of meeting participants to refine the draft Goals Statement produced in the meeting. The small group edits and wordsmiths the Goals Statement, and brings a revised draft to the follow-up meeting.

- ❏ *Implementing Key Processes.* Here it is very important for each group working with a process to list, very specifically, who will do what when in order to try the process out in the coming weeks.

- ❏ *Raising the Bar.* As with Implementing Key Processes, it is very useful for this topic to list who will try what when in order to ensure follow-through after the partnering meeting.

Overall, there is a one-word key to successful follow-up after the meeting: specificity. The more specific the action plans are in the meeting—listing peoples' names along with timelines and deliverables—the more likely it is that people will act on them after the meeting.

Between Meeting 1 and Meeting 2

In many cases, this is the most critical time period during the partnering process: Will people follow through on the action items they committed to?

It is important to plan in the initial meeting how the group will follow up on action items between the end of the initial meeting and the beginning of the second meeting. This can be done in several ways. One person or a small group of people can either collect brief updates from each of the action groups after a few weeks or contact each of the groups and request an action update.

Partnering Meeting 2

This meeting picks up the agenda items from the first meeting, but is much more focused on actions overall. If possible, it's useful before the meeting to provide participants with a brief update on the work the action groups have done since the first meeting.

The most productive agenda we have found for Meeting 2 follows. Of the five items, it is best to spend most of the time of the meeting on the last two, Implementing Key Processes and Raising the Bar:

❐ *Taking Stock.* Again, the meeting begins with a Taking Stock discussion. However, in this meeting the focus is on the partnering work done since the initial meeting. Participants discuss what's gone well, what hasn't, and what they would like to get out of the meeting.

❐ *Building Trust.* Participants discuss the observations they have made of group process since the first meeting. If the partnering work is using a personality profile, participants discuss instances in which they have observed others and themselves "acting in type"—that is, behaving in ways that illustrate their personality types. It is also helpful to discuss issues that arose since the first meeting that initially seemed like business issues but which, upon further reflection, are really more rooted in personality differences.

❐ *Clarifying Goals.* In the second meeting the group reviews the revised Goals Statement brought in by the small group that has been working on it. The larger group makes further refinements if necessary. At whatever point they agree that the statement is acceptable, they sign it.

❏ *Implementing Key Processes.* The small groups that have been working to implement action processes present brief descriptions of their work to date. The overall group listens and offers comments and suggestions to refine the processes and procedures to ensure that they are working well.

❏ *Raising the Bar.* For this topic, the group explores new opportunities that the partnership might address: quality improvements, efficiencies, innovations, and process changes.

The meeting concludes with the group planning for the long term, considering how often they should meet in order to achieve their goals, what the agenda should be, and how they can measure their progress.

Planning Your Own Partnering: A Client's Perspective

Manager of Facilities Development for EMC Corporation in Hopkinton, Massachusetts, Dominic Bisignano is a "power user" of partnering methods. He has used formal partnering efforts on five major construction projects, totaling over a million and a half square feet of space. In planning partnering, he offers this perspective:

"In planning projects, the inclination is to go full speed ahead. There's always a lot of enthusiasm to get the job done. But first it's necessary to make sure that everyone is in the boat. It's important to go slow at the beginning of partnering and make sure that everyone is on board.

"As a leader, I get pretty enthusiastic that specific issues get addressed in meetings, that we outline specific deliverables, and that people sign up for them. Everybody finds partnering meetings interesting, that part of it is never a problem. But some people are just participants in a passive way. They're just along for the ride. It's the focus on the deliverables that's important, the focus on the outcomes right from the planning stages.

"Looking to service providers who partner with us, I think SEi Companies gets it right with partnering. They are always focused on the partnership. In theory on our projects, their client is the architect, and they seem to do a good job partnering with them. What I know from my point of view is that they are always in communication with us when it's needed on the project. Whoever came out here over the course of the project, they always were informed about what was going on and they always had the relevant information with them.

"And whether it's the project manager or even the CEO of their company, when I need his input on some larger issue, they are always accessible and always part of the communications process. On top of that, they were always able to manage whatever their internal affairs might be without bringing them to the partnering. They have always been effective partners.

"Planning for partnering, that's what people should keep in mind. To focus on the outcomes and the specific deliverables of partnering, and to plan for the ongoing communications throughout the project that will make the project work."

Getting External Help/Working With a Consultant

"Can I do this myself?" is a question you may logically ask as you plan partnering work.

In many cases it is entirely possible for people to plan and implement their own partnering projects. Also in many cases, partnering effectiveness increases when it draws on external help and consultants. External help can come both from professional consultants outside your organization and from unbiased insiders who have the people and organizational skills necessary to put a partnering project together.

When people first asked us to get involved with partnering projects, we did not always understand why they needed us. As we have now worked with several hundred projects, the ways we can increase partnering effectiveness and add value have become clearer to us. The most important things our clients say we bring to partnering projects fit in four categories:

1. *Objectivity.* Many aspects of partnering involve self-criticism, awareness, and feedback. Even when people have strong egos, it can be useful to involve an external party in managing the exchange of feedback and keeping it balanced.

2. *Helps both the leader and the members.* Involving someone who is objective helps the leader of the group receive the feedback that may come as part of partnering. It also helps communicate to members of the partnering group that the leader is sincere about trying to make the partnering effort successful.

3. *Avoid problems.* Working with someone experienced with partnering can help people avoid problems made in previous partnering efforts.

4. *Identify opportunities.* More than avoiding problems, some-one who has experience working with partnering can also help identify the full potential of partnering and move the work in that direction.

In many cases in larger organizations, human resources professionals possess both the skills and the interest to participate in partnering projects as an external facilitator. If not directly involved, these people can also serve as coaches and mentors to managers who want to take a more active role in planning and leading their own partnering projects.

Working with people in your own organization has the added benefit of solidifying partnering relationships with the departments that provide help.

If you do work with someone in your organization, it is still useful to formalize their role with a written Work Plan. This may seem like a lot of work, but a few brief checklists can clear up gaps in expectations and de-velop the role of the facilitator for maximum effectiveness. Typical items worth covering include:

❐ The facilitator's role and responsibilities.

❐ Timelines and schedules.

❐ The facilitator's major tasks.

❐ Metrics and measures that define the success of the project.

❐ Metrics and measures that define the effectiveness of the facilitator.

❐ Information they will need from people in the partnering group.

❐ Roles and responsibilities of people in the partnering group.

It is useful to work with a list like this with anyone who helps in a partnering effort, whether they are from your own organization or from an external source. Also, most importantly, it is essential to clarify the anticipated outcomes of all the partnering work, not just their role and the partnering tasks. What do you expect the partnering work to produce? What should it achieve?

Maintaining a focus on outcomes, we believe it is important when working with an external consultant to structure payment in relation to outcomes, not based on an hourly or daily fee. Using an hourly or daily fee discourages the client from calling on the consultant even when a call might be worthwhile. An hourly or daily fee encourages the consultant to work slowly. Agreeing on outcomes and basing payment on predetermined meeting parameters focuses both consultant and client on achieving results.

Beware the "Subject Matter Expert" Partnering Facilitator

People who are thoroughly experienced with the issues a partnering group may encounter initially seem to be valuable resources and strong potential candidates to facilitate partnering meetings for other groups. In fact, it is important for any consultant to know enough about the partnering situation to know where the predictable issues and opportunities are.

However, people who have extensive experience with a subject that a partnering group is working on often have their own biases and come with their own solutions. This kind of intrusiveness in a group robs the group of the ability to own the solutions they come up with. Effective outside help comes with objectivity and some knowledge of the situation, but never with canned solutions. The job of the partnering facilitator is to structure the group so that it can come up with its own solutions, not to beat the group into submission so that it accepts the recommendations the facilitator makes.

Taking Action: Slowly, Thoughtfully, and With Humility

The step from planning to taking action is a big one, and it is plagued by problems not only of "succeeding," but of doing so in ways that are creative, ethical, and humane. When you are an "insider" attempting to make some improvements in your own organization, it is important to build on the experience of others who have attempted organizational change and to follow clear, ethical principles.

It is easy and understandable to become angry when you are caught in an alliance or organization that is less effective than it can be. Dysfunctional alliances and organizations can threaten your livelihood and career. Working or participating in a dysfunctional alliance or organization can compromise your values and ethics, and trigger deep-seated anger. We offer both a set of cautionary notes and principles to follow as you move from planning to taking action.

Cautionary Notes

You'll be more effective if you are aware of what you're up against when you attempt any kind of organizational change. We offer these notes not to discourage, but to inform and, hopefully, to strengthen your efforts:

❑ *The track record of many worthy attempts to improve organizations is unimpressive at best.* The bookshelves in business school libraries are filled with stories of failed attempts at change and improvement, and often in the cause of improvements far more worthy than the ones you are working on. One of our favorite books on this subject is the historian Elting Morison's *Men, Machines And Modern Times.* Morison chronicles the U.S. Navy's rejection of steam propulsion, the French government's resistance to pasteurization, and the unraveling of numerous attempts at computerization. Though based at the California Institute of Technology, Morison tends to side with the organizations conducting the resistance, pointing out the validity of their reasons and motives.

❑ *Improvement programs of any kind, even highly effective ones, come and go.* At the height of the quality improvement movement 15 years ago, we led a series of national seminars on "Teambuilding in Manufacturing" for *Inc.* magazine. In every program, participants told the same story: "We had a program. It generated results. Now it's gone." Programs ended because their executive sponsors left, and new executives with their own programs came on board. Ultimately, we came to believe that the programs ended because they were programs, generating results, but sitting outside the mainstream of the organization.

❑ *It's difficult to be an effective change agent.* Don't take it personally, it's not you. People resist change. One conclusion that clearly emerges from the business school readings is, very simply, that many people dislike, distrust, and resist change of any kind. Many managers and employees at all levels, people who are intelligent, sensitive, and creative, park in the same space every day. Changing their space would annoy them, triggering at least a few hours of lost focus and productivity. These are the people that every attempt at organizational change must work with.

❑ *It's difficult to be an ethical change agent.* The dilemmas may be difficult to recognize when people are resisting your efforts, but it's important to steer clear of two traps: coercion and discretion. No matter how compelling and "right" you may think your partnering efforts are, it's essential to never coerce or intimidate others into participating. With discretion, it is important to protect others' rights to privacy. As a change agent, you are likely to hear information from others that they want you to know in order to address the issues. You may want and need to bring this information to the whole partnering group, but you must be careful to check with the person sharing the information to ensure that doing so is all right with them. Don't become a "confessor" figure and repository of others' secrets and grudges; that sort of role breeds dependence on you and disengagement within the group. Encourage people to share what they think, but never violate their privacy.

❑ *It's even more difficult to initiate change when one is an insider.* As an insider, you have two strikes against you. First, because you are an insider, others in the organization don't value your perspective. The biblical wisdom on the way people distrust prophets from their own ranks is all too accurate for today's organizations. Second, beyond the other people, your own place in the organization, your biases and interests, color your perceptions in ways that compromise your objectivity.

Principles to Follow

These principles provide a foundation for the Partnering Solution strategies and methods described throughout the book. It is useful to keep them clearly in mind when moving from thinking about partnering to taking action:

❑ *Suggest, but never force.* Forcing change not only ensures that it will be ineffective, it also violates an ethical principle, bordering on harassment and the violation of others' rights.

❑ *Encourage open dialog, but maintain discretion when asked.* Many people love to complain about others, but shy away from speaking with those others directly. An effective change agent strongly encourages open, direct dialog, but also always maintains discretion and protects privacy.

☐ *Go only as far as the work itself dictates.* In the teambuilding and sensitivity group movement of the early 1960s, success depended on "breaking people down." The success of this kind of teambuilding was measured by the percentage of people at a retreat who cried and the volume of tears they produced. Some partnering work may in fact produce tears, but tears and breakdowns should not be the driving force. The work that is being done provides the driving force. If it produces tears or smiles, so be it.

☐ *Reach out to the people with whom you are in conflict.* Often, simple conversations and outreach can be as effective as formal partnering. Too often, when people first encounter conflict, they retreat and plan a more aggressive assault for their next encounter. Before attempting any kind of formal partnering with groups, it is often useful to keep the conflict simple and reach out and work with people at an individual level.

☐ *Embrace disagreement.* Simple disagreement has powerful effects on many people, either immobilizing them or triggering instant upscaling of the argument. Being an effective change agent requires that one respond to disagreement with more thought than emotion. In most cases, we find that disagreement contains the seeds of solutions to problems. Thus it's useful to work on building a response to disagreement that blends appreciation, respect, and enjoyment.

☐ *Pay equal attention to what the group is telling you and what you yourself believe.* Groups can be both perceptive and blind, innovative and resistant, argumentative and prone to avoid conflict. There really is a "wisdom" in most groups and teams, but this wisdom can coexist alongside strong dysfunctional tendencies. Work to see both the assets and weaknesses of your group, and work to balance these with your own convictions. Balance your perceptions, insights, and values with humility and engagement with what the group is offering.

☐ *Sharpen your facilitation and collaboration skills.* Often, partnering groups fail to resolve problems not because the problems are difficult, but because they lack the conflict resolution and facilitation skills. Go back and reread the chapters in this book on improving one-on-one skills and improving meetings. Practice in low-risk situations. Build your collaboration and facilitation skills, and difficult problems will suddenly seem much easier to resolve.

❏ *Work from the outset to move partnering from a "program" to "the way we do business."* Starting a change program of any kind can be exciting and motivating. However, achieving long-term partnering success requires that programs end and transform into "the way we do business." Companies that want to partner more effectively with their customers may well not need another program of any kind, but they will probably benefit significantly from a more effective client engagement meeting when starting new projects. Departments "at war" with other departments may not benefit from a program, but they will probably make significant gains if they regularly survey their internal customers and use the survey data to develop more effective, ongoing processes.

For further inspiration on what partnering can achieve, go back and reread the chapter on Raising the Bar. The group may be conflicted, negative, resistant, and hostile, but if you can plan it, structure it, facilitate it, and then get out of the way, it can also be a source of innovation, creativity, and enlightenment.

Moving From Planning Partnering to Taking Action

The track record of many worthy attempts to improve organizations is unimpressive at best. Improvement programs of any kind, even highly effective ones, come and go. It's difficult to be an effective change agent. It's difficult to be an ethical change agent. It's even more difficult to initiate change when one is an insider. Suggest, but never force. Encourage open dialog, but maintain discretion when asked. Go only as far as the work itself dictates. Reach out to the people with whom you are in conflict. Embrace disagreement. Pay equal attention to what the group is telling you and what you yourself believe. Sharpen your facilitation and collaboration skills. Work from the outset to move partnering from a "program" to "the way we do business."

In summary, the Partnering Solution will achieve maximum results for the organization and the most satisfying experience for the change agents if you keep three things in mind:

a. Try for numerous "singles and doubles" instead of "swinging for the fences."

b. Work at ongoing, incremental change instead of a one-time "big fix."

c. Persistently raise your own expectations for what the group can achieve.

Suggested Reading

We provide a detailed list of suggested reading for readers who are interested in the classic organizational themes and theory that provide the foundation for the Partnering Solution. We are also interested in readers' favorites, so please let us know online at *www.thepartneringsolution.com*.

Chapter 1. The Babel Problem, the Partnering Solution

Five classic texts provide useful foundations for understanding how the Babel Problem takes root between departments in the same organizations:

Graham T. Allison's *Essence of Decision* (Boston: Little Brown, 1971) uses a detailed case study of the U.S. response to the Cuban missile crisis to illustrate how decentralized organizations struggle to make clear decisions.

John Child's *Organization* (N.Y.: Harper & Row, 1984) details the far-reaching impacts of different kinds of organization structures and design. Organization design is invisible, intangible, but the lines of communications, power, and authority it defines have tangible outcomes.

Robert Michels's *Political Parties* (N.Y.: Free Press) debuted in 1911, a landmark study in the field of organizational sociology. Expecting to find ideal operations in the Socialist Party he studied, Michels instead discovered internal conflict and discord between members and professional managers.

Robert Townsend's *Up The Organization* (N.Y.: Fawcett, 1984) chronicles the dysfunctional tendencies of large organizations in an informative and entertaining way.

Frederic Brooks's *The Mythical Man-Month* (Reading, Mass.: Addison-Wesley, 1995–20th anniversary edition) describes in interesting, amusing, and sometimes painful terms how the conventional wisdom about managing projects in complex organizations is often mythically misguided and off-base.

While it's useful to understand the depth and range of the problems that plague organizations, it is also important to keep in mind the full potential that organizations can achieve. Two books in particular provide perspective in that direction:

Chris Argyris and Donald Schon's *Organizational Learning* (Reading, Mass.: Addison-Wesley, 1978) paints an intriguing portrait of the different and extensive types of learning possible in which organizations can engage.

Jim Collins's *Good to Great* (N.Y.: HarperCollins, 2001) describes organizational "greatness" in clear, measurable terms. His *Built to Last* (N.Y.: HarperCollins, 2002) identifies the factors that contribute to organizational success over the long term.

Three references provide practical insight into the ways that the Babel Problem evolves in mergers and acquisitions, along with advice on how to address the issues:

Timothy Galpin and Mark Herndon, *The Complete Guide to Mergers and Acquisitions* (San Francisco: Jossey-Bass, 1995).

Alexandra Reed-LaJoux, *The Art of Successful M&A Integration* (N.Y.: McGraw-Hill, 1997).

Harvard Business Review on Mergers and Acquisitions (Boston: Harvard Business Review Press, 2001). This collection of articles provides insight into the organizational as well as the financial issues involved in mergers and acquisitions.

A number of other books provide valuable insight on partnering:

Stephen Dent, *Partnering Intelligence: Creating Value for Your Business by Building Strong Alliances* (Palo Alto: Davies-Black Publishing, 2004). Dent introduces the useful concept of Partnering Intelligence and provides the PQ instrument to help readers assess their own partnering intelligence.

Larraine Segil, *Measuring the Value of Partnering: How to Use Metrics to Plan, Develop and Implement Successful Alliances* (N.Y.: AMACOM, 2004). Segil provides valuable insight into how to assess alliances.

Neil Rackham, Lawrence Friedman, and Richard Ruff, *Getting Partnering Right: How Market Leaders Are Creating Long-Term Advantage.* (N.Y.: McGraw-Hill, 1995). This work focuses primarily on partnering in supplier relationships.

Harvard Business Review on Strategic Alliances. (Boston: Harvard Business Review Press, 2002). Compendium of HBR articles on alliances focuses on senior executive insights and applications.

William Ronco and Jean Ronco, *Partnering Manual for Design and Construction* (N.Y.: McGraw-Hill, 1996). Our early work on partnering provides a step-by-step guide on conducting effective partnering for design and construction projects.

Much of the writing and thinking about partnering involves rethinking the nature and meaning of partnering with customers, redefining the crux of customer service. Two authors have particularly valuable ideas in this area:

Larry Wilson, *Stop Selling, Start Partnering* (N.Y.: John Wiley, 1994), targets his message to traditional sales organizations and sales professionals.

David Maister, *Managing the Professional Service Firm* (N.Y.: Free Press, 1991) and, with Charles Green and Robert Galford, *Trusted Advisor* (N.Y.: Free Press, 2001) takes the notion of customer service to entire new levels of performance and depth. These are the books we recommend most often to our clients who are professional service providers of any kind.

Chapter 4. Taking Stock

Writing on strategic planning provides useful insight on the importance of and methods for measuring organizational performance:

Leonard Goodstein, Timothy Nolan, and J. William Pfeiffer's *Applied Strategic Planning* (N.Y.: McGraw-Hill, 1993) provides useful insight into the complex subject of strategic planning and contains an excellent chapter relevant for Taking Stock, titled "Performance Audit."

Robert Kaplan and David Norton's recent classic *The Balanced Scorecard* (Boston: Harvard Business School Press, 1996) uses performance measures in a "balanced" approach both to assess organizational performance and plan thoughtful growth.

Many good books are available to help readers design and implement surveys. We like Terry Vavra's *Improving Your Measurement of Customer Satisfaction* (Wis.: ASQ Press, 1997) because of its emphasis on and detail of accurate survey methods. ASQ Press is the publishing arm of the American Society of Quality; the book reflects the Society's interests in accurately and objectively documenting quality improvements of all kinds.

Chapter 5. Building Trust

M. Scott Peck's *The Road Less Traveled* (N.Y.: Touchstone, 2003—25th anniversary edition) sold millions of copies in the 1980s because it offers practical insight into the nature of personal growth. His chapters on the nature of healthy relationships are essential reading for understanding the roots of trust.

David Maister, Charles Green, and Robert Galford's *Trusted Advisor* (N.Y.: Free Press, 2001) thoughtfully examines the nature of trust in professional relationships.

Numerous books explain and apply the Myers-Briggs Type Indicator in interesting ways (MBTI and Myers-Briggs Type Indicator are registered trademarks of Consulting Psychologists Press, Palo Alto, Calif.) Three Myers-Briggs books especially relevant for the topic of partnering are:

David Keirsey and Marilyn Bates's *Please Understand Me* and *Please Understand Me II* (Del Mar, Calif.: Prometheus Nemesis Books, 1984) are the classic, core Myers-Briggs books. They provide in-depth understanding of the theory and each of the types. This is the book to get—and learn—in order to acquire basic literacy with the concepts.

William Bridges, *The Character of Organizations* (Palo Alto: Consulting Psychologists Press, 1992). Bridges applies MBTI concepts to whole organizations and introduces the concept of "types of organizational character." This work is particularly valuable for partnering work in outsourcing, strategic alliances, and mergers in which the success of the venture depends in large part on the blending of differing values and cultures.

Paul Tieger and Barbara Barron-Tieger's *Do What You Are* (Boston: Little Brown, 2001) uses Myers-Briggs insights to provide advice on career choice and development. The concepts are useful for partnering because they describe organizational cultures in different types of work.

William Ronco and Jean Ronco, *Partnering Manual for Design and Construction* (N.Y.: McGraw-Hill, 1996). In one chapter, we use Myers-Briggs to explain several of the classic, recurring conflicts and miscommunications in many design and construction projects.

Chapter 8. Raising the Bar

Partnerships that want to explore developing social responsibility components of their work can find useful information in two references:

David Batstone's book *Saving the Corporate Soul and (Who Knows?) Maybe Your Own* (Jossey-Bass, 2003). Batstone outlines eight areas for addressing ethical and social issues that apply to many partnerships:

1. Leadership: really bought into the success of the stakeholders.
2. Integrity: business operations are transparent to shareholders, employees, and the public.
3. Community: company thinks of itself as part of a community as well as part of a market.

4. Customers: represent products honestly to customers.
5. Workers: treated as valuable team members.
6. Environment: treated as a silent stakeholder.
7. Diversity: strive for balance, diversity, and equality in relationships with workers, customers, and suppliers.
8. Globalization: strive for balance, diversity, and equality in relationships with workers, customers, and suppliers.

A new publication, *Worthwhile Magazine* is a second useful resource for partnerships interested in developing social and ethical dimensions. For example, the magazine's debut issue included an article by David Hessekiel titled "Cause and Effect." Hessekiel notes, "There's an endless number of causes out there, but a far smaller set that can help create a win-win partnership…'Cause marketing' has the power to make one plus one equal three. By working with a cause, a company can imbue its brand and culture with emotional qualities that traditional messaging can't deliver. By working with a company, a nonprofit can gain access to human and in-kind resources in addition to the cash."

Hessekiel suggests that organizations thinking about finding a cause consider two factors:

1. Logical fit: Does the cause obviously fit in with the goals of the partnership?
2. "Glocal": Does the cause have big, global concepts that can be localized?

Chapter 10. Improving Meetings and Group Communications Skills

Several books provide useful references for this chapter.

Jon Katzenbach and Douglas Smith's *The Wisdom of Teams* (Boston: Harvard Business School Press, 1991) describes the potential of teams and provides strategies and skills to improve team performance.

Patrick Lencioni, *The Five Dysfunctions of a Team* (San Francisco: Jossey-Bass, 2001) and *Death by Meeting* (San Francisco: Jossey-Bass, 2004) provide great insight into the issues teams struggle with.

Since 1972, Pfeiffer and Associates (now published by Jossey-Bass in San Francisco, formerly published by University Associates) has published annual handbooks for group facilitators—collections of teambuilding exercises carefully annotated so that managers of all kinds can use them for their own purposes. These workbooks are excellent resources for team managers and members who want to try their own hand at teambuilding work.

Chapter 11. Improving One-on-One CommunicationsSkills

Many people trying to build their competencies in this area find these books useful:

Thomas Gordon, *Leader Effectiveness Training* (N.Y.: Berkely Publishing, 2001). This updated version of Gordon's classic provides clear instruction and numerous business case illustrations.

Robert Bolton, *People Skills* (Englewood Cliffs, N.J.: Prentice Hall, 1979). This book also provides clear insight and instruction.

Roger Fisher and William Ury's *Getting to Yes* (N.Y.: Penguin, 1983) provides perspective on maintaining a cooperative approach to communications.

Adele Faber and Elaine Mazlish's *How to Talk So Kids Will Listen and Listen So Kids Will Talk* (N.Y.: Harper, 2002—20th anniversary edition) covers the same skills and perspective as the three books mentioned previously but adds a useful teaching tool: cartoons. At a practical level, many managers tell us that it is useful to work with the same skills on both the family and work fronts.

Chapter 12. Partnering Leadership

Many excellent books on leadership are widely available. Three that we find especially relevant for partnering situations are:

Jim Collins's *Good to Great* (N.Y.: HarperCollins, 2001). With its combination of humility and focus on results, Collins's notion of "Level 5 Leadership" is an approach that is particularly well suited to partnering situations.

Stephen Covey, *Principle-Centered Leadership* (N.Y.: Free Press, 1992) and *The Seven Habits of Highly Effective People* (N.Y.: Free Press, 1990). Both books describe leadership principles and practices that are particularly effective in partnering situations.

James MacGregor Burns's *Leadership* (N.Y.: HarperCollins, 1978). This book won the Pulitzer Prize in 1978, and with good reason. Burns points out the potential of all leadership not only to make fair trades and transactions, but also to transform both follower and leader. Important to keep in mind when the going gets tough.

The typical MBA text *Organizational Behavior* (Merrill Publishing Co., 1984), by Jerry L. Gray and Frederick A. Starke, provides extensive information about leadership theories and their evolution over time.

Laurie Beth Jones provides practical, usable instruction for the complex task of writing a personal vision statement in *The Path: Creating Your Mission Statement for Work and for Life* (Hyperion, 1996).

Index

A Note for Readers Groups

The Partnering Solution is well suited for use with Readers Groups in two ways. First, and primarily, the book provides step-by-step insight and support for groups of people attempting to make improvements in their own partnering situations. Second, the book can be a useful focus for Readers Groups interested more in the content of its ideas than their application. (These groups should focus on the following general issues questions.)

From the outset, we envisioned people working in groups, using the Partnering Solution as a kind of guidebook for their own efforts to improve partnering situations. The group begins by reading the whole book in order to understand the idea and approach. Then, the group would work its way through the five steps of the Partnering Solution, adapting the methods in each chapter to its own interests and needs—Taking Stock, Building Trust, Clarifying Goals, Implementing Key Processes, and Raising the Bar. Any group planning to take any kind of action in any organization should also read and discuss pages 264–269 of this book. These pages provide insight and guiding principles for taking action thoughtfully.

For reading groups using the book as a guidebook for their own partnering efforts, it will likely be useful to address these general issues:

1. In what ways have people in the group encountered the Babel Problem in the organizations and alliances they have worked with?

   a. What kinds of miscommunication and misalignment have they observed in their own organizations and alliances?

    b.   Which if any of the specific types of Babel Problems described in the book accurately describe the situations readers have encountered?

    c.   What do group members ascribe as the root causes of the Babel Problems they have observed?

2. What do group members think will happen if they attempt to apply the Partnering Solution?

    a.   What do group members think are the risks and rewards of attempting to implement any of the partnering methods? What outcomes do they think the methods could achieve? What problems and risks concern them? If they do apply any partnering methods, what can they do to reduce their risks?

    b.   In what ways do the concepts in the book reinforce observations group members had already made before reading it? Which, if any, aspects of the book do group members disagree with?

    c.   What aspects of the partnering methods do group members anticipate will be easy to implement? What aspects of the partnering methods do they anticipate will be more difficult and challenging? What could they do in applying the partnering methods to increase their chances of success?

Beyond these general issues, it is also worthwhile for groups using the book as a reference for their own partnering work to begin their efforts by reading the chapter on improving meetings and using the principles in this chapter to strengthen their own meetings.

Following that, it will be worthwhile to address these questions in their work with each of the five pieces of the Partnering Solution—Taking Stock, Building Trust, Clarifying Goals, Implementing Key Processes, and Raising the Bar.

1. What outcomes is this piece of the Partnering Solution aimed at achieving in general?

2. What outcomes could this piece of the Partnering Solution achieve in their own partnering situations?

3. What are the risks and problems of trying to use this piece of the Partnering Solution in their own situations?

4. What can they do to minimize their risks and maximize their chances for success in applying that piece of the Partnering Solution?

After the group has tried one piece of the Partnering Solution, it is very useful to conduct a thorough "Lessons Learned" discussion before moving forward:

1. What aspects of the group's efforts worked well? What aspects did not?
2. Based on the group's efforts thus far, what changes or principles should we follow moving forward?

About the Authors

DR. WILLIAM C. RONCO has helped clients improve partnering results in hundreds of projects in a broad range of applications: technology, professional firms, construction, scientific, government, outsourcing, healthcare, and education. President of Gathering Pace Consulting in Bedford, Massachusetts, Dr. Ronco also consults on strategic planning, business intelligence, leadership development, and teambuilding. He earned his B.A. at Rutgers University, his Ed.M. at the Harvard Graduate School of Education, and his Ph.D. at the Massachusetts Institute of Technology.

JEAN S. RONCO has pioneered the development of effective partnering methods and leadership development practices in numerous organizations. Chief operating officer of Gathering Pace Consulting, Jean has focused on consulting practices that enable clients to achieve their full potential. She was formerly vice president of human resources at Thomson & Thomson, Inc. Jean earned her B.A. at Boston College and her Ed.M. at the Harvard Graduate School of Education.

The authors invite you to contribute your stories and opinions about partnering on their Website, *www.thepartneringsolution.com*. The Website also contains updated information on partnering best practices. For additional information on their consulting and training on partnering, strategic planning, and leadership, the authors invite you to contact them through their Website or by telephone at Gathering Pace Consulting (781) 275-2424.